Unsettled

Unsettled

The Culture of Mobility and the Working Poor in Early Modern England

PATRICIA FUMERTON

The University of Chicago Press
Chicago and London

Patricia Fumerton is professor of English at the University of California, Santa Barbara. She is the author of *Cultural Aesthetics: Renaissance Literature and the Practice of Social Ornament* and the coeditor of *Renaissance Culture and the Everyday*.

The University of Chicago Press, Chicago 60637
The University of Chicago Press, Ltd., London
© 2006 by The University of Chicago
All rights reserved. Published 2006
Printed in the United States of America
15 14 13 12 11 10 09 08 07 06   5 4 3 2 1

ISBN (cloth): 0-226-26955-8
ISBN (paper): 0-226-26956-6

The University of Chicago Press gratefully acknowledges the generous support of the John Simon Guggenheim Memorial Foundation toward the publication of this book.

Library of Congress Cataloging-in-Publication Data

Fumerton, Patricia.
    Unsettled : the culture of mobility and the working poor in early modern England / Patricia Fumerton.
        p.   cm.
    Includes bibliographical references and index.
    ISBN 0-226-26955-8 (cloth : alk. paper)—ISBN 0-226-26956-6 (pbk. : alk. paper)
    1. Working class writings, English—History and criticism.   2. English litera-
ture—Early modern, 1500–1700—History and criticism.   3. Merchant
mariners—Great Britain—Biography—History and criticism.   4. Ballads,
English—Great Britain—History and criticism.   5. Barlow, Edward, b. 1642.
Journal of his life at sea.   6. Working class—Great Britain—Intellectual life.
7. Working class—Great Britain—Historiography.   8. Migrant labor—Great
Britain—Historiography.   9. Working poor—Great Britain—Historiography.
10. Migration, Internal, in literature.   11. Seafaring life—Historiography.
12. Working class in literature.   13. Autobiography.   I. Title.
    PR120.L33F86   2006
    820.9'920623—dc22   2005017841

For Alan Liu

Contents

Illustrations

Preface: Making Space for the Working Poor

This study began as an act of scholastic penance. In my academic youth, I must confess, I was raised on the select, refined bread of canonical Renaissance literature, and I found it fully satisfying. Even during the heady early days of new historicism—during which I eagerly sampled strange and unconventional cultural dishes—I persisted, like other historicist critics of the time, in turning for literary sustenance primarily to high court culture. Worse on my part, in *Cultural Aesthetics,* I joined the early modern aristocracy in savoring its especially trivial, useless, and ornamental morsels: miniature paintings, give-away children, out-of-the-way rooms, banqueting sweets (or "voids"), and trade in superfluities such as spice and sugar.[1] I sought out profligate trifles at every turn, delighting in holding up for examination the lavish delicacies out of which the early modern aristocracy attempted to construct itself into a delicious, sustainable whole. But in doing so—however much I believed and still believe in my thesis (and still secretly delight in its delicacies)—I represented but some 10 percent of the early modern English population and effectively disenfranchised the rest. As penance for such exclusive high-mindedness, I first thought to turn in this project to the most neglected, lowest sector of early modern society: the down-and-out vagrant. Here, I thought, I could sample plain and simple, if not particularly expansive, fare.

But I soon realized that vagrancy in the early modern period, as perhaps in all periods, was anything but simple—or limited in its reach. The more I sought out vagrants, the more I also found itinerant poor workers, and a lot of them. The working poor were subject to arrest as they moved geographically along various lines of gainful employment: same-kind itinerant labor (for example, chapmen, peddlers, carriers, entertainers, tinkers, wire-drawers, button-makers), changing from one like job to another (harvest workers, wage laborers), or switching between entirely different jobs (such as the Wiltshire man arrested in 1605 for vagrancy and listed as "sometimes a weaver, sometimes a surgeon, sometimes a minstrel, sometimes a dyer, and now a bullard").[2] What to make of all these labeled "vagrants," I asked myself, who were in fact itinerant workers? In striving to answer that question, I discovered, to my surprise, a large and growing number of mobile and casually employed laborers in early modern England. These included in their ranks not only the many itinerant and multitasked workers listed above, but also huge numbers of servants, apprentices, journeymen, and soldiers/seamen. Not all of these mostly poor migrants would have been arrested for vagrancy or peremptorily whipped before being hurried out of town, as was the custom of treating undesirable "strangers" after the late 1590s. As Joan R. Kent finds in her study of the Midlands, 1611–40, chastised vagrants in fact formed a small subset of a much larger pool of destitute travelers who often received alms rather than punishment.[3] Nevertheless, the 1572 act that attempted to define who exactly constituted the vagrant, hashed out over much hot debate, was deliberately broad in its scope, leaving considerable room for interpretation. As a result, the "legitimate" destitute traveler not only rubbed elbows with the "illegitimate" vagrant, but also risked at any moment being identified as such. When it came right down to it, the impoverished mobile poor who did escape correction did so at the discretion of authorities who could often confidently distinguish them from the "true" vagrant only by the thin paper passport clutched in their hands authorizing their travels and perhaps their right to beg.[4]

Of course, all classes to a certain extent partook of physical, economic, and even social mobility in the early modern period, as Lawrence Stone has shown.[5] Even the upper sort—specifically, wealthy merchants, yeomen, and gentry—engaged in extensive "improvement" mobility. But those of privileged social "place" are not my primary concern. I am particularly focused on the larger practice of need-driven, subsistence mobility of actual vagrants and—even more—of their look-alikes: itinerant laborers, who could from time to time find themselves treated like or, as importantly, feeling like vagrants. These latter poor migrants constituted a growing class of workers in the late sixteenth and seventeenth centuries. As Steve Hindle reports, the proportion of dispossessed laborers in the rural population alone increased from 20–30 percent in 1520 to around 50 percent by 1650. By the beginning of the eighteenth century, wage laborers constituted some 60 percent of Britain's people.[6] With the act of settlement of 1662, such mobile workers were for the first time officially recognized as a class separate from the vagrant. The law explicitly instructed that the undesirables among such laborers—that is, those migrants thought "likely to be chargeable" to the parish—should be returned to their "home" parish or last place of abode without suffering the kinds of physical punishment typically allocated to the vagrant.[7] But the law at the same time continued to discourage lower-order mobility, and those unfortunates who were deported, whether physically punished or not, would still have been subjected to spatial and emotional unsettledness.

The process of tracking the large numbers of such displaced workers in early modern England has expanded the vision of this book considerably beyond my original focus on the legally vagrant. At the same time, it has extended not only numerically but also spatially my earlier study of aristocratic subjectivity in *Cultural Aesthetics*. In that work and again here, my concern is with tracing the emergence of a new kind of secular subjectivity in the period, one that was not solely God-based but that could—even while perhaps anchored by the godly "eye"—at the same time sense a more modern notion of singularity and disconnection. Such a subject must always be recognized to be interpellated or socially determined, and in this sense "subjected"; but the notion of such a subject also posits the possibility of a "free" individual or detached self, even in the face of its actual or felt impossibility. In both projects, while addressing two very different socioeconomic groups in the early modern period, I began with the same question: what form(s) did the notion of selfhood take, and what are the means by which we can recover that sense of self, given the historically intervening filters of interpretative and aesthetic assumptions through which we must read the representational "I" in past texts?

Pursuing this question in *Cultural Aesthetics,* I found that the early modern aristocratic subject had the means and will actively to seek out detachment and privacy. But to achieve this sensibility, the aristocratic subject depended on sited physical artifacts. That is, the "discovery" of aristocratic subjectivity (whether in a sonnet, a miniature painting, the perspective scenery of a masque, an architectural site, or a delicious tidbit) required the physical layering of the self (through screens of conventional rhetoric, ornament, rooms, or other such sweet artifice), so that the self could be felt to be penetrated into and experienced as enticingly "interior" and singular. The *less access to the means of creating identity* itinerant and working poor, by contrast, appear less actively self-fashioning and more elusive subjects. They also, importantly, had little if any access to prized sited artifacts. Such a subject thus could not discover himself or herself (however illusory the discovery) as exquisitely interior, singular, or otherwise placed. He or she was without place. ———> *and so outside of community & society*

It is therefore crucial that in tracing the topography of lowly mobile workers, we liberate our thinking from the insistent critical dialectic (typically attributed to new historicism) of "low versus high," "margin versus center," "subversive versus contained."[8] This sometimes nuanced but ultimately dead-end dialectic is dependent on a *placed* universe (that is, one in which the voices of the low must be measured relative to the voices of those who have a "place" in society). But truly to understand the "low," we must track them in their own space—a spaciousness of itinerancy, fragmentation, disconnection, and multiplicity that produces a very different topographical mapping of societal relations than those determined by place. By *space* and *spaciousness,* I should stress, I do not mean to imply such "high" and positively coded notions as "roominess" or "luxuriousness" (as when an elite hotel room is touted to be "spacious"). Rather, I wish to connote the geographical *expansiveness*—sometimes positively, but more often negatively or ambivalently coded—of lower-order mobility. I also mean in my use of these terms to draw upon sociological and philosophical studies of space that help us to reflect in new ways upon such mobility.

Following the movements of poor lower-order subjects of early modern England, then, this study necessarily escapes traditional notions of place. It makes room for exploration into a new, fluid economy and a new notion of "low" subjectivity that was truly spacious, that is, in every sense mobile. In essence, this unfixed, or what might be better termed "unsettled," subject was at all times an apprentice or journeyman. Shifting from place to place, relationship to relationship, and job to job, such a subject apprenticed in a range of different identities, or "role speculations," without ever attaining the "freedom" of a whole and stable identity. Since many of the poor lower orders were vulnerable to such economic and spatial mobility, furthermore, unsettled subjectivity had a potentially wide reach, capable of being experienced (if only occasionally and provisionally) not only by the itinerant but also by the housed.

But why stretch our reach to touch even the housed? Do we not thus risk making too elastic or too fuzzy the notion of unsettled subjectivity? Do we not leave far behind the truly mobile poor? Speaking literally and focusing only on the snapshot moment, we very well might. But thinking metonymically and gazing over a longer expanse of time, we do not. Though we clearly must be careful so as not to lose the "ground" of our unsettled subject, however shifting that ground might be, the housed poor deserve consideration because they were themselves vulnerable by association and in actuality over time to a similar experience of unsettledness as the itinerant laboring poor. I am thinking here not only of servants and apprentices, who, as we shall see, were especially liable to instability and displacement. I am also thinking of poor householders from the lowest depths of the amorphous "middling sort" who were at any time susceptible to unsettling change (indigent husbandmen, small craftsmen, and petty traders in the poorer occupations, such as glovers, weavers, carpenters, fishmongers, fruiterers, and the like). These were the workers most prone to periods of unemployment, multiple or serial employment, desperate indigence, and physical mobility. They were the unstable working poor, and depending on varying geographical and economic conditions, they constituted from 30 to 50 percent of the early modern English population.

Not all of these workers necessarily experienced makeshift employment, spatial displacement, or psychological unsettledness. But we need not adopt an all-or-nothing position here. As Paul Griffiths, Adam Fox, and Steve Hindle urge in *The Experience of Authority in Early Modern England,* we should not look for a single lower-order identity but rather should be sensitive to the multiple possible subject positions of those "making do" in early modern society: "The ideas and actions of a single individual or group might alter greatly according to situation," they caution, adding that most people were capable of assuming "multiple identities" with a facility that "defies their easy categorization."[9] The larger notion of lower-order subjectivity developed in this book by definition admits, indeed demands, the possibility of a single individual's experiencing multiple or serial identities of which the unsettled experience, as it is more narrowly defined here, might not be one. Rather than seek an *entirely* or even a *mostly* lower-order identity, then, we might pursue (to adopt A. L. Beier's term about poverty) a *potential* one.[10] Unsettled subjectivity, that is, might be experienced by some, if not all, of the housed poor, if only on a one-time or intermittent basis. Such a potential for experiencing unsettledness is more understandable given the "life cycle" of poverty, by which individuals and whole households over time might periodically become dependent on poor relief and by-employments, or even become physically displaced due to sickness, dearth, accident, or old age. Given their potential for desperate poverty and mobility, some of the housed poor attempting in makeshift ways to just get by might even feel by imaginative association—however momentarily or casually—a kind of kinship with the lowest sector of unsettled subjects: the down-and-out vagrant. Such a susceptibility to the imaginative experience of unsettled subjectivity concerns me as much as the physical *fact* of vagrancy or mobility.

In pursuing unsettledness, then, I examine a porousness or interpenetration between a range of lower-order subject positions, the opposite ends of which might be thought to constitute entirely separate groups: the disciplined vagrant, the succored migrant, the laboring itinerant, the housed poor, and the indigent householder. My original determination to focus on the vagrant, in reaction against the exclusiveness of my earlier study of aristocratic subjectivity, has indeed opened up my perspective both numerically and spatially.

It has at the same time required me to expand my terminology. Terms such as *vagrant* and *rogue* are useful for this study because they reflect laws and labels that were applied to the itinerant and even to some housed but masterless poor. They thus tell us a lot about how authorities and those well placed in the period thought about the laboring poor. But we must be careful not simply to ventriloquize official terminology and thus perpetuate the misconception that masterless labor always equaled idleness or (in its rogue version) deceit. More often than not, the "vagrant" was not shiftless, but a shifting or mobile worker, moving from job to job as well as place to place. Therefore, though I cautiously continue to use the term *vagrant* as a recognized legal label of the time, I embrace as more accurate and spacious the less emotionally charged descriptor *unsettled.* The term *unsettled* allows us to escape knee-jerk thoughts of "loafer," "vagabond," or "rogue" and more readily to entertain images of the poor as mobile but gainfully employed and as not only physically but also psychologically unfixed.

In pursuing lower-order unsettledness, I have also found my earlier concept of periodization challenged. Traditionally, literary critics and historians have tended to view the English seventeenth century as divided by a kind of impassable mountain created by the Civil War. Studies of the "Renaissance" or "early modern period" usually stop at around 1640, or at the latest 1660. But alongside acceptance of this cultural divide, there has been a new interest in pursuing continuities rather than radical breaks between pre- and post-Restoration England, as is evident in Paul Griffiths and Mark S. R. Jenner's recent edited volume, *Londinopolis.*[11] Though much fine work on vagrancy and poverty has looked for conclusion to the traditional midcentury end point (seeing in England a pattern of crisis years, running from the late sixteenth century to 1650, followed by a period of relative improvement), here too there has been an accompanying new trend—in the work of Margaret Pelling, Paul Slack, and others—to recognize the merits of thinking through the seventeenth century as an uninterrupted continuity, not as two separate halves.[12] My work in this book fully supports this claim.

Certainly, in addressing poverty, makeshift employment, and lower-order mobility, especially in how these penetrate the space of the home, there is much to be said not only for focusing on the depressed years that punctuate the late sixteenth up to the mid-seventeenth century (especially the severe economic slumps of the 1590s, 1620s, and 1630s), but also for taking a longer view. As both Slack and Beier have observed, economic crises caused by dearth, war, pestilence, or other local factors occurred throughout the seventeenth century (and extended into the eighteenth century as well).[13] Improved living conditions beginning around 1650, due to a fall in population and in some prices, to extended cultivation of the land, and to an increase in domestic industries, allowed the country as a whole to cope better with such disasters. The devastating famines of the earlier years were mostly averted. But the poor remained highly vulnerable. Indeed, Beier questions whether the apparent recovery in the second half of the seventeenth century went deep enough to reach the very poor: though wheat prices fell markedly, he notes, the prices of other consumables did not, and wages at the lowest level hardly rose at all. Conditions for the bulk of the wage-earning population, Beier concludes, "could hardly have progressed."[14] The divide in the mid-seventeenth century fully collapses if we follow Slack's distinction between "shallow" and "deep" poverty. While deep poverty bodes starvation, Slack explains, shallow poverty threatens less radical destitution—for example, the lack of fuel or clothes. As he projects, "Over the seventeenth century as a whole, it seems probable that the number of people in deep poverty—those in danger of starvation—markedly declined, while the number in shallow poverty—those who might be described as 'poor'—increased by at least as much."[15] Evidence of the growth in shallow poverty over the latter half of the seventeenth century can be detected in the noticeable proliferation at this time of casual or extraordinary payments to the poor (rather than long-term pensions), as discovered by Jeremy Boulton in his study of the parish of St. Martin-in-the-Fields.[16]

One development that helped sustain the many living in subsistence poverty during these years, and which particularly bears on the question of mobility, was the increase in domestic industries. Requiring little financial outlay or training and no specialized place of production, the manufacture of such commodities as pins, stockings, and buttons allowed the poor to supplement their incomes so as to raise themselves above starvation levels. Of course, by-employments were not a new phenomenon to the seventeenth century, or even to the sixteenth. But as Joan Thirsk has observed, they became an increasingly important part of England's domestic economy in the seventeenth century,[17] and they were especially important to the poor. Not only did domestic industries promote networks of itinerant chapmen and peddlers throughout the country—well documented by Margaret Spufford[18]—but they encouraged "at-home" mobility in the form of makeshift employments, for both men and women. Women's involvement in such casual labor (spinning, stocking-knitting, street vending, etc.) was especially crucial to supplementing the family income and parish poor relief—sometimes it was the family's sole livelihood—and thus to keeping poor households from destitution.[19] The extent to which women engaged in such activities both inside and outside the home reveals the porous nature of the house or private sphere in this period, as well as the extent to which the idea of "household" itself was unsettled, multiple, and mobile.[20] And here lies the rub. Though serial, multiple, and "out-of-place" labor epitomized by the patchwork employment of women mobilized the poor in a positive sense, giving them not only sustenance but also an emergent class identity as wage laborers, such unstable, makeshift work was a cause for great anxiety in the period. Women were the flash point. Not only was women's work often not acknowledged as legitimate labor, but, as we shall see (particularly in the studies of Paul Griffiths), women who independently engaged in such marginal work—especially when practiced outside the home—were liable to persecution and even arrest for vagrancy.[21]

When considering by-employments and makeshift work within and outside the home, "mobility" takes on a more subtle meaning, to be sure. In the case of women, it might mean simply the freedom to shift employments or to move outside the home in unpredictable and uncircumscribed ways. But such local acts of mobility—however much they are a "fact" of life—do not negate the potential for a resulting feeling of unsettled subjectivity. Given the suspicion with which such activities could be viewed, when practiced by women in particular, we should consider the extent to which a laborer's engagement in such multitasking, in the effort to sustain herself and her family, might well produce not only suspicion on the part of authorities, but also the felt experience on the part of that laborer of being out of place or unsettled, however relatively scripted or localized such work might in actuality be.

To summarize: my book, in its expanded conception, entertains the instabilities of place not only for the homeless and itinerant, but also for housed lower-order subjects, including women, as part of the process of pursuing a culture of mobility among the working poor in England from the late sixteenth through the seventeenth century. Additionally, the book investigates the extent to which the straightforward "facts" of lower-order mobility might result in a subjective interiorization of unsettledness, or what I have termed "unsettled subjectivity."

The first two chapters of part 1 set the scene. They build upon the wealth of recent studies of vagrancy and poverty by adding consideration of the fine new work on apprentices, servants, and women in the early modern period and placing all in the light of a new domestic economy of mobility for the laboring poor. What takes shape in the process is an expansive, interlocking image of lower-order unsettledness. Such a historically grounded, if fluid, picture of the laboring poor, both itinerant and housed, allows us then to uncover in chapter 3 the lie behind literary representations of the vagrant in rogue pamphlets of the period, which were marketed for the middling sort. Thomas Harman's early but influential pamphlet, *A Caveat for Common Cursitors Vulgarly Called Vagabonds,* might lead us far astray from thoughts of a workforce of dispossessed wage laborers if we were to buy into the "type" of the unsettled subject Harman promulgates. Capitalizing on middle-class anxieties about displaced labor, Harman suppressed the fact of a makeshift labor force by redressing it as disguising. That is, the laboring poor, rather than shifting from job to job, were reimagined by Harman and his followers as donning disguise after disguise. Harman's tract stands as a "caveat" against too readily accepting representations or "official" descriptors of the poor in any period (significantly, Harman was a sometime judicial officer). Building instead upon our encounters with the mobile poor of the previous chapters, however ultimately representational and thus subject to interpretation they may be as well, I conclude part 1 with an alternative story of the nature of unsettled subjectivity as a lived experience available—if only occasionally or intermittently—to the lowly homeless and housed alike.

To track mobility that was more literally spacious, the second half of my book returns to the physically itinerant male laborer who was beginning to emerge as a recognized class in the second half of the seventeenth and into the eighteenth century. The settlement act of 1662 included some acceptance of mobility for working men, and in 1697 another settlement law even encouraged migration to areas where there was a demand for labor.[22] In this period of "shallow poverty," one might say, the unsettled sensibility arising from multitasking, by-employments in domestic industries, and wage laboring becomes more deep-rooted and "acceptable," at least for men. But the accompanying fact that such encouragement was controlled by strict rules—as detailed by the settlement laws of the later seventeenth century—is a sign of the still-felt nervousness about the mobilized poor, whatever the sex of the traveler. With the general improvement of economic conditions in the latter half of the seventeenth century, long-distance mobility and pauper migration may have decreased.[23] But clearly, the poor were far from spatially settled.

Peter Linebaugh and Marcus Rediker have argued that these poor, unstable, itinerant wage laborers of the seventeenth century can be seen as the beginning of an emergent class of proletariat, which is epitomized in the period by seamen.[24] We can indeed see incipient industrialism in the system of putting-out and other large industries such as brewing and shipbuilding. According to Linebaugh and Rediker, the seaman is one of the most fitting symbols of this trend. The seaman was also a point of fixation for the nervousness in the period about the mobile worker. Proclamations and acts in the sixteenth and seventeenth centuries were repeatedly directed toward containing the feared potential for instability from seamen and soldiers once released from duty onshore. The sheer numbers were daunting. Seamen formed a massive and growing class of wage laborers in the seventeenth century. In the mid-sixteenth century, around three to five thousand Englishmen were seamen. By 1750, the number was more than sixty thousand.[25] These seamen were non-landholding, free wage laborers and constituted both the alienated and collective workers of a new global economy. Without tools or a craft, they held their labor as a commodity, and despite the language evoking patronage or apprenticeship, they mostly stood outside the social economics of master-apprentice relationships. If anything, the ship was a kind of factory in which the worker's physical labor was his tool and his price. Adrift aboard a factory, seamen were acutely conscious of themselves as unsettled and yet as occupationally (or at least collaboratively) defined. Theirs was a paradoxically settled and unsettled sense of self.

In part 2 of my book, I include a consideration of seamen generally (in chapter 6), but I also offer an individual poor seaman as a case study of an unsettled subject who at first appears not fully to fit the bill of either the displaced laborer or the new seaman proletariat. His name is Edward Barlow (no relation to his contemporary by the same name who published on coastal tides). My desire to look closely at this one man responds to the similar concern of Tim Hitchcock, Peter King, and Pamela Sharpe in *Chronicling Poverty* that statistics can blind us to the persons behind the numbers.[26] We need to seek out the individuals behind the statistics and to listen for their different voices. Edward Barlow gives us the rare opportunity to hear and see how the laboring poor represented themselves, as opposed to how they were represented by their social superiors. Barlow was a most interesting and, in terms of his writing, a most vocal person of the early modern period, caught in many ways between an old and a new age, apprenticeship and free labor, stability and unsettledness. On the "settled" hand, Barlow very deliberately observed the apprenticeship system in becoming a seaman. He was also a law-abiding and, at least to a certain extent, family-conscious man. But on the other, "unsettled" hand, Barlow could never form a collective cohesion with his co-workers—in this sense he was an atypical seaman—even though he became a kind of advocate for poor seamen as collectively oppressed. Most significantly, he suffered from a deep-rooted unsettledness. He was someone who from youth experienced detachment from place, family, friends, and even his co-workers.

Edward Barlow, in sum, is an example of a poor, lower-order subject who was not legally unsettled (in the official sense of vagrant) but who nevertheless

at times experienced unsettled subjectivity. After a time of doing odd jobs
around his hometown, he left home poor and illiterate at the age of fourteen
and set upon a course of continual displacement: shifting from job to job, apprenticeship to apprenticeship, and place to place, thus enacting what he often refers to as his "unsettled mind." Eventually Barlow settled as an apprentice in the "calling" of seaman. But given the intimate associations in the
period between seamen and vagrants, which we shall pursue, such a "settling
down" was often the equivalent of vagabondage. Barlow's manuscript journal-
cum-autobiography of some 225,000 words (he somehow attained literacy
during his travels) and 147 pages of self-made illustrations—mostly of ships
arriving at or departing from ports—extensively and vividly charts a subjectivity both occupationally settled on seaman and psychologically unsettled as
perpetual journeyman or "nowhere man." Barlow's unsettled subjectivity, in
effect, sails alongside (and as the dark side of) his fixed seaman self. He
typifies unsettled subjectivity as experienced occasionally, if not all the time,
by the working poor of early modern England.

I conclude, in part 3, by extending the discussion of Barlow's private and
"historical" journal to consider public and fictional representations of seamen that were marketed primarily to the lower orders: specifically, broadside
street ballads. The preoccupation of the seventeenth century with seamen is
evident in the burgeoning of seaman ballads, especially in the second half of
the century. Here we witness the period's anxiety about seamen as workers
that were both essential but also threateningly unstable, an anxiety that was
part of a general wrestling with the strengths and feared weaknesses of lower-
order mobility. What we find through an exploration into ballads about seamen is an insistent and comforting touting of placed constancy or settledness
as most profitable (psychologically, socially, and—for both buyers and sellers of ballads—economically). But at the same time, these ballads acknowledge the concomitant profitability of representing the facts and even the
delights of change or mobility. Indeed, the ballads offer their lowly audience
inconsistency and unsettledness at "no cost." They provide a smorgasbord of
perspectives, roles, and voices, which the audience—listening or singing
along in the streets, the alehouse, or elsewhere—can vagrantly sample at will,
whether or not they ever pay the penny or halfpenny to buy the ballad.[27] Ballads in effect market multifarious, dispersed, and provisional identities. They
sell "free" unsettled subjectivity. And in so doing, they point us to a future
study of lowly street literature—what one might call the "spacious voices"—
of early modern England, as much as to a new class of unmoored and global
workers.

Acknowledgments

The making of this book has itself been a practice of unsettled labor, not only in the intellectual trajectory the project has taken but in my actual travels in pursuing research. I have especially benefited from archival research at the Huntington Library in San Marino, California, and—during one particularly intense and memorable summer—at the National Maritime Museum, Greenwich; the British Library, London; and the Pepys Library, Magdalene College, Cambridge. The feeling of unsettledness—of utter displacement from "home"—was never more forcefully brought home to me than when, at the end of that season of far-flung research in 2001, my gaze fixed in total stillness on a television screen in a Greenwich hotel lobby on September 11.

For their support over the years, I'd like to thank Leah Marcus, Deborah Harkness, Lena Cowen Orlin, Paul Alpers, Jean Howard, Rich McCoy, Pat Parker, Andrew McRae, Sean Shesgreen, Don Wayne, and all the Early Modern Center faculty and graduate students in the English Department here at my home institution, the University of California, Santa Barbara. Special thanks go to Chris Nelson (the department's former staff manager), Mark Rose (its former chair), and David Marshall (dean of UCSB's Division of Humanities and Fine Arts) for their unfailing support in my time of illness, and beyond. And extra special thanks go to Richard Helgerson, who read more versions of the manuscript than I'm sure he cared to and who is, quite simply, the best colleague one could ever have.

During a year at the Huntington Library, I was aided in my research by Roy Ritchie, Director of Research, as well as by Mary Robertson, Curator of Manuscripts (British History). Subsequent aid was kindly and promptly provided by Stephen Tabor, the Huntington's Curator of Early Printed Books. During my visits to the Caird Library at the National Maritime Museum, Greenwich, to study Edward Barlow's manuscript (as well as during subsequent correspondence with the library), I was kindly assisted by Jill Terrell, Head of Library and Manuscripts, and her knowledgeable staff: Daphne

Knott, Manuscripts Archivist; Andrew Davis, Curator of Manuscripts; and Anne Buchanan, Library Assistant. Brian Thynne, Curator of Hydrography, and David Taylor, Picture Librarian, were also attentive guides at the NMM.

I am further indebted for help during my early thinking on Barlow to a fruitful seminar exchange at the Huntington in which Mark Burnett, Cynthia Clegg, J. P. Conlan, Ron Bedford, and Douglas Brooks participated. Also instrumental were the insights that (along with a special edition of *English Literary Renaissance*) emerged from my participation in a session of the North American Conference on British Studies on the topic of rogue pamphlets with Lee Beier, Arthur Kinney, Linda Woodbridge, and David Harris Sacks. Stephen Greenblatt's keen comments assisted with finishing touches on the manuscript.

The research that underlies this book could not have been accomplished without the help of many. Thanks to Jayne Stevenson of Red Rose Research for her resourceful inquiries into Edward Barlow's life and family; to Andrea Cordani, webmaster of East India Company Ships (http://www.eicships.info), for great tidbits about Barlow's last voyage; to Roze Hentschell, for early help hunting down books and facts; and to Yanoula Athanassakis, for sanity-sustaining assistance in producing the bibliography of the completed manuscript. A special thanks must go to Alan Thomas at the University of Chicago Press for holding steadfast to his belief in my abilities over the long and sometimes rocky haul; to Randy Petilos for keeping me on track in the busy last stages of manuscript production; and to Nancy Trotic for her keen copyediting.

Financial support for my study was provided by the National Endowment for the Humanities, the University of California Office of the President, UCSB's English Department and Division of Humanities and Fine Arts, and the John Simon Guggenheim Memorial Foundation. The Guggenheim officers were extraordinarily flexible and caring in response to an unexpected need for flexibility over when to take the award; they are a humanities foundation that deserves, in the fullest sense of the term, the title "humane."

A version of chapter 3 was published as "Making Vagrancy (In)Visible: The Economics of Disguise in Early Modern Rogue Pamphlets" in *English Literary Renaissance* (2003) and reprinted in *Rogues and Early Modern English Culture*, edited by Craig Dionne and Steve Mentz (University of Michigan Press, 2004). Early versions of parts of chapters 1, 2, and 4 appeared together as "London's Vagrant Economy: Making Space for 'Low' Subjectivity" in *Material London circa 1600*, edited by Lena Cowen Orlin (University of Pennsylvania Press, 2000).

Finally, I must turn with thanks to the harboring presence of my family. At all times drawing me home, whatever the nature of my journey—sometimes with self-demanding fixity—is my daughter, Lian Fumerton-Liu. Both intellectual stay and fellow traveler in my studies is my husband, Alan Liu. Husband, partner, friend, colleague—Alan provides me with the intellectual guidance and emotional stability that allow me always to find "home." It is to him that I dedicate this book.

A Note on the Text

In all titles and quotations throughout the text of this book, spelling and, where helpful for clarifying meaning, aberrations in orthography and punctuation have been regularized to modern American usage. This is true of citations from both older and modern works. In addition, I have not preserved the seemingly erratic capitalizations of words in texts by seventeenth- and eighteenth-century authors, nor the changes in the font of ballads made by early modern printers to distinguish titles, proper names, places, refrains, and printers' imprints—changes that nineteenth- and twentieth-century editors often, though irregularly, indicate through italicization. Such italicization has been dropped because it places undue emphasis on words. Finally, abbreviations have been silently expanded.

For convenience in locating original texts, however, titles of texts in the notes and in the selected bibliography are provided in the original spelling (with the exception that u's and v's, long s's, and i's as j's are regularized) and, with less rigor, in the original punctuation. Thus, titles will be modernized and Americanized in the body of the book but not in the notes or bibliography.

Dates in parentheses indicate the year that a work was first published, unless otherwise indicated. If multiple dates are given, they indicate successive editions of the work. If publication was considerably delayed or never occurred, the date in parentheses is the estimated date the work was composed. Published ballads, in addition to usually being anonymous, are often not dated, and their publication dates can be very difficult to pin down. In all cases of uncertainty, dates are given in square brackets and are usually based on information provided in Pollard & Redgrave's *Short-Title Catalogue* (1475–1640), Wing's *Short-Title Catalogue* (1641–1700), and the *Early English Books Online (EEBO)*.

꘎ PART ONE ꘌ

Unsettled Subjects

Mobilizing the Poor

In 1594, Thomas Spickernell was listed by the town clerk of Maldon, Essex, as among those disaffected toward the Puritan magistracy and was described as "sometime apprentice to a bookbinder; after, a vagrant peddler; then, a ballad singer and seller; and now, a minister and alehouse-keeper in Maldon."[1] "Minister," taken in the religious sense (as clergyman or, more generally, agent of a faith), would seem to be the key appellation in this list of occupations—given the intent of the clerk to indicate spiritual deviance. But the title is arrived at through the loosest of temporal connections—"sometime," "after," "then," "now"—and fails to achieve a culminating position of prominence in the list of occupations. Rather, "minister" is displaced from such a preeminent seat by the highly secular nomen "alehouse-keeper" (with which "minister" shares syntactical as well as temporal and geographical space). One might at this point even heretically question the spirituality of the term "minister" and conclude that it is not meant in the religious sense at all, but in the secular meaning of "servant," "attendant," or "administrator"—of ale, not faith.[2]

Such a deviant slippage from sacral to secular place, whether consciously made by the clerk or not, may well have been inspired by the lone descriptor in the sequence of occupations: "vagrant." No matter what the clerk's prioritizing intent, no occupation in his list can necessarily follow another, and none can achieve sole preeminence, because all are versions of the same perceived lack of acceptable occupation: *a profession of vagrancy*. This is the real heresy posed by Spickernell (so insidiously that it has infiltrated the clerk's own logic). As a "sometime apprentice," Spickernell was "masterless," free of the binding terms and regulatory "freedom" of a company. Given that most printers/bookbinders were in London, Spickernell's former master was probably of London's Company of Stationers. The casualness implied by "sometime" suggests that Spickernell did not finish his term, which was, indeed, the case with 60 percent of the apprentices in London at this time.[3] He was thus unsupervised, unplaced, and socially vagrant. As a peddler wandering from place to place selling his wares, he was not only socially but also physically and legally vagrant (hence the specific designation as such in the clerk's list). "Peddler" or "petty chapman" was included among the illegal occupations detailed in the vagrancy acts of 1572 and 1598, and although in 1604 peddlers and tinkers were omitted from a new vagrancy act, they continued to be harassed. Thus, in 1637 the petty chapman Thomas Bassett found himself accused of "wandering as a vagrant" and "selling false and counterfeit jewels" by the Salisbury authorities; he was subsequently punished.[4] The type is imaged in figure 1. In addition to necklaces, pins, lace, gloves, and other such trinkets, the "vagrant" peddler would almost certainly carry pamphlets, chapbooks (cheap books) and/or ballads for sale, perhaps singing snatches of the latter to advertise his wares. As "ballad singer and seller" alone, Spickernell would not have been officially labeled vagrant but would have nevertheless often been treated as such (Prys Williams, for example, was punished in 1616 for being "a ballad-singer and vagrant")[5] and would have frequented the same places as the peddler: street corners, fairs, markets, theaters, bear-baitings, wakes, and anywhere else people congregated. As unsettled print trades, Spickernell's alternative occupations ("sometime apprentice to a bookbinder," "vagrant peddler," "ballad singer and seller") are essentially interchangeable.

To be "now" an alehouse-keeper was to site provisionally, and thus suspiciously, all three of the above "professions," since unsettled laborers (including runaway apprentices and servants), peddlers, and ballad singers would all frequent the alehouse for food, lodging, sales, and the hope of finding service.[6] Finally, all such groups also came together under the nomen of disaffected "minister" in the term's secular sense (the alehouse-keeper "ministering" ale to his customers), as well as—at least in the minds of many authorities, such as Maldon's clerk—its religious meaning. On the latter score, officials often suspected the unsettled of being recusants, radical Protestants, or irreligious— especially when gathered together at ungodly assembly points such as alehouses—not because many itinerants were indeed such religious dissidents, but because by the very nature of their mobility, they were considered wholly deviant.[7] From the perspective of authority in a patriarchal and theoretically static society, the laboring poor who moved from job to job and place to place were tremendously threatening and subversive, whatever their actual religious or political position might be.

What begs for exploration here is the connection—or, more accurately, the heretical disconnection—in early modern England that linked makeshift "professions" (such as those undertaken by Spickernell and like poor workers) and the lower-order subject.[8] As an end point to such an investigation, my study aims to make space for a new notion of "low" subjectivity—economic, social, psychological, and metonymic—that escaped the "bound" and made a home of homelessness. An originary trace of such an unbound subject can be detected in a newly emergent economy characterized by mobility, diversity, alienation, freedom, and tactical (as opposed to strategic or *authorized*) craft. Traced through this unsettled economy, the largely invisible laboring poor glimpsed in the case of Spickernell emerge as distinctive subjects but with potentially extensive reach. Indeed, they have the potential to embrace metonymically many of the lower orders (not just the indigent and homeless) of early modern England: mobile wage laborers, on land and at sea; unstable servants and apprentices; and even some of the multitasked poor household-ers of the period, both men and—perhaps even more so—women. Our gaze is thus low but elastic: it extends beyond the legally vagrant/itinerant poor and the crisis years in which they emerged during the late sixteenth and early seventeenth centuries to include consideration of how such crises might subtly and sometimes insidiously penetrate the home and extend into the deep substructure of the later seventeenth century. In order to make visible such an elastic connectedness, however, we need to rethink not only our traditional theories of place as hierarchical and stable, but also our traditional notions of subjectivity as "high" or erudite and as unitary or consistent. We must make more class-specific the totalizing language of exchange and theatricality, or self-fashioning, that has—as Christopher Pye rightly sees—marked (and marketed) new historicist notions of early modern subjectivity.[9] The first part of my book thus concludes by positing a theory of "low" subjectivity that is itself unsettled: a subjectivity that could invest in multiple types of "selves" (whether additionally, intermittently, or provisionally) and that itself might be only casually or occasionally held.

My goal, then, is to open up our perspective of the low to consider a large body of physically and psychologically unsettled poor, not just those determined in the period to be legally vagrant. But the judged vagrant remain vital to this study because so many of them were in fact itinerant laborers. There is further value in looking at those labeled and arrested for vagrancy as a group if we read the evidence about them as representations rather than simply facts, because study of the arrested "vagrant" renders transparent the contemporary preconceptions and misconceptions about the unsettled poor in general. We shall, then, begin at rock bottom—however slippery or shifting the ground—and trace the unmooring of the poorer subject in the tide of labeled "vagrants"—however inaccurate or misleading the term—that appeared to overrun late sixteenth- and early seventeenth-century England. This will be the focus of the present chapter.

Many factors—none of which were singularly "new" in the period[10]—conspired to create a proliferation of dispossessed laborers in Elizabethan and

Jacobean England and, more importantly, a contemporary sensibility that vagrancy had reached new crisis levels. Heather Dubrow has studied two frequent causes of homelessness and migration: the loss of parents and the loss of dwellings due to fire or property disputes.[11] The list goes on: rising population and unemployment (especially in the economic depressions of the 1590s, 1620s, and 1630s), decreases in noble households and hospitality, rising rents (to 1650), the conversion of copyhold tenures to leaseholds (fueling property disputes), high agricultural prices, and low wages. All were among the many significant factors contributing to an increase—and, more importantly, a *felt* increase—in the number of dispossessed poor. Anxiety over the perceived rise in physical unsettledness manifested itself in a number of ways: the escalation of official proclamations and statutes against "Rogues, Vagabonds and Sturdy Beggars"; the upsurge throughout the country in alehouses, which catered especially to the poor and homeless; contemporary impressions of an epidemic of masterless men; the expansion of slum tenements and suburbs in cities; dramatic increases in mandatory and spontaneous roundups of perceived vagrants; and the massive proliferation of beggar and rogue literature, to name but a few.[12]

In actuality, towns (such as Maldon) bore the brunt of the problem of the displaced and impoverished, and by the 1620s many towns felt overwhelmed.[13] During crisis years, we find, the numbers of indigent in urban societies could rise to 20 percent or more, far outstripping the usual 5 percent slated for poor relief.[14] Those unprovided for, or inadequately provided for (mostly members of the laboring poor struggling all along to stave off penury), necessarily resorted to begging, theft, and/or migration to other towns in search of food, lodging, and opportunity. But many towns strictly enforced the Tudor poor laws, ejecting poor migrants of recent date, which often compelled the migrant to become perpetually unsettled.[15] Driven (and sometimes whipped) from town to town, the urban mobile poor occupied not so much a place as a *space* of alienation. A caveat: the conditions that might open up such an alien space of unsettledness were widely variable (dependent on such factors as originary status, family size, gender, and locality), as were the different ways the space of unsettledness might be inhabited. The latter was especially the case for those wage laborers or housed poor who might only metonymically associate themselves with the unsettled subject, as we shall see most clearly in the life of the seaman Edward Barlow. But even among the legally vagrant, there was no cast-iron type. Vagrants were not all identical or interchangeable. There were, however, some typical features to the unsettled experience that allow us to formulate the following broad, if tentative, generalizations.

First and foremost we might stress the common detachment of the urban itinerant from any sense of stable community. The myth of a vagrant subculture, promulgated in the contemporary rogue literature of Thomas Harman, Robert Greene, and Thomas Dekker, among others, has been debunked by recent historians of vagrancy. Peaking in the 1590s and early 1600s, when itinerancy was on the increase because of severe economic depression, such rogue literature depicted the unsettled as professional criminals organized in gangs of an alternative culture replete with hierarchy and canting language. Little historical evidence supports this imagined criminal community. When the mobile poor engaged in crime other than vagrancy, it was most often petty and impromptu. The average English itinerant traveled alone or with one other person. And gatherings—such as occurred at markets, fairs, or alehouses—were mostly spontaneous. Indeed, as Paul Slack points out, the physically unsettled

> might have their familiar haunts in a local ale-house, an isolated barn, or a lodging-house like that of John Matthew, a Salisbury hosier, but whether they relied on petty crime or persuasive begging for their livelihood, or were genuinely seeking work, their chances of success depended on their relative solitude. They also often depended on a certain anonymity, hence the frequency of aliases in these records.[16]

The Salisbury register of arrested vagrants, 1598–1669, which provides us with one of the fullest surviving records of the physically unsettled in the early modern period, is peppered with such aliases adopted by itinerants in their efforts (often vain) to cover their tracks: "John Heyward *alias* Chrowche *alias* Hancock, an idle vagrant person was punished," notes the entry for January 26, 1599; "Margaret Legge *alias* Jackson *alias* Smyth was found wandering as a vagrant, not giving any reason or account of her wandering" (nor presumably of her change of names), declares an entry on January 11, 1610. Whatever her "real" identity, we know that Margaret escaped whipping because she was pregnant.[17] The inability or refusal of officials to fill in more information about these arrested vagrants and their various identities contributes to our unsettling sense of an anonymous and—in the sequential listing of aliases—displaced identity.

Solitary wandering and a kind of anonymity marked the unsettled subject's detachment not only from any stable community but also, as in the case of Margaret and her unborn child, from any complete family. "Family structure among vagrants," remarks A. L. Beier in *Masterless Men*, "is a story of fragments, of individuals cut adrift from kin and masters."[18] Under economic duress, husbands deserted their families—in such numbers that a vagrancy statute of 1610 stipulated "that all such persons so running away, shall be taken and deemed to be incorrigible rogues"[19]—while abandoned wives often took to the roads to seek them out and/or to beg. In 1582 Anne Smyth, sadly, was twice so deserted by her husband, and the second time cheated by him as well. Apprehended in Warwick, she explained that she dwelled in Lincoln but that her husband had left her about six weeks earlier.

> And she following after to seek him found him here at Warwick on the fair day the first day of May last. And he brought her to an alehouse where he left her and willed her to tarry there until he came out of the market and then he would keep her company and so with fair word went away from her and took from her a cloak and since then she did not see him.[20]

The proliferation of "ands" in this report (no fewer than seven), with few subordinating clauses, verbally enacts Anne's bleak experience of displacement: one event follows and replaces another, with little change but in the details, such as the loss of a cloak. But such loss does not deter Anne's determined wandering. Cloakless, she continues searching for her husband. Many such deserted wives wandered from town to town in the late sixteenth and early seventeenth centuries. Despite the increase in displaced married women, however, most of the physically unsettled at this time were children, adolescents, and young adults. Whether leaving home because of a parental loss of the kind Dubrow so feelingly describes, or to help relieve family poverty, or to hide a pregnancy, or as punishment for the deed, the majority of these youths were single and unattached. About half were single men; a quarter were single women.[21]

Liaisons, licit and illicit, were formed among this generation of unsettled youths, but they were mostly unstable and short-term. For this reason, traditional terms such as *family* or *household* seem highly inadequate to describe the kind of social ties itinerants formed; "modular affective units" might be a more accurate, if too clinical, phrase.[22] In this context, physical separation was not so much a breaking of the marriage tie as an expected part of it. Such fluid bonding characterized even the marriages of laboring peddlers and petty chapmen, who often came from the ranks of unsettled youths and were likewise often persecuted for vagrancy. In her extensive study of these itinerant salespersons, Margaret Spufford provides numerous accounts of wives separated from husbands for long periods of time, each partner wandering as if they occupied parallel, unplaceable universes (some were not even able to name what town they were in when "arrested" by authorities). Bernard Barrye was typical: "terming himself a petty chapman," he was arrested in Salisbury on September 8, 1612, for "wandering as a vagrant," and he had "a wife and child wandering about Dorchester." Such marital *dis*-union, Spufford posits, suggests "the possible lightness of attachment represented by marriage, particularly amongst the very poorest" of these traders.[23] Findings of an increase in "quasi-uxorial" relationships between migrant women and single male employers in late sixteenth- and early seventeenth-century urban environments (by Michael Roberts) and of a high incidence of remarriages of expediency among the Norwich poor (by Margaret Pelling) would seem to support Spufford's hypothesis.[24] The Salisbury register included many such chapmen and peddlers, together with lists of other young couples temporarily coming together and disbanding in loose sexual/affective relationships. Officials carefully noted such laxity, or, as they termed it, "lewd living." Slack provides a tally of the entries:

> There were 17 couples . . . described as "living lewdly together, being unmarried"; ten single women were spared punishment because they were pregnant; another 17 were sent back to their husbands, while one man alleged that he "travelleth from place to place to seek his wife who is departed from him, and here he persuaded one Felton's daughter that he would marry her."[25]

When one considers how little information was usually recorded by authorities about those arrested for vagrancy, this is an especially impressive list.

Of course, officials themselves played a significant part in fragmenting sexual/affective bonds among the unsettled. Again and again we hear of "couples" who claim they are married but "on examination" by authorities admit they are not. Their common fate: punishment and then separation, each directed to their individual birthplaces or last dwellings. Usually such partners were sent far afield from each other, even to opposite reaches of the realm and beyond. When on March 24, 1601, for instance, "Ralph Johnson, a vagrant, was found with Joan Maddocke in a kind of lewd life, alleging her to be his wife, which on examination appears untrue," Joan was first punished and then given a passport to St. Albans, Hertfordshire; Ralph was sent via Bristol to Ireland. And so ended that "marriage."[26] Hoping to ward off the financially debilitating oxymoron of a "vagrant family," parishes would go so far as to separate parents from children and break apart not only casual alliances but also legal marriages of long-term residents if such unions were made by poor wage earners (the group most vulnerable to destitution in an age of high prices and low wages). As Ian W. Archer points out, for example, by the late 1590s some parishes in London "required the poor to remove their own offspring because of the threat of an extra burden on the rates." So, too, the justices of Oxford, Slack observes, "made vagrants distribute their children in the parishes where they happened to have been born and had a settlement, while the parents were ordered elsewhere."[27] The right to seize a "beggar child," if between the ages of five and fourteen, and to compel the child into service or apprenticeship—with or without the parents' consent—was written into the vagrancy statute of 1547, regularly reiterated in subsequent laws, and institutionalized with the parish apprenticeship system of 1598.[28] Pursuing a more drastic line of forced separation and employment, the Virginia Company in 1619 transported several hundred poor children from London's Bridewell to serve as laborers in the New World. In 1627 another fourteen to fifteen hundred were shipped out, and in 1653 four hundred Irish children were, in the words of a contemporary, stolen "out of their beds" and likewise exported.[29] These were extreme measures of forced separation and servitude. But all such interventionist laws and actions, even when well-intentioned, "quite deliberately broke up families," as Slack notes.[30]

Particularly striking is the case of the wage laborer Anthony Adams, cited by Alice Clark. In 1618 Adams complained to the justices that he was born and bred in Stockton and had

> taken great pains for my living all my time since I was able and of late I fortuned to marry with an honest young woman, and my parishioners not willing I should bring her in the parish, saying we should breed a charge amongst them. Then I took a house in Bewdley and there my wife doth yet dwell and I myself do work in Stockton . . . and send or bring my wife the best relief I am able, and now the parish of Bewdley will not suffer her to dwell there for doubt of further charge. . . . I most humbly crave your good aid and help in this my distress or else my poor wife and child are like to perish without the doors: . . . that by your good help and order to the parish of Stockton I may have a house there to bring my wife and child unto that I may help them the best I can.[31]

Though treated by the officials of Stockton and Bewdley as a high risk for ending up on poor relief, Adams clearly perceives himself as a hard, if poor, worker, forced by the local parishioners into a situation of risky unsettledness—working in one place and commuting back and forth to his family in another. He implies that without the justices' aid, he will be further forced by the towns of Stockton and Bewdley to realize their worst fears: to abandon his young wife and child to a certain death as homeless, "without the doors." He would thus unwillingly become yet another deserting husband of the time.

Adams's only other option—one that was frequently taken by families in times of prolonged economic crisis, especially in the early seventeenth century—was emigration to another town.[32] But as the response of the town of Bewdley suggests, to attempt to move to another town was to start down a road of almost certain homelessness and, finally, family fragmentation. Passed from town to town (no town wanting to accept them for fear of draining the parish poor-relief fund), such families could not hold themselves together. "Persons departed," Beier observes, "sometimes never to return, or only to meet many years later."[33] The dissipation of the Coxe family, as told by Slack, is typical: "Thomas Coxe, his wife, and two children had an apprentice with them when they were whipped as vagrants and sent from Salisbury to Gaddesden, Hertfordshire, in March 1624. . . . Eleven months later the family was taken in Salisbury and whipped again, but the apprentice and one of the children had by then disappeared. The household," Slack concludes, "was gradually being fragmented and degraded."[34]

Among the unsettled of the sixteenth and seventeenth centuries, then, we find a large population of urban youths necessarily forming only "modular affective units" (whether legally bound together or not). Extending in the early seventeenth century to include even "established" families and households, such as the Coxes, such affective ties were subject to rupture, fragmentation, and dispersal, to being detached from any stable community or cohesive family structure. The mostly young itinerants so affected wandered from place to place, tentatively forming and re-forming relationships, enacting their alienation from any settled whole. When we follow these unsettled subjects to London—the favorite destination of the itinerant poor—our understanding of such alienation is mirrored, intensified, and expanded in new ways.

What emerges particularly clearly on the London scene is the "economy" of unsettledness implied in my narrative above, an economy supported by peddlers and petty chapmen like Barrye and Spickernell (in one of his roles), wage laborers like Adams, and mobile craftsmen like Coxe (who, notably, had an apprentice in tow). Such a mobile economy involved not only the legally vagrant, but also the "respectable" yet unstable servant and apprentice classes; it even touched poor householders, especially women. For as "shallow poverty" spread in the course of the seventeenth century, the housed poor were increasingly forced to mobilize their labor in a makeshift, grab-bag fashion—resulting in a kind of "at-home" unsettledness.

London's Economy of Unsettledness—and Beyond

London bore the brunt of the problem with the unsettled poor in early modern England. The city grew rapidly over the course of the late sixteenth and seventeenth centuries (from about 120,000 in 1550 to 200,000 in 1600, 375,000 in 1650, and 490,000 in 1700), and the numbers of the dispossessed grew even faster, at least up until the 1650s. According to A. L. Beier and Roger Finlay in *London, 1500–1700*, while London's population quadrupled from 1560 to 1625, the vagrancy rate rose twelvefold. Such burgeoning numbers are unlikely to have fallen off during the severe economic depression of the 1630s, which drove whole families onto the roads. Indeed, many of London's unsettled poor came from the swell of immigrants that flooded the city and its suburbs—on the order of some ten thousand a year.[1] About half of these new immigrants were apprentices,[2] though increasingly in the seventeenth century, apprentices and the larger, growing class of servants (and servant women) came from areas closer to hand: from neighboring southeastern England or from within the city or suburbs of London itself. Most interestingly, such "housed" apprentices and servants, whether imported or home-grown, made up the largest body of persons arrested for vagrancy in London.[3] This points to a resonant possibility: that over the course of the seventeenth century, displaced labor became more "at home"—more part of a makeshift economy and lived experience of lower-order unsettledness. That is, the poor, even poor householders, increasingly found themselves living in an unstable state of subsistence poverty in which they had to hustle in multiple, shifting by-employments to just get by—a kind of placed mobility.

In a way, of course, the idea of "native" unsettledness conspicuously comments on the metropolis as a whole. For there is a sense in which displacement, transience, and instability were inherent or native to early modern London. For many, to be a Londoner in the late sixteenth and seventeenth centuries was to experience a degree of unsettling alienation and anonymity. As Beier and Finlay observe, in the city of London

> almost everyone was a migrant; the operation of the labor market, together with child-care by nurses, meant that many people lacked family ties or any sense of belonging. Relatively poor communications made it very difficult to keep in touch with relatives; there was no Post Office until the later seventeenth

century. In periods of peak alien immigration, language and dialect problems would also have been encountered.

"All this," they conclude, "provided the conditions for a sense of isolation and insecurity with possible psychosocial effects."[4] Margaret Pelling finds further evidence of such unsettledness in an everyday "mode of metropolitan living which was mobile, the effect of constant movement in and out of the city on a periodic, even daily basis." Business, pleasure, and the pursuit of health lured and drove Londoners back and forth, into and out of the city, to the extent that they might be termed "skirters" ("town-dwellers following patterns of living which involved avoidance of, as much as commitment to, urban environments"). Subject to such constant mobility, households could periodically find themselves divided apart.[5] As late as 1659, the newly apprenticed seaman Edward Barlow, on the verge of sailing away from London after migrating there from Lancashire, seemed momentarily overwhelmed by the feelings of estrangement that such unsettledness could arouse. London stretched out before him as a great place of leave-taking and personal rupture. He wrote poignantly of

> leaving that famous city of London, where many, both rich and poor, have taken a farewell both of their friends and country, little thinking that it would be the last time that they should see them. Here hath the husband parted with the wife, the children from the loving parent, and one friend from another, which have never enjoyed the sight of one another again.[6]

Barlow's grand vision of London as the site of massive fragmentation of families and friends (occasioned, in his biased view, by departures for destinations overseas) finds earlier expression by a London parish parson at a more local level, reflecting his own circumscribed, landed position. The parson, writing between 1587 and 1590, commented that every twelve years or so, "the most part of the parish changeth, as I by experience know, some going and some coming." This situation, Lawrence Stone remarks, resembles nothing so much as modern-day Los Angeles. Even in seventeenth-century English villages, Stone continues, some 30 to 40 percent of the population migrated in any given ten-year span.[7]

We will hear from Barlow again later in this chapter, and most extensively in the second part of this study, where as a seaman he exemplifies the landless and mobile wage laborer of a new proletariat emerging in the course of the seventeenth century. Furthermore, though he is an (eventually) occupationally defined subject, Barlow evinces signs of a deeply ingrained unsettled subjectivity. But for the moment we should resist overemphasizing his expressed feelings of severance—he was, after all, on the point of his first overseas

departure ("not knowing what dangers might befall me as I was now going to
seek my fortune in the ocean of seas and in foreign lands"), a critical parting
that might well have triggered an intense but momentary sense of generaliz-
able isolation.[8] Furthermore, as Ian W. Archer cautions, we need to recognize
that "the obligations of neighborhood were taken seriously" in London,[9] even
in the face of intense fragmentation and mobility of the kind Barlow and the
London parson describe.

Jeremy Boulton's study of the seventeenth-century suburban district of
Boroughside, in the parish of St. Saviour's, Southwark, corroborates Archer's
qualification: coexistent with high mobility in the area, Boulton finds, operated "a network of neighborly obligations and interactions." In fact, his
figures present a slightly different vision of mobility than that of the whole-
sale changeover described by our London parish parson. Records for Boroughside show that in a ten-year period in the early seventeenth century,
roughly 75 percent of heads of households there shifted residence, a figure
that would largely substantiate the parson's sense of change. But Boulton also
finds that much of this mobility occurred within Boroughside itself, often at
a very local level (e.g., across the street or one or two blocks over). Of course,
the district of Boroughside was much larger and more prosperous than many
London parishes and thus could more easily contain change. Furthermore,
much of Boulton's evidence of neighborliness comes from the wills and official
services of the more stable and affluent sorts. Such established contemporaries, as Boulton himself observes, generally associated prosperity with stability; and, in fact, those making repeated moves tended to be of the poorer sorts
(for instance, recent arrivals hoping to escape official notice or locals suffering from economic hardship).[10] A tally of these intensively unsettled poor
would increase substantially if we focused on a suburban district less wealthy
than Boroughside (such as St. George's parish) or added to their numbers
those persons excluded from the registers of Boroughside householders,
upon which Boulton relies: namely, the unhoused local poor and the many
transients just passing through the district, as well as occasional inmates
(renters, whom most households harbored) and the detachable dependent
members of households. The latter includes children who left home, for
whatever reasons, as well as shifting servants and apprentices. It is especially
to the last workers that we must look if we are fully to pursue the experience
of unsettledness. For a sense of urban instability and disassociation would
have been intensely felt by many within these housed ranks of London's service orders.

Of course, in many important ways servants and apprentices little resembled the unsettled poor, especially those who would be subject to arrest as

vagrants. Servants and apprentices occupied important economic places in the city, constituting the majority of its dependent workforce—a third to a half of the labor force, according to the burial records of three seventeenth-century parishes. Though the number of apprentices declined in the latter half of the century, they remained an important sector of the urban population. In Beier's accounting, "apprentices are thought to have numbered 20,000 in London between 1640 and 1660, and domestic servants were probably several times more numerous." Drawing on the statistics gathered by D. V. Glass, Beier further calculates that by the 1690s "the two groups may have accounted for 121,000 people . . . or about a fifth of London's total population."[11] Apprentices, in particular, occupied not only sanctioned economic but also social positions in the city. They belonged to an elaborate guild system aimed at disciplining and socializing youth. Although this ordered structure placed apprentices "low" within its hierarchy, it held out the prospect of future advancement. Indeed, however "lowly" their status by virtue of being apprentices, many youths at the time of their apprenticeships could claim "high" family connections in the middling ranks and, increasingly in the seventeenth century, in the gentry.[12]

Paradoxically, though, such elevated social ties situated some apprentices in highly problematic "nowhere" positions—simultaneously high and low—which could destabilize a sense of secure place. Even more importantly, despite the trappings of "place," servants and apprentices in London in fact made up the group most liable to arrest for vagrancy, as noted above. Authorities especially suspected the unsettled inclinations of our "placed" apprentices. William C. Carroll notes that in official documents, " 'apprentices' was usually a term of contempt equal to, and essentially identical with, 'masterless men.' " Thus, disturbances involving apprentices, such as those that occurred in 1595, triggered an intensive roundup of suspected vagrants.[13] In *Youth and Authority*, Paul Griffiths attributes such suspicions about apprentices specifically to their "youth," which he describes as a "contested territory" whose dark side was envisioned by contemporary moralists to be unsettled, licentious, irreligious, rebellious, and dominated by a "vagrant will." Griffiths further investigates the criminalization of vagrancy and of "masterless" young people as part of efforts by authorities in the period to regulate youth.[14]

One of the fascinating discoveries of Griffiths's study of such youths is the equivalent intolerance in late sixteenth- and early seventeenth-century Norwich of, on the one hand, the out-of-town homeless and, on the other hand, locally housed but "masterless" youths who lived at home "out of service." Beginning in the seventeenth century, this intolerance extended especially to single young women who were living at home or independently "at their own hand." Crackdowns against such housed but masterless women occurred at the same time as heightened prosecutions against vagrants—during periods of economic hardship, for example in the years 1609–10 and 1630–36.[15] Merry Wiesner adds that "unmarried women working and living on their own were the most mistrusted" of these unsettled youths.[16] Unplaced female labor— standing outside the traditional contractual and male-supervised economic system—not only drew money away from the regularized work of apprentices and householders, but flaunted untoward female liberty (hence the frequent charging of women living independently with sexual offenses as well). Thus, whether working or not, whether housed or not, these usually poor women were liable to arrest. The daughter of widow Bensley, living at home with her mother, was charged for being "out of service" in December 1628 and December 1630, and was in just as much, if not more, trouble when she was found working "at her own hand" in 1634.[17] The young woman may well have been laboring in makeshift jobs in her mother's home all along. But since she was neither contracted, apprenticed, nor married, her labor was "out of place," in the sense both of being unsettled and of being unsettling. It caused, rather than cleared her of, the charges.[18]

Supervision by a widow rather than by a male householder—a common situation among those poor women arrested for being masterless—compounded the problem; as an independent woman, the widow could not sufficiently sanction or place the girl's position. Indeed, the widow was herself in a tenuous position of authority, as Griffiths points out. Not only was widow Bensley considered "not able to keep" her daughter, but "herself had been presented for 'lewdness and ill rule,' 'for frequenting the company of bearers of the infected,' and for lodging 'masterless' people."[19] These masterless people harbored by the widow would have included not only itinerant poor laborers but also, as the charges make clear, Bensley's own laboring daughter.

Though residing in their parents' or in their own independent lodgings, then, "at-home" youths, especially women such as Bensley's daughter—even when engaged in labor—were vulnerable to being labeled "vagrants" and to prosecution by officials as if they were just such idle tramps: they might be driven out of town or, more likely, incarcerated in a bridewell, put to supervised work, and instructed to find service, apprenticeship, or, in the case of women, a husband.[20] What is so intriguing about such prosecutions (which more often verged on persecution and shall hereafter be referred to as such) is that in the minds of contemporary authorities, the vagrant experience did not need to involve physical mobility or even homelessness. It was marked by being out of place, which included engagement in irregular or unsettled labor. We will want to consider more fully the association between housed but unsettled labor and poor women in the seventeenth century. But for the moment I propose that we cast our net farther. I propose that we pursue the idea of a metaphorical (or, perhaps more accurately, metonymic) experience of unsettledness implied in persecutions of "masterless" residents of either gender, specifically as the concept relates to the large constituency of "housed" servants and apprentices.

What I suggest is that, even without becoming physically displaced, members of the huge body of servants and apprentices, both male and female, in London and in other urban centers could very well have experienced conditions of unsettledness within their designated social, economic, and physical positions. In the most basic sense, such youths would have shared the sense of estrangement associated with London life that we have also identified with the physically unsettled poor. Like many other Londoners and the displaced poor, most servants and apprentices were immigrants, detached from local communities upon traveling to London for service. Also, like many other Londoners and itinerants, they were separated from their parental homes and were overwhelmingly young and single.[21] But, unlike other Londoners—yet especially like the physically unsettled—servants and apprentices were encouraged to remain unattached. As Beier remarks, "celibacy and sexual abstinence were written into apprenticeship indentures, and among servants it appears to have been exceptional, if not unheard of, for them to marry and have children while in service."[22]

Not only detached from their originary communities and homes but also barred from establishing their own families, such workers were caught in what amounted to a state of rupture. The extent to which an individual servant or apprentice might have experienced such dislocation or experienced it as a state of distress would have depended on many other aspects of his or her position. As Beier observes, "of servants in husbandry and domestics, a half to two-thirds . . . seem voluntarily to have changed masters each year, forsaking the security of steady employment, room, board and clothing."[23] By the end of the sixteenth century, it was increasingly difficult to tie both master and servant down to an annual contract. Not only was casual labor becoming financially preferable from the employers' viewpoint, but many servants appear to have embraced the resulting insecurity. Michael Roberts cites the example of the York servant Anne Godfray, "who owned only the clothes 'which she had upon her back,' and of whom her employer, a tiler's wife, said, 'she is but my servant for a while, and I cannot tell when she will go away, for she will be here tonight and away tomorrow.'"[24] Instability and dislocation, it would appear, were an accepted, perhaps even a desired, way of life for Anne Godfray and many other servants who found themselves in like conditions.

Among apprentices, we find a more complicated picture. Some apprentices, especially those from more well-to-do families and placed in lucrative trades, would have probably felt less unsettled, or might have regarded any insecurity they experienced (such as could have been elicited, for instance, by possible status tensions) as a transitional or temporary condition on the road to an established and settled socioeconomic position. Others might have accepted, even embraced, the fact of unsteady employment as "normal," as was perhaps the case with the servant Anne Godfray. Yet others might have felt more bleakly vulnerable. This would likely have been the case especially with parish apprentices taken from families desperately fractured by parental death, desertion, or destitution.

Certainly, the experience of service was fraught with potential fissures. The contracted term of apprenticeship was no security. Up to the mid-seventeenth century, service tended to be of short duration, and apprentices were at all times subject to layoff if a master died, suffered a financial setback, or left town. Disease was often the culprit. During outbreaks of plague or smallpox, householders routinely divided their households and fled the contagious city with the healthy. Contaminated servants and apprentices might thus find themselves left behind, abandoned. Indeed, Pelling argues that "smallpox was a major factor in eroding the conventions of service and apprenticeship" in the course of the seventeenth century, "especially those specifying the duty of care owed to the apprentice by the master, and the tight conventions about the breaking of indentures which were predicated on masters and apprentices living under the same roof."[25] Whatever the particular causative factor, violations of the seven-year apprenticeship term were so common, Beier points out, that "a contemporary singled out short apprenticeships and early marriages as causes of poverty and vagrancy." We know that 60 percent of London's apprentices in the early seventeenth century (and an even higher percentage of apprentices in other major cities, such as Norwich, Bristol, and Salisbury) never completed their terms.[26] Certainly, some of these apprentices profited from early termination, themselves breaking their indentures in order to return to their homes with their newly acquired skills, as Steve Rappaport conjectures. But given the large numbers of apprentices among those arrested for vagrancy, a less rosy picture of broken terms emerges on the urban scene.[27]

The case of a runaway apprentice arrested in the town of Warwick in the 1580s shows how easily a severed apprenticeship could devolve into unsettled labor and even vagrancy. The apprentice, Richard Fletcher, aged 13, was clearly from a family of some stature (he had lands in feoffment, and one of his friends, though of questionable character, was able to draw the interest of some gentry to his case). After the decease of the boy's mother (the father had died earlier), Fletcher had been apprenticed to Thomas Cook, a botcher, who mended clothes. In the course of the bailiff's interrogation of Fletcher—riveting for the sheer determination with which the boy insists "he would never serve" his master, despite entreaties, imprisonment, and threats—we learn that Fletcher (and his sister as well) has made a habit of casting off jobs. Townsend, the family friend entrusted with the children's care by their father, asserts "that he [Townsend] hath been a means both to place the boy and his sister divers times and hath done so. And that they will never tarry." This fault of not tarrying is attributed in part to Fletcher's mother, who married a poor man after her husband's death and "suffered the boy to go at large, who hath taken such a wandering as now will hardly be tied to tarry in any place." Given Fletcher's unsettled history, his friends and family as well as the authorities reiterate the same fear: that the boy will "roam at liberty." Such roaming might take the form of vagabondage or, as in Fletcher's history so far, a mode of unprofitable shifting between labors rather than settling on a single "honest" trade. His friends allege "that if he should be now suffered to roam at his plea-sure the boy would never fall to any trade but roam at liberty and so for lack of some honest trade or occupation or otherwise should in the end neither have stock of his rent nor land left to maintain him." The bailiff concurs; if the boy were released from his indenture, he asserts, "it might be a scope of fur-ther liberty." Townsend soberly adds, "If he should be suffered to go at large now the boy would be lost." Meanwhile, the boy himself insistently reiterates, "I will never serve him."[28]

The narrative, frustratingly, breaks off abruptly in the clerk's record, so we never learn Fletcher's fate. But the account, though only a fragment, shows how "placement" of a youth—even when that youth was relatively well-off and supported by a circle of family friends—could easily slide into libertine "placelessness" or roaming from job to job. It also throws some light, in Fletcher's defense of himself, on how problematic master-servant relations could be. The boy complains of abuse: both that deadly vermin in Cook's house threatened his health (Cook counters that the boy arrived infested) and that "everybody was his master" there, even the maids who chided him for fouling his bed (which the maids may well have shared with him).[29] This last comment points to potential gender tensions in addition to status tensions in apprenticeship positions. Edward Barlow, who went "a-liking" (on a two-week trial period) in a number of apprenticeships and other positions of service, con-sistently complained about his bossy mistresses. Indeed, in the apprentice contract, the apprentice was legally placed under the authority of both his master and his master's wife. Such an overturning of traditional gender roles could be complicated if there were unsettling relations with the master as well. Theoretically, and especially in the case of apprenticeships, masters were to provide an alternative family for their dependent laborers, guiding and instructing them as father figures. Surely many masters strove to realize this ideal. But as court records testify, mistreatment and violence were common (Fletcher complains of the former, and Barlow accuses one master in the trade of "whitester," or cotton bleacher, of both kinds of abuse).[30] Sexual relations between master and servant posed another threat. This problem evidently increased for young female servants in the course of the seventeenth century (as their numbers also grew). As Tim Meldrum notes, some advice manuals from the late seventeenth and early eighteenth centuries aimed at women as mistresses or servants hinted at the problem: unlike earlier literature, which idealized master-servant relations, these later manuals "displayed some ambivalence in their representation of ideal relations between master and maid, even if they sometimes reflected the earlier period's injunctions to reciprocity." The end result of the ideal gone awry could be devastating—physical displacement, prostitution, even suicide.[31]

The master-servant bond was thus at best insecure and at worst subject to gross violation, unmooring apprentices and servants from any secure social, economic, or physical place (however insubstantial such security had been all along). Dependent workers that were so cut loose—and we should remember that early in the century, some 60 percent of London apprentices never completed their indentures—might "roam at liberty" indeed, as all those concerned with Richard Fletcher of Warwick feared. But such roaming most likely took the form of continuing and displaced labor, a course of job-shifting in which Fletcher was already preliminarily engaged. That is, the liberated apprentice or servant might take to the suburbs or the back alleys of the city proper and practice a craft illegally and surreptitiously, without the "freedom" of a company. Such craft work outside the guilds became more common in the course of the seventeenth century, as the decline in numbers of those apprenticed testifies. Even more likely, though, an apprentice or servant at "liberty" might craftily take up and cast off jobs as they came to hand: at one point practicing a trade, next working as a wage laborer, next hawking ballads, pamphlets, or brooms, next shining shoes, begging, or stealing, next just roaming the streets, shops, and market stalls of London.[32]

It should be stressed that such shiftless trade-shifting was not solely a male prerogative. Although the scope of female labor was more restricted, women, such as Fletcher's sister, might also take up and cast off various crafts (spinning, stocking-knitting, lacework), hawk sundry goods on the streets, and, of course, sell themselves as prostitutes. Sara Mendelson and Patricia Crawford, in *Women in Early Modern England,* recount the nearly sixty-year saga of

Annis Cowper's unsettled labor within London, which begins with apprenticeship (an opportunity increasingly closed to women in London of the late sixteenth and early seventeenth centuries) and ends in suggestions of begging:

> Annis Cowper, the daughter of an embroiderer, was born about 1560. Her father died when she was young, so she lived with her stepfather, a cap-maker. At around 11 or 12 years of age, she was apprenticed in the same trade to William Giblett, with whom she served nine years, then worked for another cap-maker for eleven years. When Annis was about 30 years old, "the trade of capping then decaying," she lived in London with another woman, a costard monger (an apple seller), for twelve years. Subsequently she worked in an unspecified occupation with a Dutchman for six or seven years till he went abroad. A single woman aged 50, Annis then labored as a charwoman for two or three years, moving to live with an almswoman of the Salters' Company, Goodwife Goose. Later she worked with a poulterer, who ran away after a week leaving the rent unpaid. . . . some claimed that she had begged daily with the poulterer's wife.

The authors point out that "witnesses' accounts did not confirm all the details of this history." "Nevertheless," they add, "the picture is still one of vulnerability and recourse to a series of expedients."[33] In the case of Annis Cowper, her path of unsettled labor was apparently not caused by early termination of her apprenticeship, but by fluctuating fashion ("the trade of capping then decaying"). The net result, however, was the same: displacement from place to place and job to job. That Cowper so often sought lodging and labor with another man or woman suggests both the need for cooperative work among the very poor and Cowper's fear of being charged of living independently "at her own hand" or "out of service." Claims that she had been begging on the streets with the poulterer's wife are as much a product of Cowper's unstable situation as a reality. By virtue of her displaced, unsettled labor, she was subject to suspicion of vagabondage or beggary. Both women and men could in fact end up wandering far afield from their home town in their unsettled labors. Any one of these more nomadic laborers might have crossed paths with the industriously unsettled Thomas Spickernell, with whom we began, or his many look-alikes, who ended up wandering beyond London itself (one determined London master tracked his wayward apprentice all the way to Norwich).[34]

The case of London apprentices and servants thus allows us to reimagine the displacement of the poor both metonymically and expansively. In the previous chapter, we witnessed the formation of an experience of alienation in the detachment of itinerants from a stable or cohesive community and family. Here we have seen such an experience generally approximated in the nature of being a Londoner and more intensively in the socioeconomic group of London's servants and apprentices, whose often fractured and uncertain place as dependent laborers could render them psychically (if intermittently) unmoored, even while housed—that is, without becoming unsettled physically. What the special situation of London servants and apprentices "at large" further offers us is a way of understanding such a state of alienation and instability not only in terms of community and family, or of a metonymic association of shared feelings of displacement, but also, more literally and expansively, in terms of a new, fluid economy that produced, and was reliant upon, mobile and intermittent labor. Here the itinerant laborers, whom we have all along found grouped together with the vagrant by authorities of the period, come to the fore.

Many an apprentice who terminated his indenture or was terminated, as we have seen, joined this nomadic labor pool at the risk of being accused of vagrancy. Paul Slack provides the example of Edward Yovell. "A vagrant taken in Salisbury," Yovell "had been born in London and begun wandering after ending an apprenticeship in Worcester. Twice in two years he took up casual work back in London, where he had friends, then helped with the harvest at his uncle's in Surrey, next worked at various inns in Chichester, and finally returned to Worcester via Salisbury, Bristol and Gloucester, where he might hope for casual work, or charity." Ilana Krausman Ben-Amos cites a host of other such mendicant laborers among early modern youths, with examples extending well into the eighteenth century. One youth born in 1745 worked at various times as an errand boy, a domestic servant, a gunmaker's apprentice, a pitman, a coachman, a driver, an agricultural laborer, a beggar, and a gardener.[35]

It is but a side step from such diversely employed youths, dispersed spatially as well as economically over the English landscape, to the peddlers and chapmen of all ages who increasingly in the seventeenth century linked town and country in a network of exchange. So necessary were these tradesmen to the dissemination of consumer goods that the new vagrancy law of 1604 omitted them from the list of the legally vagrant (though, as we have seen, they continued to be persecuted well into the late seventeenth century).[36] Spickernell was seizing an opportunity and capitalizing on a demand when he shifted from being an apprentice for a bookbinder to working as a peddler. Peddlers and petty chapmen specialized in trading in the diverse cheap luxury goods of a burgeoning domestic economy, discussed at length by Joan Thirsk. The late sixteenth and seventeenth centuries, Thirsk notes, saw the rise of new goods that capitalized on surplus labor. Lacework, stocking-knitting, the making of pins and buttons, and the distilling of aqua vitae were all such new trades.[37] That they were conceived of not only as requiring few start-up costs but also as occupying a space outside the traditional labor force is suggested by the setting up of arrested vagrants to work in such trades in institutions designed during this period for employing the poor. Among the twenty-six "Arts, Occupations, Labors, and Works, to be Set Up in Bridewell" in London, for instance, were included such new domestic labors as the making of nails, gloves, combs, "inkle and tape," silk lace, pins, points, bays, and felts, as well as the knitting of hose, spinning of linen yarn, and "drawing of wire."[38]

Also suggestive of the marginality and unsettled character of this new kind of domestic labor was its frequent association with women. Because the production of domestic goods required minimal start-up costs or training, and could be done "on the side," single and married women (together with their children) often undertook it casually and intermittently alongside their other household work of cooking, cleaning, and caring for children.[39] Here the practice of physical displacement and serial labor, which we have so far traced in following apprentices and servants "at large," takes the "at-home" form of unsettled multiple labor. Improvised, diversified, and occasional labor, not simply a general upswing in the economy, was instrumental in allowing families to move from "deep" to "shallow" poverty in the latter half of the seventeenth century. This would help explain the evident decrease in long-term poor-relief pensions meted out by the local parish at this time but also the overall increase in expenditure in the form of casual and extraordinary payments to the poor, as noted by Jeremy Boulton in his study of the parish of St. Martin-in-the-Fields.[40] More families could now *most of the time* get by with help from by-employments of various kinds. In many cases, it was a poor woman's involvement in such various patchwork labor that formed the ragged, thin line separating her family from destitution—especially in the 20 percent of households that, according to Bernard Capp, were headed by women.[41] Women in poor households were heavily involved in the new trades of button-making, pin-making, bone-lacemaking, and stocking-knitting. Of the 13 percent of laborers and paupers estimated to be involved in stocking-knitting, for example, some one woman in every fourth laboring household was so employed.[42] As with men, the kinds of labor women undertook would depend on their locale and stage of life. In addition to periodic by-employments, women in towns were typically employed as servants in youth, as needleworkers in middle age, and in charring, washing, nursing, and hawking in old age.[43] Successive employment ran alongside the simultaneous multiple labors that characterized women's "at-home" work. Testifying in a court case, Isabel Dodd documented the latter: she said "she winds silk and knits and washes and scours whereby she maintains herself." Jane Steere, similarly, "buys fruit and sugar and brandy from seamen and their wives and sells the same and winds silk"; she may also have worked as a laundress.[44]

Not all of these labors were new domestic trades. Widows, wives, and daughters within households moved freely and opportunistically between whatever employment was available. But such freedom of movement and casual investment in unsupervised labor rendered their work suspect, as we have seen in the cases of women arrested for living independently "at their own hand," or in the suspicion that Annis Cowper, moving from job to job, might also be begging. Women who occasionally left the confines of the home and took to the streets were especially vulnerable. Water bearers, fishwives, fruit sellers, herb women, and female hucksters of all kinds were subject to persecution as idle, lewd, unruly, dishonest, or out-and-out "vagrant."[45] The irony is that as new opportunities for labor became available to household women in the course of the seventeenth century, especially in the new do-mestic trades, more such women were out and about laboring in makeshift jobs outside the home. Furthermore, however much most women's space remained relatively circumscribed within a contained radius of the home (house, porch, common well, and market), their various labors, especially those of working poor women, were intensely mobile in the sense that their work was multiple, makeshift, intermittent, and occasional. Women's labor was in this way both unsettled and unsettling. As Roberts remarks, contem-poraries struggled to reconcile the ideal of the household as the wife's settled domain of domesticity with "the wayward but necessary improvisions of working women."[46] Pelling posits, furthermore, that another societal ideal—that of constant male occupational identity—may have been "prompted more by the fragility of fixed occupational identity for men, than by its strength."[47] Women were thus the point of fixation for anxiety about unsettled, diversified labors that were becoming the norm across the gender divide, especially for the poor. By the end of the seventeenth century, as we shall see, such anxiety became more muted as those in authority recognized the value of diversified labor and of passing work through many hands.[48]

To be sure, many in the lower spectrum of society in seventeenth-century England—not just the physically unsettled and women in poor households—were increasingly engaged in by-employments of these kinds in addition to their "established" trade. Holding down more than one job was becoming the norm, despite the "official" ideal of a single, settled occupation and the settled sixteenth-century belief that "no man should gather diverse men's livings into his hands."[49] As Thirsk points out, "poorer men had two and three occupa-tions at once. Licensed alehouse keepers in Staffordshire, for example, were also tailors or weavers, shearmen or wheelwrights, husbandmen, shoe makers, dyers, or joiners."[50] As with women's diverse domestic labors, such multitasking was the geographically placed equivalent to the other common practice of shifting from job to job (into which simultaneous multiple employment easily converted) that especially characterized wage earners and other laboring poor. As Boulton observes in his study of Southwark, laborers could be variously described as "porters, ostlers, tapsters, husbandmen, carmen, draymen, chamberlains and servingmen," reflecting the various kinds of employment they typically undertook. "One Henry Ducklyn was therefore identified as laborer, servingman and chamberlain; Richard Beldam as a servingman, laborer, horsekeeper, husbandman and victualer."[51] North Norfolk laborers, A. Hassel Smith finds, developed such a "multi-faceted fringe economy" of job-switching that they sometimes neither could nor would make themselves available for seasonal hire in local husbandry. "Hence," Smith concludes, "the comments by seventeenth-century authors—writing from the viewpoint of would-be-employers—about the shiftlessness of the laboring poor and their disinclination to work. 'Work' meant something quite different for each of the parties concerned."[52]

Voicing a later period's suspicion of the kind of work that involved job diversity, even when safely circumscribed by place, Adam Smith imagined such changing of trades as making a worker idle or lazy:

> The country weaver who cultivates a small farm must lose a good deal of time in passing from his loom to the field and from the field to his loom. When the two trades can be carried on in the same workhouse, the loss of time is no doubt much less. It is even in this case, however, very considerable. A man commonly saunters a little in turning his hand from one sort of employment to another. The habit of sauntering and of indolent careless application, which is naturally or rather necessarily acquired by every country workman who is obliged to change his work and his tools every half hour, and to apply his hand in twenty different ways almost every day of his life, renders him almost always slothful and lazy, and incapable of any vigorous application, even on the most pressing occasions.[53]

If only for relatively fleeting moments in each day—the moments when passing from job to job—the multitasked worker became, in the mind of Smith, "indolent" and "slothful and lazy"—that is, what early modern authorities would deem "idle" or even "vagrant." How much more would this be the case for the wage laborer or other itinerant worker of our period, in much wider spatial movement, at the moment of being officially arrested between jobs?

That the sixteenth and seventeenth centuries also worried about such irregular labor can be seen in the 1598 and 1601 acts, which ordered that people who "use no ordinary and daily trade of life to get their living by" should be put to work.[54] But what was an "ordinary and daily trade of life to get their living by"? Despite the widespread fact of multiple, serial, and occasional labor among the working poor, authorities had difficulty recognizing such diffusion of labor as "ordinary and daily." This can be seen not only in prosecutions for vagrancy of poor women "living at their own hand" or out on the street hawking goods, but also in the conceptual problem officials faced when listing the "occupation" of those arrested for vagrancy. Typically, as with the occasionally and serially employed Wiltshire man arrested in 1605—described as "sometimes a weaver, sometimes a surgeon, sometimes a minstrel, sometimes a dyer, and now a bullard"—the itinerant laborer would be accused of having "no trade to live by."[55] The more subtle version of this refusal to recognize displaced labor as legitimate work was the tendency of authorities to describe the diverse labors of poor housed women as things they "do" rather than occupational identities they have; while men typically *are* something, Pelling observes, women *do* something.[56] And much of what poor laboring women do is multifarious but unacknowledged work. For instance, in the Norwich census of the poor, Margaret Baxter, a widow of 70, was said to "spin her own work in woollen and worketh not." Similarly, we are told that Agnes Welles, a widow of 76, is one of those "who do no work but help others that have need" (a typical labor of poor women); and another Norwich widow "worketh not but stylleth [distills] aqua vitae" (one of the new domestic trades).[57]

Behind the conceptual block against multiple or serial and occasional employment as legitimate work (especially when practiced by women) lay yet another obstacle: resistance to the notion that work and need could go hand in hand. The idea of a new category of poor—neither the deserving impotent nor the undeserving sturdy rogue, but the deserving, sturdy indigent who sought but could not find enough work—did slowly seep into the official consciousness. The 1572 vagrancy law, for instance, though severe against offenders, included for the first time a proviso for itinerant harvest workers and for servants who had been turned away or whose masters had died. And later statutes, following the lead of Norwich, attempted to employ resident "able" poor by providing for parish apprenticeships and workhouses (though both projects ultimately failed).

The settlement act of 1662 in this respect marked an important new turn in the history of the laboring poor: recognition of a need on the part of employers themselves for mobile wage laborers. The act accepted some mobility for working men, and the law of 1697 even encouraged migration to areas where there was a demand for labor.[58] In this period of "shallow poverty," the fact of mobile wage laboring as an "ordinary and daily" need became so much of an economic reality, so deep-rooted, that it was officially accepted, at least for single young men. "Those removed under the settlement laws," Slack observes, "were overwhelmingly women and men with families—not young male employable laborers."[59] Decreases around this time in the persecution of poor women engaged in multitasked by-employments as part of their household work would also suggest more acceptance of the makeshift economy of women's domestic labor, as part of a general recognition and acceptance of the value of economic diversification. Nevertheless, the need for what were still called settlement *laws* in the later seventeenth century suggests a still-felt anxiety over the unsettled poor, whatever the sex or physical range of mobility of the laborer. In *From Reformation to Improvement,* Slack further argues that it was such anxiety, rather than confidence, that generated the literature on political economics of the 1670s—which included the new idea that the urban and rural poor were a public resource that could be harnessed, as opposed to parasites that depleted the country's reserves.[60] For all the well-meaning efforts of political reform, however, authorities continued to have difficulty distinguishing the unemployed, the underemployed, and the multitasked or in-transit laboring poor from the incorrigibly "idle" or "sturdy" beggar.[61]

One can see how such a category crisis could fuel fears and hostilities on the part of authorities. During the heyday of official "hysteria" over the physically unsettled poor in the late sixteenth and early seventeenth centuries, attacks (proclamations, statutes, roundups) against "vagrancy" proliferated. And although the vagrancy laws might appear to have softened as the sixteenth century progressed—as punishments shifted from ear borings and death to (more typically) whippings—such "leniency" was in fact aimed at widening the punishing reach of the law.[62] Like stocks, whippings were an attempt to put the unsettled in their place through degradation and ridicule, as Linda Woodbridge argues. Woodbridge has insightfully pursued this "comic" rendering of the homeless by those in the period for whom deprivation and mobility were particularly threatening (proponents of humanism, Protestantism, nationhood, social stability, domesticity, etc.). The literary expression of such dark comedy, she argues, was the jest book, within which genre she includes the wildly popular rogue pamphlets of the time.[63] But the fact is that no such representational or physically coercive tactics could put the unsettled in their place, precisely because mobile labor was produced by, and in large part supported, an economy that resisted familiar categories and stability. Anxiety over an unclassifiable economy of unsettledness, as much as over the threat of insurrection, prompted authorities in the late sixteenth and early seventeenth centuries to single out for persecution wandering able-bodied men (whereas in the late seventeenth century, when the new economics of mobility were more recognized, these itinerant workers usually escaped official notice).[64] The same anxiety turned official attention to independent women laboring "at their own hand" in the early seventeenth century and—in linking female freedom with lewdness and the illegitimate labor of birth—led to a hard line against illegitimacy in the act of 1610 and the act of 1624 against infanticide, which bitterly condemned the activities of "lewd women."[65]

How much did the "common man" share the authorities' fears and antagonisms toward the unsettled poor? It is hard to say. Certainly, many would have also experienced the conceptual problem and anxiety of officials over "placing" the itinerant. With the rise of whipping posts all over London in the 1590s, the "man on the street," in the form of the lowly constable, took on the primary responsibility of inflicting punishment for the "crime" of vagrancy.[66] But as Steve Hindle notes, "historians have underestimated the sheer difficulty experienced by parish constables in identifying poor migrants."[67] The common man could be a not only confused but also unwilling participant in persecutions—as is evident in complaints by officials such as Edward Hext, a Somerset justice, about the low rate of apprehension, conviction, and punishment for vagrancy and related crimes.[68] The 1547 vagrancy act attributes the failure of previous such laws to an incorrigible habit of "loitering" on the vagrants' part, but also to the "foolish pity and mercy of them which should have seen the said godly laws executed." As if anticipating this reluctance, all such statutes enumerate what fines should be levied against officials and inhabitants who neglect or hinder their enforcement. The vagrancy act of 1604 (continuing the spirit of widening the law's prosecutorial reach) thus declares that "every person or persons shall apprehend or cause to be apprehended such rogues, vagabonds and sturdy beggars, as he or they shall see or know to resort to their houses to beg, gather or receive any alms, and him, her or them shall carry or cause to be carried to the next constable or tithing man, upon pain to forfeit for every default ten shillings."[69] The fine here is as much a testimony to civilians' resistance to implementing such massive prosecution as it is an incentive to enforce the law. Even the order-driven officials of Salisbury showed a reluctance fully to implement the rigor of the 1604 act and brand incorrigible offenders, as the law prescribed, rather than just whip them.[70] And yet proposals to badge, if not brand, the poor continued late into the seventeenth century.[71] It would seem that contemporaries generally experienced a confusing mixture of attitudes—fear, antagonism, sympathy—in thinking of the unsettled poor and in their own unsettled thinking.

Such conflicted feelings were no doubt further complicated by the extent to which residents profited from the migrant laboring poor—employing them for occasional work, benefiting from a needed craft they might supply while in residence (as tinker or weaver, for instance) or taking rent money from them. And, of course, such attitudes were also inflected by the extent to which contemporaries actually saw themselves in such impoverished itinerants and, closer to home, in the "placed" version of mobile labor: makeshift by-employments of the housed poor. Woodbridge notes a widespread fear in the Renaissance that "*anyone* might suddenly become poor," whatever their social or economic or moral station.[72] But some—a sizable group—were evidently more vulnerable than others. Gregory King estimated that in 1688, some 51 percent of the population of England was poor. While that calculation has since been subject to considerable downward revision by historians, Beier cautions against applying in reaction too low a definition of poverty: out-and-out destitution. A householder could be taxed and poor at the same time. And not all of the poor are visible in the official records, especially the elderly and those many youths aged 16–30 who left home to help relieve family finances but in doing so entered a path of economic uncertainty (about 30 percent of them would eventually become poor).[73] It should also be noted that a large percentage of householders did not pay poor rates but were not on poor relief (44 percent in Warwick in 1582, for instance; 43 percent in Boroughside, Southwark, in 1618; 50 percent in Aldenham, Hertfordshire, in the early seventeenth century; and about 28 percent in St. Martin's Salisbury in 1635).[74] These unrelieved householders were able—though just able—to maintain their families in "normal" years, with the help of the makeshift labors of their wives and children. They were also the householders who increasingly needed extraordinary payments in the course of the seventeenth century to keep themselves above destitution. They generally came from the poorer trades (petty craftsmen, manual laborers, minor retailers)—though we must remember, as Boulton notes, that huge discrepancies in social and economic situation can be found within any given occupation, especially in urban society. We might call such independent poor "middling," as does Boulton.[75] Certainly, some of them would have fit one modern definition of this class: "independent trading households." As recent studies of the middling sort have shown, however, the category, while not invalid, is highly elusive. Ascription of middling status varies with such diverse factors as locale, occupation, politics, wealth, birth, gender, and age, so that the category can, in the words of Jonathan Barry, be separated "into a thousand different categories."[76]

My concern here is not so much with sorting through such nuances in the interest of status identification as it is with viewing these poor householders in the light of certain shared habits or experiences of living and working that

embraced large numbers of people. Whether we call these people "the poorest of the middling sort," "the low," or just "the poor," we can recognize that
they constituted a significant group just above those on parish relief and the
vagrant. "By 1650," declares Hindle, "the poor had emerged 'as a class, and as
a considerable class at that.'"[77] This was the class most prone to unemployment, multiple employment, desperate indigence, and mobility. Largest in
their numbers were dispossessed laborers, who constituted some 50 percent
of the rural population alone by 1650.[78]

Such destabilizing poverty had not only a wide but especially an unpredictable reach when considered within a family's "life cycle," as Hindle explains.
In the parish of Aldenham, Hertfordshire, for instance,

> correlation of family reconstitution and poor law records suggests that of the
> sedentary families, thirty-five per cent were recorded as poor at some period
> during their marriage. Only fifty per cent of families were wealthy enough
> to be assessed for contributions to the parish poor rate. More significantly,
> different families appear to have been relieved or assessed in different phases
> of the life-cycle, rather than one group of families always rich and another
> relatively poor.[79]

Indeed, in the life cycle of poverty, there was considerable overlap between
those small ratepayers who made decisions about poor relief and those who
received relief.[80] Given the unexpected and intermittent nature of poverty's
embrace, one would expect that, especially for the lowest sector of housed
society, uneasy identification with the unsettled migrant and laboring poor
could have been very strong. Especially for the middling "low," then, the space
of unsettledness—geographical, social, psychological, and economic—would
have been variously and at times ambivalently inhabited.

To conclude, the special situation of London servants and apprentices
opens up this ambivalently regarded unsettled space—with all its inherent
alienation and instability—by extending the terms of our study from community, family, and psyche to the market. Such a market, as characterized by
Jean-Christophe Agnew, took the form of a market *process* rather than a traditional market*place*.[81] That economic process could further take the form
of "at-home" mobility—engagement in multiple, makeshift, and occasional
labor—for many of the housed poor, especially women. But at any moment,
such a multitasked but geographically placed worker could be compelled to
"move on" and experience the market's workings more spaciously, in the
form of displaced labor. The unbound or "freelance" apprentice can be seen
as a landed type of this new itinerant worker. When an apprentice's indenture
was terminated and he became a wage laborer, or when he was accepted into

the freedom of a company and—as in 50 percent of the cases of those who so completed their terms—became a journeyman,[82] he entered an unsettled economy that had a wide reach. The wage laborer and journeyman joined huge numbers of other itinerant and variously employed workers, including servants, painters, soldiers, purveyors of medicine, entertainers, tinkers, masons, carpenters, carriers, hawkers, and chapmen, that formed the shifting "ground" of an increasingly unsettled economy.[83]

Perhaps the best representative of the displaced laborer in his capacity as a member of the newly emerging proletariat, however, was the seaman. William Hogarth saw the connection between unsettled or "idle" apprentice and seaman in his depiction of Tom Idle, "the Idle 'Prentice," as he is "sent to sea" (fig. 2). If the displaced apprentice was a type of landed itinerant worker, his counterpart on the seas was the unsettled seaman. We shall later follow just such a laborer "at sea" in the case of the poor seaman Edward Barlow. An itinerant worker whose labor was his price and whose ship was his factory, the seaman epitomized the seventeenth-century economy of unsettledness that capitalized on wage labor. For that very reason, the seaman was a focus of both anxiety and economic value for the early modern period, as can be seen in the proliferation of seaman ballads addressed primarily to the lower orders.

But before going to sea and turning to lowly representations of the unsettled poor, we will pause to consider landed itinerant labor as represented by the middling and more established sort, focusing specifically on the influential rogue pamphlet of Thomas Harman, *A Caveat for Common Cursitors Vulgarly Called Vagabonds*. First published in 1566, Harman's pamphlet is an early response to the threat of an economy of unsettledness, but one that shaped representations of the unsettled poor for some forty years. His response was to translate displaced and makeshift labor into disguisings. Rather than shifting from job to job and place to place, Harman's vagabonds and rogues shift from disguise to disguise. He thus makes invisible (or barely visible) the unsettling economics that were to dominate the seventeenth century, willy-nilly.

Unveiling Harman's disguised laborers, which hide the unstable and exchangeable *investment* of the mobile laboring poor in diverse employments within a new market economy, will allow us to revisit the psychic space of unsettledness and hypothesize more fully the character of the persons who inhabited it. As we shall see in the final chapter of part 1 (before going to sea in part 2), the unsettled subject in its most extreme form, detached from a secure community, family, or even marketplace, takes on the contours of a truly spacious—one might even say *virtual*—subjectivity. Such an open identity could have been occasionally and provisionally shared by others, such as the middling poor discussed above, who might be similarly or closely (if not identically) positioned socially, economically, and/or geographically. For, as we have seen, one did not need to be vagrant to be treated like a vagrant or to feel unsettled. The experience of unsettledness was truly spacious. But first we must unveil the middling disguise of the laboring poor in order to reveal their "true" identity.

Disguising the Working Poor
Harman's *Caveat*

Assessing the stories of Nicholas Blount, alias Nicholas Jennings (or Genings), introduced in Thomas Harman's *A Caveat for Common Cursitors Vulgarly Called Vagabonds* (1566, lost edition; 1568, two editions; and 1573), William C. Carroll remarks that "in the various accounts, Genings plays many roles; foremost is the Counterfeit Crank [one who feigns epilepsy] . . . but he is also an Upright Man [high in Harman's hierarchy of vagabonds], a Mariner or Whipjack, a hat-maker, a serving man, a rogue, an artificer, a parody of himself [in picture], and finally 'a moniment' in Bridewell."[1] This multiply roled man—who was arrested, according to Harman, as a vagrant—captured the imaginations of Harman's audience (leading to textual and visual embellishments of his story in subsequent editions) as well as of modern cultural critics of Harman's work, including Stephen Greenblatt, Elizabeth Hanson, Paola Pugliatti, and (most fully) Carroll.[2] All of these critics, together with scholars of rogue pamphlets in general, focus on the various roles that named vagrants such as Jennings are said to play; and all inevitably turn to a discussion of some theatrical work, the favorites being Shakespeare's *King Lear* (Carroll in *Fat King, Lean Beggar*; Linda Woodbridge in *Vagrancy, Homelessness, and English Renaissance Literature*), Shakespeare's *2 Henry VI* (Carroll; Pugliatti in *Beggary and Theater in Early Modern England*), and Shakespeare's *Henry V* (Greenblatt in "Invisible Bullets").[3]

This is not a naive move. Although the unquestioning conflation of the history of "vagrants" with the literature of roguery characterized early writers about rogue pamphlets, later critics have attempted to separate fact from fiction. Nevertheless, they characteristically adopt a sequential pattern of analysis that itself suggests convergence: that is, they typically trace a narrative line that leads, as if necessarily, from historical vagrants to rogue pamphlets to drama or theatricality.[4] Such would seem the logical direction to take, given the rogue pamphleteers' own obsession with the role-playing of rogues, which was bolstered by the government's 1572 inclusion of itinerant players on its list of the legally vagrant. But I urge that we resist the push toward theatricality. For so many of the "roles" that Harman says Jennings and other "vagrants" played—mariner, hat-maker, serving man, artificer—could be "played" by an unsettled laborer in earnest. These "roles" typify the newly

mobile economic network that we traced in the previous chapter: an unsettled economy, constituted out of multiple, serial, occasional, and displaced
employment that unmoored traditional notions of fixed spatial and occupational identity. If the displaced workers of such an unsettled economy necessarily *speculated* in different work roles, they were not, nor could they afford
to be, role-*playing*. And yet that is precisely how Thomas Harman's tract—
suppressing the reality and at the same time setting legal, historical, and critical precedents—portrays them, as Pugliatti most recently underscores.[5] In
Harman's and subsequent rogue and cony-catching pamphlets, the newly
emerging unsettled labor market of late sixteenth- and seventeenth-century
England was deliberately *mis*-represented as manifold disguising.

We might once again pause to assert our own "caveat" in regard to our use
of the term *new* as a descriptor of the late sixteenth- and seventeenth-century
economy of unsettledness. Mobility, job diversity, and displaced poor were
certainly not entirely new to late sixteenth-century England, when Harman
was writing. As we have seen, however, contemporaries experienced a feeling
that there was a burgeoning of such phenomena around this time, which created anxieties that resulted in legislation aimed at restricting the movements
as well as (somewhat ironically) the labors of the unsettled poor—especially
those involved in what was perceived to be irregular employment, such as
itinerant serial labor or "at-home" makeshift work, particularly by single
women living independently "at their own hand." By the end of the seventeenth century, we have also seen, by-employments and job diversity had become so prevalent as to be partially, if still nervously, recognized as necessities
to the nation's fluid economy; this was evidenced in the acts of settlement
of the time, which, while upholding the idea of fixed place, allowed certain
itinerant labor for single young men.

Harman's tract, then, marks a relatively early phase in the reaction to
London's economy of unsettledness. Furthermore, Harman speaks in this
work from a relatively privileged position: he was an esquire, a member of the
country elite in Kent; he bore arms of heraldry (and had them stamped on his
pewter dishes); and he appears to have served in the elevated office of Com-
missioner of the Peace. Despite his relatively high social standing, however,
Harman writes in a genre—the pamphlet form—that was priced to attract
not only the elite but, more importantly, the larger, though less affluent, purchasing body of the middling sort. Indeed, priced at the reasonable rate of five
pence, Harman's pamphlet would have been available to all but the poor.

This is not to say that some of the middling purchasers of Harman's work
would not themselves be vulnerable to poverty or unsettledness in one form
or another at some point in their lives. Given the large percentage of the

middling to lower orders who did not pay into the poor rates but who also did not receive poor relief (from 30 to 50 percent of the population, as we have seen, depending on locale, economics, and age), and given the increasing need for extraordinary relief payments in the course of the seventeenth century— despite heavy investment by families in occasional by-employments to supplement household incomes—we should be careful in terming Harman's audience "comfortable." We might, indeed, recall Woodbridge's observation that there was a widespread fear in the period "that *anyone* might suddenly become poor," whatever their social or economic or moral station.[6] Middling status was no sure sign of security. Thomas Harman's readers were thus a mixed bunch, some perhaps feeling relatively secure, others more prone to uneasy instability.

Harman, and the pamphleteers who followed him, capitalized on this fact. He in essence evoked while at the same time assuaged any fears the middling sort had about an unsettled economy in which they themselves were heavily—if uneasily—invested. Even if not vulnerable to physical or occupational unsettledness, after all, the middling sort profited from a fluid market and its displaced wage laborers. Craig Dionne, in "Fashioning Outlaws," pursues this latter connection further. He offers a more solidly middle-class perspective on how rogue literature mirrored the boundary-breaking features of emerging capitalism. Specifically, he sees rogue pamphlets as playing out an ambivalent fantasy of unlicensed urban economics for a newly emerging corporate hegemony. "These pamphlets," Dionne argues, "promoted an image of otherness that was on the surface inimical to the legal and economic practices of a new group of merchants and shareholders whose cultural affinities had yet to develop into a coherent form of class solidarity." But at the same time, he adds, "this image of outcast criminals who shared intense fraternal bonds with freedom from legal strictures provided a powerful fantasy for a group of businessmen and merchants whose own economic practices of investment and foreign trade maintained an ambivalent position in relation to the established medieval traditions of domestic production."[7] Dionne's reading offers what one might call a "top-down" vision of the rogue pamphlets. It focuses on the affluent "corporate class,"[8] which profited from the new economics of unsettledness. I am more interested in a lateral or angled reading of the works. My concern is the perspective of the middling sort who were more vulnerable and thus more anxiously involved in this new unsettled economy, as well as the perspective of the physically and occupationally mobile lowly workers who formed its unstable ground. The more lowly of the middling sort at times might well have identified uneasily and even fearfully with the latter unsettled poor. Precisely for this reason, I argue, unsettled labor is made virtually to disappear in Harman's tract. Harman, that is, assuaged fears of displaced labor by transforming the *fact* of an unsettled economy grounded on a shifting mass of itinerant labor into the *fiction* of role-playing rogues. At the hands of Harman, the itinerant laborer becomes thinly disguised as a deceitful rogue. Instead of changing jobs or holding multiple jobs, the diversified worker is imaged as donning various disguises. But the itinerant laborer, and the unstable or unsettled economics that he or she serves, continually peeks out from behind Harman's role-playing masks.

Indeed, despite his agenda of suppression, Harman repeatedly points to a fluid money market in what he clearly sees as a disturbing insistence on the part of the various rogues he catalogues on *selling* the food they acquire through begging, stealing, or vending wares. If the Upright Man "be offered any meat or drink," Harman says, "he utterly refuseth scornfully, and will naught but money" (117). Others, such as Palliards and their Morts, will travel separately and beg food as well as alms, but "what they get, as bread, cheese, malt, and wool, they sell the same for ready money" (125). The Abraham Man is of like mind: "These beg money; either when they come at farmers' houses they will demand bacon, either cheese or wool, or anything that is worth money" (127). Indeed, the Demander for Glimmer—one who feigns having been made destitute by fire—sounds very much like a peddler, with her pack of mostly foodstuffs that she trades for money (although peddlers did not as a rule carry perishables). She travels, Harman informs us, "walking with a wallet on her shoulders wherein she put the devotion of such as had no money to give her; that is to say, malt, wool, bacon, bread, and cheese. And always, as the same was full, so was it ready money to her when she emptied the same, wheresoever she traveled" (134). In Harman's view, the fact that these itinerants beg for money or sell wares—especially food—for money proves them to be undeserving. The truly deserving poor would exist on a subsistence level and thus be forced to eat any food they acquired. They would not have the luxury of selling it. But the very fact of acquiring and selling food suggests that these people are products of and participants in the new money market, where money freely circulates along with goods and where value is transferable. Such a system of acquiring an income included in its ranks not only rogues but the laboring, unsettled poor who worked as well as begged and did accumulate some cash, if only in small amounts.

Indications that such laboring poor lurk behind Harman's rogues are everywhere evident in his tract. For example, Harman refers to the formerly employed life that some rogues are said to have led before they became idle wanderers: one Abraham Man was Lord Stourton's man until the lord was executed (128); and Dells (virgin young women) "go abroad young," often because of "some sharp mistress that they serve"—so they "do run away out of service" (144). We might recall not only that abrupt termination of service was common around this time but that casual as opposed to contracted labor was coming to be preferred by masters (and mistresses) as well as by servants. Harman's tract, however, refuses to acknowledge such general economic instability and dislocation. To the extent it is portrayed here—in the running away from service of young women—it is projected as solely one-sided, as the servants' wayward desire to escape difficult work ("some sharp mistress that they serve"). But the trace of a more general economy of unsettledness can still be discerned behind such forsaking. Most significantly, for all Harman's determination to show such ex-workers as now turned roguishly idle, we also see them as laborers in the here and now.

Priggers, for instance, "will also repair to gentlemen's houses and ask their charity, and will offer their service. And, if you ask them what they can do, they will say that they can keep two or three geldings, and wait upon a gentleman" (124). Interestingly, this claim is neither denied by Harman nor turned into an act of roguery. So, too, Raffe Kyteley, although listed under "Rogues" in the appendix to Harman's tract, is described thus: "A lusty and strong man, he runneth about the country to seek work, with a big boy his son carrying his tools as a dauber and plasterer, but little work serveth him" (148). Does "little work serve" Kyteley because he cannot work or because he will not work? Harman would appear to mean the latter, but the former meaning is most prominent given the rest of his description. Even drunken tinkers are grudgingly granted work by Harman: "Thus with picking and stealing, mingled with a little work for a color, they pass the time" (133).

Peddlers are the most problematic: "These swadders and peddlers be not all evil, but of an indifferent behavior," Harman begins ambivalently. But he gains conviction:

> These stand in great awe of the upright men, for they have often both wares and money of them. But forasmuch as they seek gain unlawfully against the laws and statutes of this noble realm, they are well worthy to be registered among the number of vagabonds, and undoubtedly I have had some of them brought before me when I was in Commission of the Peace as malefactors for bribing and stealing. And now of late it is a great practice of the upright man, when he hath gotten a booty, to bestow the same upon a pack full of wares, and so goeth a time for his pleasure because he would live without suspicion. (133–34)

In Harman's mind, the problem with peddlers is that they are legally vagrant, and therefore they must be in cahoots with rogues. But at the same time, Harman recognizes their "indifferent behavior"—indeed, that they "be not all evil." Woodbridge, in her essay "The Peddler and the Pawn," goes further and notes a close connection between respectable merchants and the lowly peddler. Both, she argues, were engaged in an economics dependent upon an unsettling mobility. But the socially and economically "placed" merchants were uncomfortable with this connection, hence the scapegoating of peddlers in the service of respectable merchants.[9] Reflecting his own ambivalence, or perhaps confusion, over the position of peddlers within his nation's mobile economy, Harman obliquely acknowledges that the potential "respectability" of these itinerant laborers could serve to sanction even the most roguish Upright Man. Working for a time as a peddler, Harman says, the Upright Man could "live without suspicion."

Women are also veiled unsettled laborers in Harman's tract. The Walking Mort (a woman who travels pretending to be a widow) defensively affirms to Harman, "How should I live? None will take me into service. But I labor in harvest-time honestly" (139). Harman himself adds that Morts "make laces upon staves and purses that they carry in their hands, and white valances for beds" (139). Most industriously, Bawdy-Baskets (a kind of female laborer/peddler) work in many of the new domestic trades. These latter women "go with baskets and capcases on their arms, wherein they have laces, pins, needles, white inkle, and round silk girdles of colors. These will buy conyskins and steal linen clothes off of hedges. And for their trifles they will procure of maiden-servants, when their mistress or dame is out of the way, either some good piece of beef, bacon, or cheese that shall be worth twelvepence for twopence of their toys" (137). Harman goes on to note that these women also casually "trade" themselves, as was common among poor street women: "As they walk by the way, they often gain some money with their instrument, by such as they suddenly meet withal." So the trade in wares becomes, by the end of his commentary, a "trade" of "their lives in lewd, loathsome lechery" (137). His moral condemnation translates into roguery all the multifarious ways these women are invested in the new domestic economy. But clearly, the women are foremost transient workers, not rogues.

Like the unsettled men in Harman's pamphlet, these poor women laborers are on the move, physically displaced as they engage in a fluid economy of trading in different wares. Yet they also display a marked connection to the placed mobility of poor housewives, who, as we have seen, resorted to various occasional and makeshift labors within a relatively circumscribed space ("the home") in order to help support their families. Harman's tract obliquely recognizes this uncanny connection between the displaced itinerant and the placed householder in the workings of an unsettled economy. He observes that, in an effort to avoid losing everything to the rogues they meet on their travels, Walking Morts often place their money in the surety of householders: "They leave their money now with one and then with another trusty householder, either with the goodman or goodwife, sometimes in one shire, and then in another, as they travel" (139). In the process, loose ties with the placed householder are formed. Coming "once in two years" (141) into one area, for example, a Walking Mort formed a friendship with a local wife whose husband tries to force the Mort to have sex with him in exchange for helping her get unstuck from a beach hole (into which she fell, pregnant, while looking for oysters and mussels to satiate a craving). "His wife my good dame is my very friend," protests the Mort to Harman in telling her story, "and I am much beholden to her. And she hath done me so much good ere this that I were loath now to harm her any way" (140). In the end, the Mort tells the wife all, and the wife arranges, with the help of her neighboring gossips and the Mort, to take her revenge: on the point of the husband's having his way with the Mort in the barn, the masked gossips jump out from hiding, bind the husband by his hose, blindfold him, and beat him soundly.

Harman's story of the Walking Mort is told as a humorous tale, a fine example of the jest form at work in the rogue pamphlets, which Woodbridge has so well demonstrated.[10] Harman gets caught up in the fun of the events, despite his moral condemnation of the Mort, and fails to think deeply about her close ties to the other housewives in his tale—a connection to an economy of unsettledness that his tract works so hard throughout to suppress. Women on the move in Harman are funny, immoral, and enticing; they are not particularly threatening. By contrast, when Thomas Dekker writes in the early seventeenth century, his tone, while at times still ambivalent, is generally more shrill. Itinerant laboring women, in particular, are perceived to be much more dangerous than in Harman's work, perhaps reflecting the period's developing intolerance and fear of independent women who lived "at their own hand." In Dekker's *The Bellman of London* (1608), for instance, which draws heavily on Harman's catalogue of rogues (and is interspersed with stories from Robert Greene's rogue pamphlets), Dekker describes the full array of Harman's itinerant women laborers/rogues. But unlike in Harman, the Walking Mort in Dekker raises ire. Dekker begins by repeating Harman: Morts, he says, "travel from country to country, making laces (upon staves) and small purses, and now and then white valance for beds." He also repeats the idea that these women leave money with local householders—now specified as female—in order to prevent the Upright Men from stealing it: "They leave their money (sometime five shillings, / sometimes ten shillings) in several shires, with some honest farmer's wife or others whom they know they may trust, and when they travel that way again, at half year's end, or a quarter's, fetch it to serve their turns." Like Harman, Dekker notes the vulnerability of the women to being stripped even of their clothes by the Upright Man. But while Harman is relatively mild in his judgment of the Walking Mort and clearly enjoys retelling her story, Dekker is virulent in his condemnation, so much so that the judgment seems to exceed the "crime." Directly after describing the Mort's involvement in what are essentially domestic industries, Dekker adds, "Subtle queans they are, hard-hearted, light-fingered, cunning in dissembling, and dangerous to be met if any Ruffler or Rogue be in their company. They fear neither God nor good laws, but only are kept in awe by the Upright Men, who often times spoil them of all they have."[11] In this sharp attack against Walking Morts, we hear the voiced suspicion of Dekker's time: that women working on their own in unsettled by-employments—and widows, which the Morts claim to be, were the most independent of such women—are to be feared, in large part because they are hard to keep under control. Such independent, unsettled laboring women are not yet imagined to be so dangerous in Harman's tract. It is rather the strong young men that he fears. But even these rogues, we notice, are often gainfully employed, despite Harman's efforts at suppression.

The case of the Upright Man is one of the most telling in Harman's tract. For a nasty rogue, he is quite a worker. Not only does he often "go a time" as a peddler with "a pack full of wares . . . because he would live without suspicion" (134), he also takes on many other jobs, if only through a slip of the tongue or a printing error. Harman declares that "of these ranging rabblement of rascals, some *be* serving-men, artificers, and laboring men, traded up in husbandry" (116; my emphasis). That is, they *are*, not *were*, practicers of these trades. And later, Harman again notes at length that some of these so-called rogues work honestly as wage laborers:

> And some of them useth this policy, that although they travel into all these shires abovesaid, yet will they have good credit, especially in one shire, where at diverse good farmers' houses they be well known, where they work a month in a place or more, and will for that time behave themselves very honestly and painfully and may at any time for their good usage have work of them. And to these at a dead lift, or last refuge, they may safely repair unto and be welcome when, in other places, for a knack of knavery that they have played, they dare not tarry. (118)

Rogue in some places, honest wage laborer in others: does not this shift approximate the situation of the itinerant laborer who is legally vagrant—a rogue—when between jobs, but respectable when locally employed?

We might now return to our Counterfeit Crank, Jennings. When we first meet Jennings in the second edition of Harman's work (Q2), he appears solely in the guise of one who has "the falling sickness" (128) and claims to have spent a year and a half in Bedlam hospital. Suspicious, Harman checks out Jennings's story about Bedlam and discovers it is false; then, with the help of his printer and the printer's apprentices, he has Jennings followed. This leads to Jennings's arrest and literal exposure as a counterfeit. He is stripped naked (to reveal a healthy and handsome body) and, further, made to show and hand over the hefty profit from his day's begging: thirteen shillings, three and a half pence—far above a poor man's daily earnings. Though Jennings subsequently escapes naked into the night, Harman arranges to have his "earnings" equitably distributed to the poor of the parish. Notably in this story, the printer's apprentices, who aid in Jennings's arrest, are inscribed by Harman into an ideal society: they are diligently obedient servants to their master— not, as was historically the case more than half the time, themselves subjects of unsettled and unsettling labor.[12]

In the 1573 edition (Q4), the same story of Jennings starts up again on a new note of semi-respectability. We are told that Jennings "had both house and wife in the same parish" where the money that had been seized from him had been distributed to the poor, "whereof this crafty crank had part himself" (298). Harman proudly declares that his printer at length searched out Jennings's habitation; Jennings was found "dwelling in Master Hill's rents, having a pretty house, well stuffed, with a fair joint-table, and a fair cupboard garnished with pewter, having an old ancient woman to his wife" (299). The implication, of course, is that Jennings was in fact undeserving of poor relief; but then why would he have received it from the parish in which he lived? Historically, parish officers were no pushovers in handing out relief. If anything, they erred on the side of parsimony, and they were especially reluctant to relieve a householder in any way capable of work. The "garnish" of pewter in Jennings's house, which Harman underscores in an effort to stress Jennings's high comfort level, in fact tells us little. As Woodbridge points out, owning pewter was by no means a sign of affluence in the period; it was increasingly owned by the very poor.[13]

That Jennings might be "like" a poor householder worthy of relief is underscored by the other "disguises" he adopts: he appears "in mariner's apparel" and as an unemployed hat-maker. The latter is very realistically portrayed. "I came from Leicester to seek work," Jennings tells the printer when confronted by him, "and I am a hat maker by my occupation, and all my money is spent; and if I could get money to pay for my lodging this night, I would seek work tomorrow amongst the hatters" (298). This story is more than plausible, given the huge number of migrants flooding London at the time in search of work and relief (on the order of some ten thousand a year).[14]

And though Harman takes pains to describe Jennings as exceedingly well-dressed in "a fell black frieze coat, a new pair of white hose, a fine felt hat on his head, [and] a shirt of Flanders work esteemed to be worth sixteen shillings," it seems odd that Jennings would attire himself so lavishly if his goal on that occasion was, as Harman's sentence concludes, "to beg" (298). Harman is "embellishing" somewhere here.

My point is not to discount as pure invention all of Harman's claims of roguery on the part of Jennings. As Carroll testifies, there is historical evidence that a person going by the name of Jennings's alias, "Blunt," was convicted of being a Counterfeit Crank (and punished in like manner to that described by Harman). Carroll further finds that a "Nicholas Jennings" was arrested and set free on bond in Harman's home county, Kent.[15] But even after acknowledging these "facts," it would nevertheless seem that the lines between role-playing rogue and vagrant laborer continually blur in Harman's story. And the more Harman adds to the tale, the more confusing it all gets.

Consider the woodcut that Harman placed in the chapter related to Jennings in the third and fourth editions of his book (fig. 3). This illustration was accompanied by the following verse:

> These two pictures lively set out,
> One body and soul, God send him more grace:
> This monstrous dissembler, a Crank all about.
> Uncomely coveting of each to embrace,
> Money or wares, as he made his race.
> And sometime a mariner, and a serving man:
> Or else an artificer, as he would feign then.
> Such shifts he used, being well tried,
> Abandoning labor till he was espied.
> Condign punishment for his dissimulation
> He surely received with much exclamation.[16]

"As the verse makes clear," Jean-Christophe Agnew remarks, "only the faintest of lines separated the multiple by-employments of the rural outworker from the multiple impostures of the professional rogue."[17] But, as we have seen, it was not only the rural outworker who was employed in such job diversity. It was the lower orders generally, including householders.

Harman's spelling of what has been modernized as "feign" in line 7 underscores this mingling of what is pretend and what is real. He spells it "faine" in the 1568 edition (Q3) and "fayne" in the 1573 edition (Q4), both of which renderings might mean "take to gladly" (Oxford English Dictionary), not "feign." That is, despite Harman's denouncement of Jennings as a "monstrous dissembler" earlier in the poem, one might be inclined to read the serial occupations of mariner, serving man, and artificer as jobs Jennings would be glad to have, not only as jobs he feigns. Agnew goes on to argue that "to the jaundiced Elizabethan eye, the casual laborer and the wandering rogue were virtually indistinguishable from the itinerant actor, so that few would have been entirely surprised when, in 1572, players themselves were placed under the force of the Vagabond Act."[18] But I wonder whether contemporaries seeing Harman's verse and illustration—especially those engaged in multiple by-employments or facing physical displacement or even just undergoing a period of financial unsettledness (always a threat to the poorer of the middling sort)—might have read not the professional actor, but rather himself or herself in Jennings's variously assumed work roles.

The accompanying picture reinforces this possible reading of the verse. As Carroll observes, Jennings here appears "as *two* people, standing side by side as mirrored images": "A upright man, Nicolas Blunt," whom Carroll describes as "extremely well-dressed" and "prosperous"; and "The counterfeit crank, Nicolas Genings," who, Carroll notes, is "dressed in rags, the mud/blood visible on his face, almost precisely according to Harman's description of him in the text." Carroll points out that "the two figures merge in the middle, where the walking stick of 'Blunt' seems to pass through the hand, but behind the hat, of 'Genings.'"[19] I am not sure I see the figure on the left as "extremely well-dressed," though he does look like someone from the middle ranks of society, such as the hat-maker Jennings claimed himself to be. He appears indeed to be an "upright" (as in "respectable") man—someone with whom the viewer might well identify. What, then, might the viewer make of the merging of the two figures at the center of the picture? I would argue that such merging suggests not how Jennings can "play" two roles and is thus (in Agnew's reading) equivalent to an actor; rather, it illustrates how any respectable, hardworking citizen, especially one from the lower or lower-middle ranks, can unexpectedly become unsettled, displaced, even vagrant.

Such a social and economic "declination"—which is the last word of the 1568 verse accompanying the picture (translated in 1573 into the cry of "exclamation")—is undoubtably presented by Harman in his text as deceitful roleplaying because, as many critics have noted, Harman wants to picture the sturdy beggar as willfully idle, and hence morally depraved and punishable. This vision of rogues disguising themselves seized the imagination of Harman's pamphleteering followers—and also of the authorities. Kathleen Pories, Jodi Mikalachki, and Linda Woodbridge have also shown that rogue pamphlets affected the language of legislation against vagrants. Woodbridge and Pories specifically note that the adoption of the term *rogue* in official legislation—for example, the 1572 statute against vagrancy—came *after* Harman's influential pamphlet. Mikalachki, in "Women's Networks and the Female Vagrant," looks at the legal case of a female vagrant in the 1620s, in which the participants in the trial seem to have been influenced by, or at least in dialogue with, Harman's text.[20] I would take such an impact even further and question whether some of the historical documents frequently cited for "evidence" and "facts" of vagrancy are not, in fact, Harmanesque fiction in historical guise.

I have in mind the "facts" repeatedly cited by authorities of the period about respectable persons willfully "going over" to the "sweet liberty" of vagrancy, or about vagabonds pretending to be glassmen or servants of nobles, or about shoemakers or yeomen pretending to be Gypsies, and Gypsies pretending to be tinkers, peddlers, or jugglers, and so on.[21] These "facts" so resemble the role-playing fictions of rogue pamphlets that the two become at times indistinguishable. We might take as an example the oft-quoted letter of 1596 by Edward Hext, a Somerset justice, to Lord Burghley. Lamenting the inability to effect justice against the "infinite numbers of the wicked wandering idle people of the land," who "multiply daily to the utter impoverishing of the poor husbandman that beareth the greatest burden of all services," Hext cites as one instance the problem that such "stout rogues ... will be present at every assize, sessions, and assembly of justices and will so clothe themselves for that time as any should deem him to be an honest husbandman, so as nothing is spoken, done, or intended to be done but they know it."[22] According to Hext, poor, honest husbandmen are done in by vagrants in disguise as poor, honest husbandmen. But as with such "disguising" in Harman's tract, and at the risk of sounding paranoiac—or, rather, of accusing the early modern authorities of cultural paranoia—might not the "guise" of honest husbandman be real? Given what we know of the workings of the period's unsettled economy, might not an honest husbandman become, or even at the same time be, a transient wage earner, and thus *appear* vagrant? What might seem a guise might *in fact* be a change or shift in status or occupation. This conjecture is further supported in Hext's letter by his complaint that, unlike Gypsies, stout vagrants are hard to detect because they do not travel "visibly in one company."[23] Rogues have a certain invisibility to them (as did the laboring poor). Ironically, such invisibility is made visible when it is reimaged as a disguise.

One cannot but wonder how much Hext was influenced by Harman's similar rendering of the unsettled laboring poor. Certainly, his text ends with the familiar claim of Robert Greene and other rogue and cony-catching pamphleteers that he is writing to expose these ills although his life is thus endangered: "I will not leave it unadvertised though I should hazard my life by it," Hext boasts.[24] Compare this with Greene's similar vision of himself as heroical in the face of death threats in *The Second and Last Part of Cony-Catching*, published in 1591: Greene claims that rogues have been complaining about his exposing their chicaneries in his first book and that one such villain "swears by all the shoes in his shop I shall be the next man he means to kill, for spoiling his occupation. But I laugh at his bravados."[25] (The occupation here, of course, is not shoemaker but the "trade" of cony-catching, though the rogue's reference to his shop recalls the multitasked laborer everywhere at work in Greene's lived economy.) By 1596, when Hext was writing, such a bravado stance on the author's part of exposing villainy even in the face of death was a worn convention in rogue pamphlets.[26]

What is unnerving in Hext's letter, for contemporaries as well as cultural historians, is the inability to distinguish between the invisible rogue and the invisible itinerant poor. Followers of Harman imitate his double-edged reaction to this problem in extreme forms: in their works, persons who haunt the margins of placed society are always adopting some kind of disguise or role, and at the same time, they imitate the hierarchical structures of society, especially middle-class guilds. They have apprentices, laws, even their own hall where the craft members meet. In the process, the "real" unsettled laboring poor are reduced in these works to but a trace.

But there is a medium in which the unsettled poor and the culture of mobility gain a truer representation (to the extent that a representational form can in fact be "true") than in Harman's text or the later cony-catching pamphlets, which institutionalize roguery while ambivalently playing with disguise and theatricality. Such authenticity certainly cannot be found in the actual drama about beggars and rogues of the period, such as John Fletcher and Philip Massinger's *The Beggars Bush* (likely composed between 1613 and 1622), Richard Brome's *A Jovial Crew* (performed in 1641), or Thomas Middleton and William Rowley's *The Spanish Gipsy* (1653). These plays lightheartedly embrace the opportunities of playing at being beggars or rogues, especially for those of the upper sort who seek an escape from the mundane, workaday world. All such theatricalized literary forms, by virtue of their emphasis on theatricality and disguising, reinforce the notion that the unplaced laboring poor (whether or not actually visible in these works) were also in disguise. If we are truly to *see* the mobile working poor, we must instead look to more lowly street literature. I am here thinking of broadsides, such as *The Town Crier* (1590s), and especially ballads, such as "Turner's Dish of Lenten Stuff; or, A Gallimaufry" (1612), which embraced the diverse labors of itinerant workers. Indeed, broadside ballads offer not only "realistic" representations of the unsettled laboring poor, but also undisguised voicings of their multiple role speculations (not role-playing) that were necessitated by shifting from job to job and place to place. Ballads allowed for a "no-cost," multifarious role speculation in the singing of the various parts, which was vicariously experienced by their audience in the very process of listening and, especially, singing along. Through these popular songs that were also ownable texts—the only works of the period that could really be afforded, and thus made their own, by the lower orders who were so prone to physical, economic, and psychological displacement—the voice of the unsettled subject becomes truly spacious. And if not always seen, it could be heard, *undisguised*. It is to such lowly street literature, not to rogue pamphlets or drama, that we must turn if we are to inhabit fully the aesthetic space of the itinerant working poor. This literature will be the concluding focus of this book.

But before making that aesthetic turn to the low, I would like to revisit the notion of the "subject" and think more fully about what it means to talk of unsettled subjectivity. Clearly, a subject who is physically unsettled in the most extreme sense—homeless—is different from a householder or a member of a household who experiences the unsettledness of multiple, occasional, and/or marginal employment, or the psychological unsettledness of simply feeling out of place, not fully accepted, or vulnerable (to physical displacement, economic instability, legal accusations, or social opprobrium). In the next chapter, I would like to begin thinking about unsettled subjectivity in its most radical form—physical displacement and serial labor—by employing other forms of unsettledness evident in housed laborers as a window for defining our terms. In the end, I hope to define not simply a range or spectrum of unsettled "low" subjectivity, but also a notion of subjectivity more generally that is itself unsettled, that is, multiple, intermittent, occasional, and displaced. We will then be in a position to look at a case study of one kind of unsettled subject—the displaced poor wage laborer—who becomes a type for an emerging proletariat in the seventeenth century, by quite literally going to sea.

Unsettled Subjectivity
The Virtual "I"

One can legitimately ask how we can pretend to "know" the lowly unsettled subject when such a subject is virtually invisible and incomprehensible not only to us, but even to many of his or her contemporaries. This is especially the case with the dispossessed itinerant poor, whether unemployed vagabonds or mobile workers, such as wage laborers, peddlers, or dabblers in serial, makeshift trades. Few such transients left written records of their thoughts or feelings. Furthermore, authorities who investigated those arrested for vagrancy tended to gather only bare-bones accounts: "Most records of vagrants," A. L. Beier observes, "give no more than a name, place of origin, date and place of arrest."[1] Rare are fleshed-out accounts of the homeless or the nomadic laboring poor— such as the petition by the wage laborer Anthony Adams, housed in Bewdley but working in Stockton, whose family teetered on the brink of nowhereness (threatened with eviction by one town and refused a home in the other); or the lengthy story of the runaway Richard Fletcher, shifting from apprenticeship to apprenticeship. Even in these cases, we are not on sure, unmediated ground. In Adams's case, we cannot trust that the letter was written by Adams himself, since, as a wage laborer, he was likely illiterate or only barely literate. He thus may well have followed the common practice at the time of hiring a local person with learning to write for him. In other words, what few feelings are expressed by Adams may well have been mediated by another. This was certainly the case with Fletcher, whose story is told by the Warwick town recorder, John Fisher. At moments we seem to hear the voice of Fletcher through his mediator—as in the insistent declaration "I will never serve him"—but such seemingly authentic voicings offer only glimpses into the boy's personality. So restricted is our vision of Fletcher that, as with Adams, we don't even know his fate.

Given the kinds of "evidence" we are dealing with, then, one could argue that any notion of what such an unsettled subject actually experienced is largely conjectural, an imaginative creation of a virtual "I." To a certain extent, this is true. In fact, one of the defining features of the vagrant outlined in the statutes of the period was an inability to give a proper "reckoning" of his or her life. In delineating legally vagrant occupations, the 1572 statute, for instance, includes as vagrants those who "can give no reckoning how he or she doth lawfully get his or her living."[2] The Salisbury records of arrested vagrants often take pains to note this particular failing. We might recall that when the pregnant Margaret Legg (alias Jackson alias Smyth) "was found wandering as a vagrant," the report confirmed her vagrancy with the addition "not giving any account or reason of her wandering." Similarly, the entry for April 8, 1605, regarding "Dorothy Grene *alias* Percye, a wanderer" concludes, "She is not able to give account of her life." And the record for April 7, 1606, of "one naming himself Thomas Carter" declares that he is "an idle person and a vagrant not able to yield any account of his idle course of life"; he was thus "punished."[3] Yet another woman, Martha Maddox, was put to labor at Bridewell in 1642 because, the Lord Mayor decided, "she is a vagrant woman [who] is out of service and can give no good account."[4] It is as if, in the minds of early modern authorities, an "account" or "reckoning" of one's life—what we might call "autobiography"—could belong only to the respectably settled. To be unable to give such an account labeled one as criminal.

Lacking such "legitimate," autobiographical accounts, we cannot penetrate the introspections of the early modern homeless and itinerant laborer. But that does not mean we are reduced to the simply imaginary. Indeed, the scarcity of introspective accounts by lower-order subjects might point not only to a lack of evidence or writing skills but also to a subjectivity that was by nature not introspective or inward-turning. The major exceptions, of course, are spiritual autobiographies by lowly Puritan nonconformists, such as Roger Lowe and John Bunyan, who were instructed by their spiritual leaders to keep a daily account of their thoughts "as a means to cultivate a holy life by the discipline of self-examination and self-revelation."[5] Even so, most religious autobiographers, as Paul Delany observes, "were priests, ministers, elders, or persons holding some kind of clerical office," that is, members of "a militant elite."[6]

Moreover, a godly definition of self—though capable of promoting a sense of introspection or inwardness, as Katharine Eisamen Maus has argued—is by its very definition not radically unsettled. Or, rather, such a subject evinces a different kind of unsettledness than is the focus of this study. The devout subject is in one way, at least, very placed: he or she is securely housed or anchored by God.[7] The inward-searching Bunyan, for instance, though often appearing to be hopelessly and damnably afloat in a secular world, is in fact by virtue of his tireless soul-searching at all times placed, however agonizingly, by the godly eye/I. At the risk of following—or being thrown down— one of Bunyan's errant paths to damnation, I would further question whether subjectivity defined primarily in theological terms may not be subjectivity at all from our modern, and an emergent early modern, perspective. Of course, one could counter that such a notion of God-based subjectivity was precisely what contemporaries were encouraged by their culture to find, which cannot be denied. But a new kind of subjectivity was simultaneously emerging in the period that speaks more to a modern notion of singularity and disconnection—a detached "I"—and unsettled poor subjects may well have had greater access to it than did their better-off contemporaries. In any case, early modern authorities may have been on to something in describing the vagrant as godless. Whether or not the itinerant or otherwise unsettled poor embraced a particular religion—and many undoubtably did—unsettled subjects were products and producers of a secular economy that resisted any centering, not even, as we have seen, on London. If we are devoted to seeking out truly unplaced or unsettled subjectivity in an emerging modern sense of the term as it might have been experienced by the mobile poor, we had best then look to a secular autobiography. This is precisely the direction we shall take in part 2, in turning to the journal-cum-autobiography of Edward Barlow, the son of a poor husbandman who defined himself quite literally as a subject "at sea." Barlow's unsettled story of himself is a rare find among the plethora of sea journals of the time: though there are many extant secular sea journals made by officers in seventeenth-century England, Barlow's is the only surviving such self-accounting made from the perspective of a poor seaman.[8]

But before turning to Barlow's journal, I propose we follow the unsettled who are "of no account" a few steps further. For although we cannot hear directly from most of these dispossessed dead, we are not reduced to silence. We can at least catch momentary voicings (as in the cases of Adams and Fletcher); and on the basis of our mappings of their disconnected, unstable, and spatially dispersed positionings within early modern society, we can begin to sketch an outline, however tentative, of what identity such unsettled poor might have formed. With the goal of reaching such a hypothesis, I propose we revisit two well-documented "groups" of the period whom we have found to be metonymically, if not identically, akin to displaced laborers: youths and apprentices. With the help of studies of these unsettled housed workers, we might gain a fuller picture of the homeless laborer, which will then enable us to return with new vision to contemplate more fully the tendrils of connection between the unsettled subject and poor householders of varied status, including women.

The work of Steven R. Smith on apprentices (whom we have found to be always precariously placed, often psychically dislocated, and frequently becoming literally displaced) is especially helpful. Drawing on Erik Erikson, Smith observes that the long and uncertain terms of apprenticeship created something of a "lifestyle" of adolescence: a "way of life between childhood and adulthood." Such an adolescent lifestyle involves a period of "free role experimentation" whereby youths search for a niche or identity in adult society and in the process establish "an adolescent subculture with what looks like a final rather than a transitory or, in fact, initial identity formation." Smith finds such role experimentation in the ballads and stories of apprentices, which depict a spectrum of characters from riotous youths to manly heroes, and sees it as being facilitated by "the vast range of opportunities in London." It was out of such role experimentation, Smith argues, that apprentices developed a subculture—replete with rituals, creeds, and programs—that assumed a permanent rather than transitory status.[9]

Ilana Krausman Ben-Amos and other historians have since questioned the extent to which apprentices or youths in general formed any organized subculture, countering this theory in the same way that the theory of a vagrant subculture has been undermined. Paul Griffiths, however, has recently countered the counter by claiming that "subculture" is too restrictive a notion. That is, he posits, we need not argue for a youth "subculture" in order to recognize a common character to the age of youth. Such an age, he argues, amounted to a complex, ambiguous, and contested territory signposted and shaped by shared formative experiences. Two such formative experiences that both Griffiths and Ben-Amos agree on were service or apprenticeship and mobility. Indeed, Ben-Amos (concurring with Martin Ingram on this subject as well) asserts that "the spatial mobility of young people was itself perhaps the most important feature of an adolescent culture in early modern English society."[10] For Griffiths, such mobility was a significant factor that allowed youths creative expression in the face of repressive households and local communities: "The high rate of migration," he contends, "was one way in which young people crossed these alleged obstacles." Griffiths further extends the notion of liberating spatial mobility to include the many "shared cultural and social moments" experienced by youths outside the constricting place of the household where they lived and served—roaming the streets, playing games on the green, indulging in alehouse pleasures, and so on—activities that adults often condoned and in which they also sometimes participated.[11]

Griffiths's flexible and open-ended characterization of the youth experience can help us further understand the experience of unsettledness as well. Rather than thinking of the unsettled poor as constituting an organized subculture or specific class, we might best think of them as sharing an array of practices or habits—foremost being economic, interpersonal, and spatial mobility. Thinking along these lines, we can return to Smith's notion of role experimentation. The common experience of mobility among the unsettled laboring poor would itself have allowed for—or, more probably, required—role experimentation similar to the kind Smith discusses, even if it did not produce a categorical sub-culture. Repeatedly moving from place to place (both geographic and socio-economic), mobile workers would most likely have adopted a casual and pro-visional attitude toward the variously undertaken jobs and relationships along the way. Furthermore, if we take away the ultimate "niche" in society that such experimentation could temporarily fill (which happened in over half of ap-prenticeship cases) we have the potential for open-ended role-playing—or, perhaps more accurately, role *speculation,* since it involved serious economic investment.

Such was certainly the situation of the radically unsettled subject—the dis-possessed wanderer—in early modern England. Traveling the byways of ur-ban and rural England, the displaced subject was at all times, one might say, an "apprentice" or "journeyman." As with apprentices embarked upon serial role speculation, the unsettled subject—shifting from place to place, relationship to relationship, and job to job—"apprenticed" in a range of different identi-ties or roles without ever attaining the "freedom" of formulating an integrated and singular subjectivity. This perpetually speculative subject would have little resembled Stephen Greenblatt's notion of a self born out of masterful acts of "fashioning" or "rehearsal." Such conceived self-determination (however ul-timately illusory and culturally defined, as Greenblatt shows) is grounded in a power structure by which the dominant creates himself—or, in the case of a class, itself—through assertion over an imagined Other.[12] The unsettled had no such empowering "place," either physical, social, or economic. This is not to say that the displaced subject would have lacked any sense of autonomous subjectivity. Indeed, displacement approximated in many ways what we have come to think of as a kind of free individualism. The itinerant was detached, solitary, and independent. To quote a male-biased cliché (though we should never forget that women could be independent as well), he was "his own man"—hence the reiterated fear that Richard Fletcher, if released from his ap-prenticeship, would "roam at liberty." But at the same time, the unplaced sub-ject occupied a spaciousness that was provisional (subjected to the vagaries of an unpredictable marketing network), multiple, and anonymous. He was "no man," or, perhaps more accurately, "many men." In the spirit of unsettled-ness, we might best characterize such a subject by a deviant coinage of our own: "multividualism."

The multividual unsettled subject in the early modern period who occupied the most extreme form of unsettledness (extensive physical displacement) can thus be seen as being composed of dispersed, serial "selves"—variously defined occupationally, relationally, or spatially—that could be taken up, adjusted, and cast off as occasion demanded. One might be tempted to equate this notion of subjectivit(ies) with theatrical role-playing (as we discussed in the previous chapter), especially because unlicensed actors were included among those listed in the vagrancy acts of 1572 and 1598, and players cohabited with the migrant and laboring poor in the suburbs and liberties of London. Jean-Christophe Agnew has made just such a connection in his excellent study of the market, the theater, and the self. For Agnew, the new, liquid money market unmoored traditional market relationships, creating a sense of distance and theatricality—even mis-representation or disguising—and a consequent feeling of the protean character of man. This argument is in many ways compelling. But it proves problematic on two counts: (1) Agnew does not take into consideration status differences, so that in his view, every early modern subject (with the partial exception of Puritans) shares the same kind of theatrical subjectivity; and (2) at the same time, he obfuscates the kind of subject such role-playing would actually represent. Sometimes persons so invested in the market appear utterly ungrounded: "liminaries poised forever on the threshold of their own exchange." But most of the time, they appear to be stable persons in disguise, that is, private individuals hiding behind an exterior "second" face, like actors on the stage.[13]

Disguise and theatricality do figure prominently in contemporary beggar and rogue literature, as we have seen. And certainly the itinerant poor engaged in undertakings or speculations that involved subtly changing guises, as well as even adopting aliases to hide their unsettled identity (ironically, thus underscoring it at the same time). But to label as "theatrical" such moment-to-moment or day-to-day shifts in identity, occasioned by spatial and occupational unsettledness, seems as askew as to apply the term "disguise" to the different roles we all must undertake in our various (and varyingly unsettled) everyday capacities as parent, spouse, child, consumer, teacher, and so on. The problem is that the term "theatrical" implies a level of disguise or fakery not necessarily a part of everyday role-playing, whether that role-playing is perceived by the practicers to be "normal" or—as I am arguing would have been the case for many of the early modern mobile poor—"unsettling." Indeed, as we try to focus on the shifting "I" of actual vagabonds and their laboring fellow itinerants, the notion of theatricality proves dangerously misleading. As demonstrated in our discussion of Harman's tract, the idea of theatrical disguising not only cloaked the harsh fact of serial or multiple labor, but allowed for official accusations of fakery and consequent punishments. Furthermore, it should be stressed that the itinerant poor could not have afforded to engage in role-*playing* in any theatrical sense of the word. Too much was at stake—too much was *invested*—in their variously adopted identities, however transitional, occasional, or casual they might have been.

Such role investment, enacted as it was through displacement, would have manifested not one or the other of Agnew's two seemingly irreconcilable senses of subjectivity, but *both*. That is, the unsettled subject was simultaneously grounded and ungrounded, independent and transient, there and not there. He or she (and I deliberately include women here, as discussed below) was an individually multiple "I." We might best think of such a subject as "performative" in an intensive and extensive version of Judith Butler's sense of the term: as variably constructed in and through acts of continual displacement.[14] This nontheatrical notion of performativity is helpful to our thinking about the unsettled poor, with the proviso that we do not lose sight of the harsh economic impositions under which the dispossessed suffered.

It is in light of such a multiply displaced identity formation that we can further expand Christopher Hill's notion of lower-order "mobility and freedom." In a section under this heading in *The World Turned Upside Down*, Hill emphasizes the independence and liberty that characterized the life of transients: whether squatters in woodland and pasture areas or, more typically, frequenters of the suburbs of towns, the homeless sought out places that were free from established and coercive authority. Hill does not ignore the high cost of such liberty—in the form of alienation and insecurity—but he nevertheless sees a certain truth in the playwright Richard Brome's description of the placeless as "the only freemen of a commonwealth."[15] Thinking less enthusiastically along similar lines, one contemporary complained that in London's suburbs, "many vicious persons get liberty to live as they please, for want of some heedful eye." Such liberty may have been the special attraction of these liminal places for "wayward" women—such as those cited by the authorities of Salisbury—who sought emancipation from the prying eyes and strong arm of their local villagers.[16]

Other cultural critics have since further focused on the "place" of liberty, most notably Steven Mullaney in his study of the theater and London's suburbs, *The Place of the Stage*.[17] But I would argue that it was not simply the *placement* of woodlands or suburbs—or, for that matter, of the open streets of London—that bestowed liberty. It was also, and perhaps even more importantly, the unattachedness and dispersal of the displaced persons who frequented them. In other words, to reemphasize my earlier point, unsettled freedom is more a matter of *space* than place. Sociological and philosophical studies ranging from the geographer Yi-Fu Tuan's *Space and Place* to more postmodern works, such as Michel de Certeau's *Practice of Everyday Life* and Henri Lefebvre's *Production of Space,* help us to conceptualize this distinction.[18] Together, these studies unmoor conventional place to make room for space: as a state of consciousness, as constructed, as mobile, and as free.

A modern example of place, in these terms, would be one's home or work-place, where familiar and predictable activities occur. Space is more strange, shifting, and malleable, more open to being differently inhabited or used, like an airport lounge area. Of course, these terms are not mutually exclusive: places can become spaces and vice versa, depending on their use.

Pursuing this notion of interchangeability, recent historical studies of women's "place" in early modern society have noted the permeability and ambiguous liminality of the feminized household, calling into question the model of "separate spheres." In the words of Laura Gowing, "The historical model of 'separate spheres,' which dates a transformation in gender relations to a reinforcement or reconstitution of the distinction between male/public and female/private to between 1650 and 1850, has been challenged in both its chronology and its terms . . . it has become quite clear that the period before 1650 did not see a 'golden age' of shared public worlds and more equal gen-der roles in politics, economy or housework." She adds that "there are [also] some problematic elisions of meanings in the model of separate spheres. One of these is the confusion between public or private *issues* and *events* and pub-lic and private *spaces*. Public events might take place in private spaces; women's participation in one kind of public realm did not give them a place in others. Nor is the relationship between separate spheres and the distribu-tion of power clear."[19] Certainly, despite affirmations of women's right to con-trol household space—which was especially articulated in the popular cul-ture of the time—when push came to shove in this patriarchal society, the man owned the house and the woman's labor (in terms of both childbirth and work). Indeed, Sara Mendelson and Patricia Crawford have coined the phrase "public housewifery" to underscore that married women from the middling and upper ranks often performed a significant portion of the labor for which their husbands were paid.[20] It would seem that the term "public housewifery" is equally applicable to lower-order housewives, whose income supplemented the householder's but also was not their own, even though they labored extensively in occasional and makeshift by-employments.

Finally, it should be stressed that women's work extended the domestic space outside the walls of the house to their liminal doorsteps—where they often worked at domestic industries, such as lace-making—and even beyond: "The town conduit or public well, the bakehouse, and the riverbank where clothes were washed were patronized mainly by women, and treated by them almost as an extension of their dwellings," Mendelson and Crawford observe.[21] Women also took goods to market and sold wares on the street. But, of course, all such extensions of the confined domestic space, though part of women's—especially poor women's—daily lives, challenged traditional notions of the female realm. Women outside the physical place of the home and especially those "at large" on the street were always vulnerable to censure, as in the 1582 complaint against "vagrant women such as commonly go up and down in the streets carrying and selling of apparel."[22] "Vagrant" is here a loaded term, suggesting the association of female labor out of the home, or as an extension of the home, with the most radical of unsettled subjects, the vagabond. The "home" was indeed an unsettled space, and extensions of the home by women through their daily chores as well as their officially unrecognized makeshift labors could be very unsettling for their male (and probably even some of their female) counterparts. The period tried to delineate the place of women, but in reality women occupied an unstable and open space.

The early modern period, I would add, understood (however suspiciously, cautiously, or enthusiastically) the kind of distinction I am making here between place and space, as Andrew McRae has shown in his study of changing attitudes toward travel in England from the sixteenth to the seventeenth centuries.[23] Furthermore, the actual terms by which we are construing this distinction would not have been foreign to contemporaries of the period. This can be seen in the common use of the word *space* in the period to designate the passage of time—as, for example, in the phrase "the space of two days." Such temporal usage of the term *space* appears regularly in the successive statutes against vagrancy of the sixteenth and seventeenth centuries, in descriptions of lengths of various punishments to be meted out to apprehended itinerants. The term *space* in these acts is associated with transience, as was the vagrant himself or herself. In official and common contemporary parlance, time is space without place; it moves.

The early modern unsettled subject who was physically displaced or homeless most fully occupied just such a transient space. Tramping the streets of London (within or without the walls), speculating in a range of affective, social, and economic roles, and thus continually remaking the spaces he or she inhabited, the dispossessed made of the city itself, in de Certeau's words, "an immense social experience of lacking a place."[24] And, of course, this unlocalized social experience, which extended to other urban and country spaces as well, was also for such unsettled subjects a psychological experience, a state of consciousness that existed from place to place and was thus everywhere and nowhere at once. The inability of itinerants to name many of the towns they passed through, as we have seen in cases of peddlers arrested for vagrancy, underscores such unplaceable "nowhereness." Anne Smyth, in search of the husband who twice deserted her and stole her cloak, began her wandering relatively grounded; but increasingly, as she confessed to the examiner, she knew not her place: "And when he came not to her again, she went out of Warwick to Kenilworth and lay there that night. The next night she lay at a town two miles beyond Coventry the name she knoweth not. And so from town to town, in and out. And one night she lay in Noneton but where she hath been ever since she knoweth not."[25] Such an expanding "nowhere experience"—ironically epitomized by Anne's last siting in "Noneton"—could finally have been at best but a "simulation" of free subjectivity in the Baudrillardian sense: an enactment for which there was no foundational reality in the background.[26] John Taylor, in his ambivalent paean to beggary, *The Praise, Antiquity, and Commodity of Beggary, Beggars, and Begging* (1621), momentarily captures just such an ungrounded simulation of unsettled "freedom":

> A beggar lives here in this vale of sorrow,
> And travels here to day, and there tomorrow.
> The next day being neither here, nor there:
> But almost nowhere, and yet everywhere.[27]

Such a free-ranging "nowhere" subject was simultaneously alienated and free. For, in the words of Tuan, "place is security, space is freedom."[28] Or, put another way, space is freedom without security. It is unsettled.

The ambiguously "free" space of unsettled subjectivity, we have said, would have been most intensely occupied by perpetual itinerants in early modern England: not only wandering beggars or rogues, but also migrant wage laborers and trade-shifters (who might at any time resort to begging or theft) in the process of continually shifting from place to place, relationship to relationship, job to job. But what about those other subjects on the margins of physical displacement—those housed but socially and psychically displaced apprentices and servants; or those many poor householders just getting by (indigent husbandmen in the country, petty craftsmen and minor traders in the city) who often held more than one job, occasionally needed poor relief, and frequently were forced to move and change jobs; or those many poor single and married women who worked in various occasional and makeshift by-employments either "at their own hand" or to supplement their husband's income, at the risk of persecution and identification with the labeled vagrant? Would not the space of unsettled subjectivity—of speculating in displaced, serial identit(ies)—have also been open, if not wholly available, to many of these poor? A percentage of such housed workers might very well have provisionally and/or partially experienced unsettled subjectivity, if not actual homelessness. Certainly not all of them; probably not all the time. But very possibly, some of them, some of the time, or at some time would have known what it meant to be an unsettled subject.

Implicit in this claim is the argument that subjectivity itself need not be consistent or singular. In other words, we need to expand our thinking about early modern subjectivity so that its conceptualization itself becomes unsettled or multiple. In recent years, many models of subjectivity have been promulgated by cultural critics of the period: from the radical debunking of the older humanistic notion of Renaissance individualism or interiority (for example, by such Marxist critics as Francis Barker, Jonathan Dollimore, and Catherine Belsey) to the currently dominant reaffirmations of subjectivity, but only as dependent on social or political constructs (as variously argued by Stephen Greenblatt, Jonathan Goldberg, and myself, among others) to the latest "born-again" visions (such as Debora Kuller Shuger's religiously construed subjectivity—which is fragmented or interior depending on whether the subject is Protestant or Catholic—or Katharine Eisamen Maus's God-based inwardness that cuts across denominational lines).[29] These works constitute an impressive corpus of investigation into the nature of early modern subjectivity and have opened up first its sociopolitical character and then, in a just reaction against such emphasized secularization, its religious character. Whatever the differences in approach, however, two problems recur: (1) these works tend to offer a universal or holistic version of the early modern subject when in fact the posited "I" derives from consideration of a select pool of early modern contemporaries who are male (Belsey's work is the notable exception here), of the upper sort or at least the educated middling sort, and great theatergoers; and (2) such a universalized subjectivity (however differently defined) tends to be treated as if it were singular and consistent.[30]

Might it not be more likely that, as Maus herself has suggested, subjectivity is in fact mobile and even inconsistent?[31] To expand upon her point: depending on many variable general factors (status, wealth, age, religion, gender, and locale), as well as on diverse shifting, particular events in everyday living, might not one and the same subject experience, say, an intense withdrawal or interior wholeness at one moment, an entirely publicly or socially constructed identity at another, an overwhelmingly self-divided or internally fractured sensibility at another, and a sacral self securely grounded by a godly eye/I at yet another? Might it not even be possible to hold two or more self-conceptions at once—say, as God-centered and as completely detached from all centers, secular or divine—in the same way that a person might hold two or more jobs at once? The poor worker whose family was crammed together into a one-room cottage or who shared his or her meager urban space with strangers within a small section of a tenement may have been denied any sense of a placed interior "I"; but he or she might still have lived through (however provisionally, partially, or ambivalently) a variety of changing, different "selves": perhaps as socially constructed, then as God-determined, and then—in the course of job diversity and mobility—as multiple and displaced.

Indeed, to conclude with yet another hypothesis, the conception of subjectivity as itself mutable and manifold might well have been most available as a "thought" in the early modern period by those lower to lower-middling poor for whom unsettledness—provisionality, multiplicity, change, and dispersal—was in varying degrees a lived experience. In my concluding chapter, where we shall turn again toward aesthetic representations of the mobile poor, we shall see that the "lowly" broadside street ballad of the period projected just such a notion of unsettled self in imaging and voicing diverse serial personae and subject positions through an anonymous, mutating, generic form. But we first need to complete our historical investigation into the unstable poor by turning to a borderline historical/literary text, the journal-cum-autobiography of Edward Barlow. Such a "case study" will allow us to test our hypotheses about unsettled subjectivity in both senses of the term: as the felt experience of being unfixed, multiple, and displaced on the one hand; and as the inconsistent and intermittent awareness of such an unsettled experience on the other.

A mobile poor wage laborer who tried out apprenticeships on land but finally became an itinerant seaman, Barlow offers another important contribution to this study. Servants and apprentices, we have seen, presented a type of landed unsettledness; seamen presented such unsettledness fully launched. By 1700, landless wage laborers constituted some 60 percent of Britain's people, and one of the largest groups among this displaced body of free workers were seamen. Indeed, if apprentices made up an ever-smaller proportion of this percentage, seamen constituted an increasing proportion.[32] As I mentioned earlier, in the mid-sixteenth century about three to five thousand Englishmen were seamen; by 1750, that number had grown to more than sixty thousand.[33] An even larger number of persons were involved in some aspect of maritime business (building and stocking ships or disseminating their imported goods). And yet, as we shall see in chapters 6 and 8, seamen were a source of anxiety as much as of opportunity in the period. This is in large part because such "spacious" workers quintessentially represented an emerging "free" proletariat born of a new economics that was no longer anchored in traditional notions of placed market or labor. Seamen epitomized the landless wage laborer, who was always, even when housed and employed, deeply unsettled.

Edward Barlow, in his unique way, fits this bill. Despite his shifting from place to place and job to job on land, Barlow was never arrested for vagrancy (though he was several times vulnerable to such arrest); indeed, he held to a very traditional work ethic at sea, refusing to break his apprenticeship no matter how annoyingly it "bound" him. And yet his journal displays a mind that occasionally inhabited—perhaps, deep within, at all times inhabited— and most definitely portrayed, *quite literally,* the space of unsettled subjectivity. In Barlow's own words, "I was not well settled in my mind."

FIGURE 1

Jost Amman, *The Peddler,* from *The Book of Trades* [*Panoplia Omnium Illiberalium
Mechanicarum Aut Sedentariarum Artium Genera Continens*] (Frankfurt, 1568).

FIGURE 2.
William Hogarth, *The Idle 'Prentice Turn'd Away, and Sent to Sea,* plate 5 of Hogarth's
Industry and Idleness series (1747), from *The Works of William Hogarth, from the Original Plates
Restored by James Heath* (London, 1835).

FIGURE 4.
Edward Barlow leaving home, with his mother beckoning in the wheatfield, 1657,
from Edward Barlow's Journal. National Maritime Museum, Greenwich, London. JOD/4: E7894.

FIGURE 5.
The *Augustine*, 1661, from Edward Barlow's Journal. National Maritime Museum,
Greenwich, London. JOD/4: B1686/37.

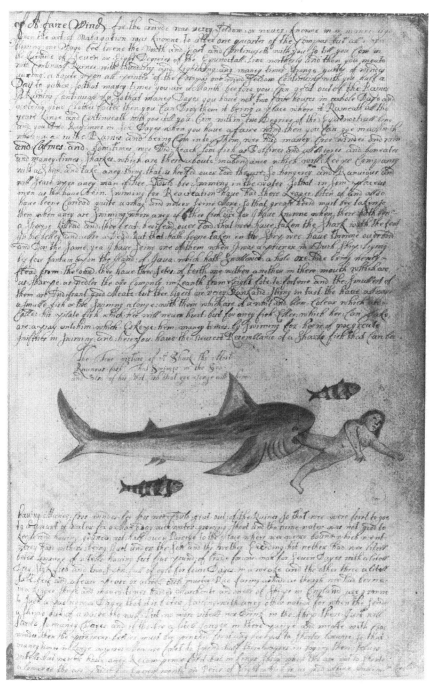

FIGURE 7.

Man-eating shark and pilot fish, 1663, from Edward Barlow's Journal. National Maritime Museum, Greenwich, London. JOD/4: B1686/50.

FIGURE 8.
Man-of-war birds, bonitos, flying fish, shovelnose shark, and views of Devard Islands
(Mayo and Bonavista), 1670, from Edward Barlow's Journal. National Maritime Museum,
Greenwich, London. JOD/4: B1686/79.

FIGURE 9.

Views of coastlines of Persia, Arabia, India (from Surat down the Malabar Coast), and Ceylon, 1702, from Edward Barlow's Journal. National Maritime Museum, Greenwich, London. JOD/4: E7897.

FIGURE 10.
Pulo Condore Island, 1702, from Edward Barlow's Journal. National Maritime Museum, Greenwich, London. JOD/4: E7898.

FIGURE 11.
Falmouth harbor, on the coast of Cornwall, England, 1664, from Edward Barlow's Journal.
National Maritime Museum, Greenwich, London. JOD/4: E7895.

FIGURE 12.

The Buoy of the Nore, off Sheerness, at the mouth of the Medway, with inset view
of Cape Agulhas, 1659, from Edward Barlow's Journal. National Maritime Museum,
Greenwich, London. JOD/4: B1686/23.

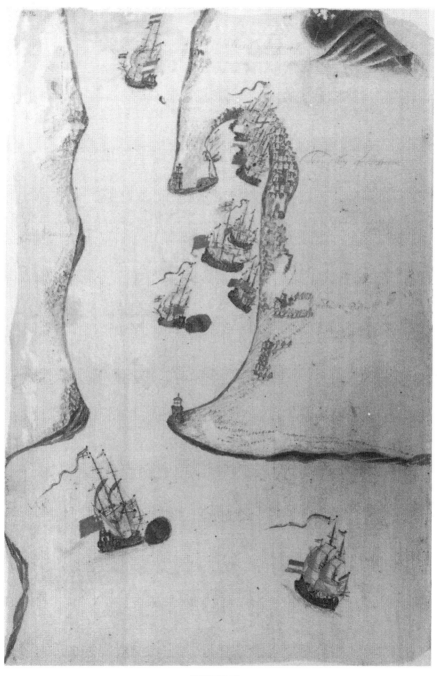

FIGURE 13.
The straits and city of Messina, Italy, with Mt. Aetna, 1668, from Edward Barlow's Journal.
National Maritime Museum, Greenwich, London. JOD/4: E7896.

FIGURE 14.
The harbor and town of Port Royal, Jamaica, 1679, from Edward Barlow's Journal.
National Maritime Museum, Greenwich, London. JOD/4: B1686/109.

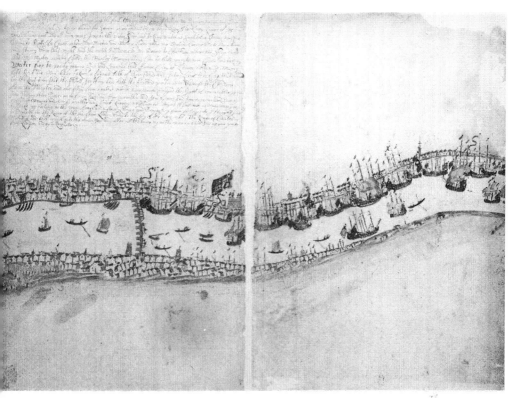

FIGURE 15.
The city of London, focusing on London Bridge and the Lower Pool of the Thames,
viewed from the south, 1659, from Edward Barlow's Journal. National Maritime Museum,
Greenwich, London. JOD/4: B1686/6 and 7.

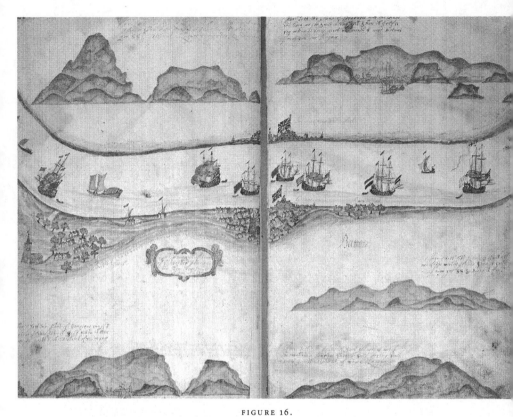

FIGURE 16.
Gravesend (center, south bank) on the Thames, with inset views of the Azores Islands
(Fayal, Graciosa, Terceira, San Jorge, and Santa Maria), viewed from the south, 1659,
from Edward Barlow's Journal. National Maritime Museum, Greenwich, London.
JOD/4: B1686/24 and 25.

FIGURE 17.
The harbor and town of Plymouth, on the coast of Devon, England, 1681, from
Edward Barlow's Journal. National Maritime Museum, Greenwich, London. JOD/4: B1686/57.

FIGURE 18.
The harbor and town of Toulon, Provence, 1675, from Edward Barlow's Journal.
National Maritime Museum, Greenwich, London. JOD/4: B1686/98.

FIGURE 19.
The harbor and town of Belopatan, on the Malabar Coast, India, with island views
of Krakatau and Bossey (?) near Java, 1670, from Edward Barlow's Journal.
National Maritime Museum, Greenwich, London. JOD/4: B1686/146.

FIGURE 20.
Exeter and the Devon coast, from an anonymous watercolor chart, ca. 1536.
By permission of the British Library. MS. Cotton Aug.I.i.39.

FIGURE 21.

Christopher Saxton, map of Hampshire (*Southamptonia*), 1575, in *Atlas of the Counties of England and Wales* (London, [1580]). By permission of the British Library. Maps C.3.bb.5.

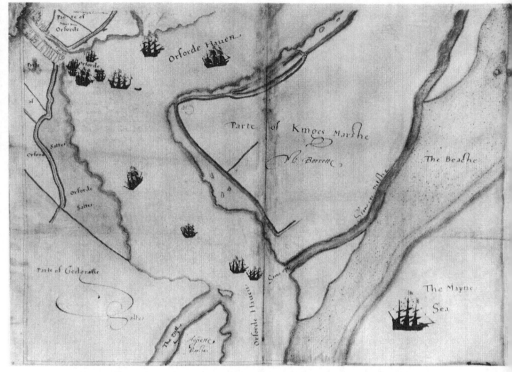

FIGURE 22.
John Norden, Orford Ness, 1601, sheet 22, from 28 colored maps in Norden's "An Ample
and Trew Description and Survey of the Manors, Lordships, Townes and Parishes of Staverton,
Eyke, Bromswall, Wantesden, Chilsforde, Sudburn, Orforde and Dunningworth
with Parcell of Tunstall in the Countie of Suffolk, Parcell of the Landes of the Right Worshipfull
Sir Michaell Stanhop." Suffolk Record Office, Ipswich, EE5/11/1. By kind permission
of the New Orford Town Trust.

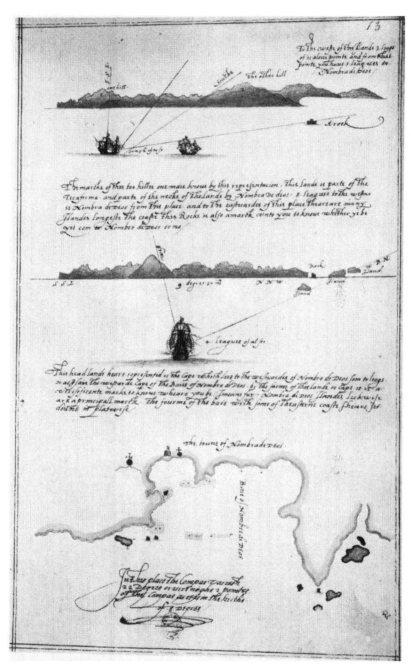

FIGURE 23.
Views of Nombre de Dios, from Sir Francis Drake's last voyage, 1595–96, Paris Profiles, f. 13.
Bibliothèque Nationale, Paris. Manuscrits Anglais, 51.

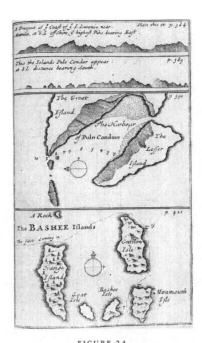

FIGURE 24.

Pulo Condore and other island views, from William Dampier's voyage of 1687,
in his *Collection of Voyages* (London, 1729), vol. 1, facing p. 384.
Reproduced by permission of The Huntington Library, San Marino, California. 121612.

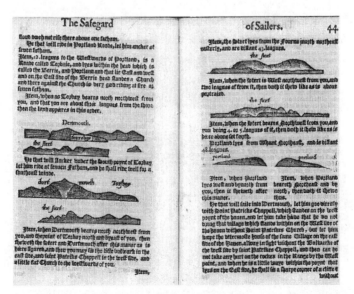

FIGURE 25.

Views of coastlines, from Cornelis Antoniszoon, *The Safegard of Sailers*, trans. Robert Norman
(London, 1587). Reproduced by permission of The Huntington Library, San Marino, California. 3394.

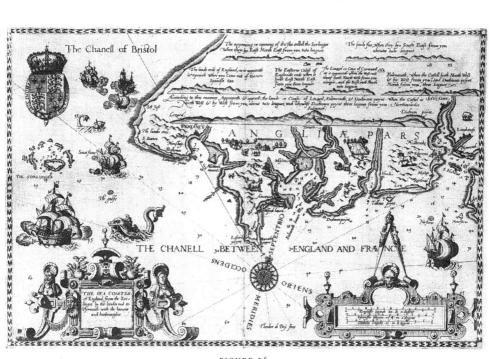

FIGURE 26.

Southwest coast of England, showing Falmouth harbor (center), from Lucas Janszoon Waghenaer, *The Mariners Mirrour,* trans. Sir Anthony Ashley (London, 1588). Reproduced by permission of The Huntington Library, San Marino, California. 69788.

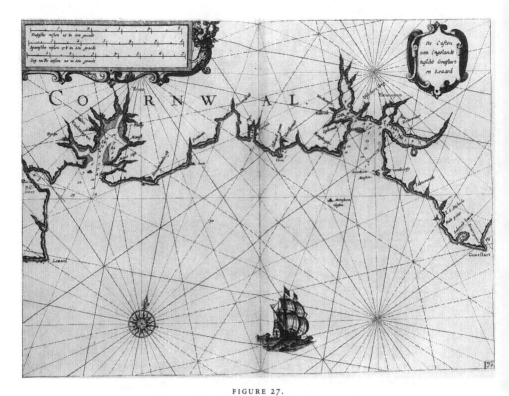

FIGURE 27.

Detail of Cornwall coast, showing Falmouth ("Vaelmuyen") harbor on the left and Plymouth
("Pleimuyen") harbor on the right, from Willem Janszoon Blaeu, *The Sea-Mirrour,*
trans. Richard Hynmers (London, 1625). Reproduced by permission of
The Huntington Library, San Marino, California. 98695.

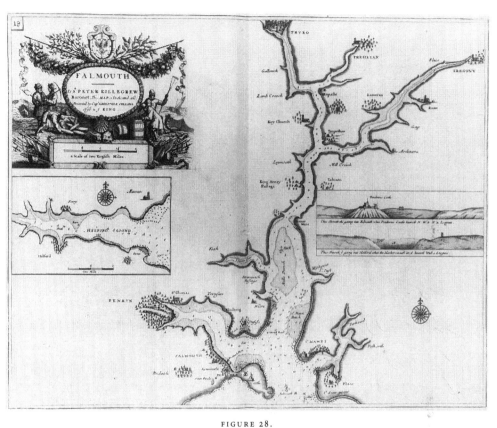

FIGURE 28.
Falmouth harbor, from Greenvile Collins, *Great Britain's Coasting-Pilot* (London, 1693).
National Maritime Museum, Greenwich, London. A1895.

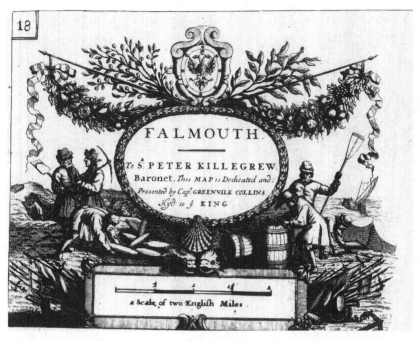

FALMOUTH.

To S.ᵗ PETER KILLEGREW.
Baronet. This MAP is Dedicated and:
Presented by Cap.ᵗ GREENVILE COLLINS
Hyd.ᵗ to ỹ KING

a Scale of two English Miles

FIGURE 29.
Detail of cartouche in upper left corner of page showing Falmouth harbor, from Greenvile Collins,
Great Britain's Coasting-Pilot (London, 1693). National Maritime Museum, Greenwich, London. A1895.

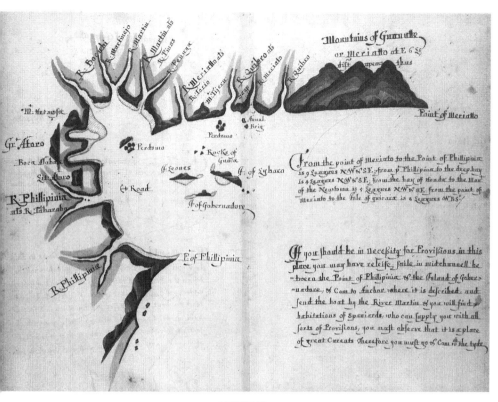

FIGURE 30.

Coastal detail showing bay between the Point of Meriatto and the Point of Phillipinia,
from William Hack's watercolor South Sea waggoner (drawn ca. 1684), p. 24.
Reproduced by permission of The Huntington Library, San Marino, California. HM 265.

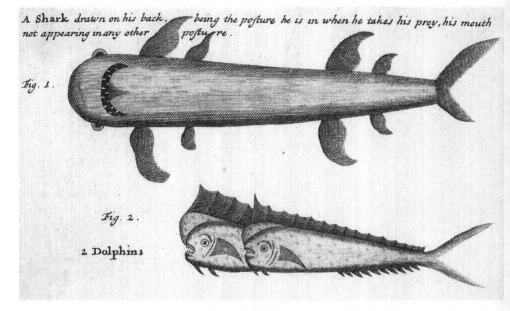

A Shark *drawn on his back,* being the posture he is in when he takes his prey, his mouth *not appearing in any other* posture.

Fig. 1.

Fig. 2.

2 Dolphins

FIGURE 31.
Sketches of shark and dolphins, from William Dampier's voyage of 1703,
in his *Collection of Voyages* (London, 1729), 4:4. Reproduced by permission of
The Huntington Library, San Marino, California. 121612.

FIGURE 32.

Map of the city of London, with company arms, viewed from the south, from John Norden,
Speculum Britanniae. The First Parte (London, 1593). Reproduced by permission of
The Huntington Library, San Marino, California. 62786.

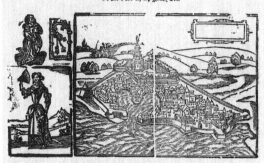

FIGURE 33.

Anonymous, "The Seamans Sorrowful Bride," from Samuel Pepys's five-volume ballad collection, 4:193.
Reproduced by permission of the Pepys Library, Magdalene College, Cambridge.

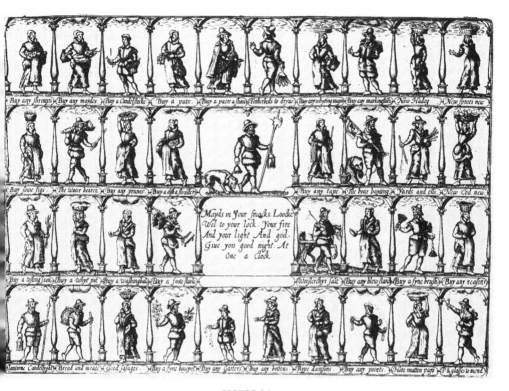

FIGURE 34.

Anonymous, *The Town Crier* (or *The Bellman of London*), ca. 1590s.
Reproduced by permission of Jacqueline and Jonathan Gestetner.

PART TWO

The Case of Edward Barlow

"Not Well Settled in My Mind"

Around age 14, in 1657, Edward Barlow, the son of a very poor husbandman, abruptly and unceremoniously left his Prestwich, Lancashire, home and struck out for London. As if such peremptory departures were ordinary happenings of the day, he first fetched a loaf of bread from the bakehouse (presumably at his mother's bidding), "and coming home," he records in his account,

> I went up into the chamber where I lay, and put on my best clothes, which were but ordinary in the country. . . . So coming down the stairs, my mother and one of my sisters being in the house and not knowing my intent, marveled to see me put on my clothes that day. Passing by them, not staring at all, I bid them farewell and came out of the house. They sat still awhile to see whither I would go, and by and bye when I was gotten almost out of call, my mother came out, and seeing that I did intend to go, called to me in the manner you see here drawn, beckoning her hand to come again, and willing me not to go I could not tell whither, and if I would go, to stay till my father came home and see what he would say to it.

At this point on the page of writing appears Barlow's drawing of the parting scene, with the caption "My mother calls to me"; above the larger building he adds, "My father's house in the wheatfield," and above the smaller, "The barn" (fig. 4). "Yet with all her persuasions," Barlow continues on the next page of the manuscript, "she could not entreat me to stay."[1]

What is so extraordinary to the modern reader about Barlow's departure as recorded is the odd casualness and spontaneity with which the momentous event (or what would seem so to us) occurs. Barlow acts as if such sudden familial severings were common. Indeed, Adam Martindale, a Presbyterian divine also living in Lancashire, records a similar exit made in 1625 by his sister, Jane. Disliking the local dress regulations, he says, Jane abruptly left home for London. "These limitations I suppose she did not very well approve," he comments, "but having her father's spirit, and her mother's beauty, no persuasion would serve, but up she would [to London] to serve a lady as she hoped to do, being ingenious at her needle." Though the report is Adam Martindale's, occurring in his diary, the phrase "up she would" seems to capture something of Jane's own words (and her liberty-seeking spirit). As did Barlow, Martindale recounts his mother's sorrow over the brusque leave-taking; "and indeed there was great cause for it," he adds, "considering how irregularly her daughter broke away from her" (mother and daughter never saw each other again).[2] The cases of Edward Barlow and Jane Martindale taken together suggest that perhaps not only leaving home but leaving home "irregularly," that is, suddenly, was not so irregular at all.

What makes Barlow's record of spontaneous departure even more notable than Jane's and other such partings is that Barlow himself *doubly* represents the moment: first textually and then visually. For all his apparent matter-of-factness in telling his story, Barlow's second recording of the event should give us pause. Perhaps the split with his family, even though a common happening, was momentous for him after all. Why else would it receive a double register? Offered as "illustration" of his breaking away from his mother, Barlow's second, visual representation emphatically underscores the idea of separation or fracture that is verbally narrated in the text. In the picture, Barlow's mother stands in the wheatfield by their house and, in Barlow's words, "called to me in the manner you see here drawn, beckoning her hand to come again" (20). The family home is imaged as oddly grandiose, considering his father's poverty, as if Barlow were imagining his mother tempting him with a comfortable and established place in which to reside. The black hat each wears reinforces the connection between the two figures. But Barlow turns away from such familial bonds. Whereas his mother advances her body fully toward her son, Barlow only partly looks back and is so far removed from her as to be almost out of the picture. Already a wide gap or fissure—occupied by the emptiness of the reaped field—separates mother and son, isolating the two figures as it also images a youth on the move. Rather than stretching his right hand out toward his mother, as she stretches hers to him, Barlow firmly grips his inanimate walking stick. The wheatfield now, on reflection (and as seen retrospectively by Barlow?), looks less like a place of sited labor than a loosely lined thoroughfare leading beyond the edges of the household property, out of the familial scene, and upward to—what? Barlow's destination is open-ended, undelimited by the constricting margins of the page. But one thing is certain: he here pictures himself as intently set upon the spacious road of disengagement.

Why does Barlow grant such prominence to the moment he leaves home? Why is this picture of familial fragmentation placed at the forefront of his account of his life? And why is it the only picture in his accounting that images a human relationship (out of some 147 pages of self-drawn sketches in the 279 extant pages of his manuscript)? As we shall see, the foregrounded scene of familial fissure instantiates but also serves as a monument or, perhaps more accurately, a marker to Barlow's enduring experience of feeling and being unsettled—not only with respect to his ultimate poor seaman's "calling" (as he describes his occupation), but also, more generally and more deeply, with respect to his lifetime commitment to spacious mobility. All of Barlow's life, foremost in his land-based youth but even in his later, sea-based age, he was unsettled and disconnected (from people, places, and even his eventual calling). Such was not a consistent but rather an intermittent and conflictual identity. Barlow, we might say, ambivalently inhabited the space of occasional unsettled subjectivity.

As we explored such space in the first part of this book, we found that the radically unsettled subject was disconnected from family and community, becoming affectively as well as economically and spatially mobile—shifting from relationship to relationship, job to job, and place to place. He or she could thus have developed only a casual and shifting investment in the various modes of identity formation assumed along the way. Such a subject could never become "master" of himself or herself as a stable, or interior, or otherwise "placed" self; s/he would forever be bound to the uncertainty and virtual identity of an apprentice or journeyman "I." Finally, we mused, since most of the service orders and many of the other multiply employed lower orders or poor were vulnerable to such economic, social, and geographic displacement—even considering the stabilizing foci of paternal masters or local gathering spots, such as alehouses[3]—many might well at times have experienced something like unsettled subjectivity (however occasionally or ambivalently), even without becoming actually unplaced. In many ways, among the housed or "placed" poor, women were the most vulnerable to such feelings of occasional displacement or unsettledness, given their marginalized work in diverse makeshift jobs both within and outside the home, which exposed them to censure and even accusations of being vagrant. This is not to say, of course, that all poor laborers or all poor women experienced an unsettled subjectivity. Rather, the state of feeling dislocated, whether physically, economically, and/or psychologically, was most available to the lower-order poor of the early modern period, particularly to itinerant youths and women.

But there is another category of unsettled laborers that we must consider, of which Barlow became one. I refer to landless seamen, who in the course of the seventeenth century emerged, Marcus Rediker observes, as "one of the earliest and most numerous groups of free wage laborers in the British and American economies."[4] Laboring without tools, without a product from their "craft," and without a fixed "home," seamen are the *ne plus ultra* of the displaced laborer, quite literally landless or "at sea." Though occupationally defined and even in a fashion "housed," they are simultaneously deeply unsettled. In the next chapter, we shall look more closely at seamen in general, specifically at the connection between seamen and both vagrants and landed poor laborers. Such an opening up of our perspective will help us further place the seaman Barlow. But for now we need to turn to Barlow's text, which deserves scrutiny as a full accounting of unsettled subjectivity precisely because it is offered not by a vagrant or vagabond, but by an occasionally placed and housed poor worker. Barlow, as we shall see, is a fine example of occasional unsettled subjectivity, which was often felt simultaneously along with a more placed or occupationally fixed self-identity.

It should be noted from the start that Barlow's work itself falls into a kind of "between" or "nowhere" category. It is neither strictly autobiography nor strictly journal. It is both and neither. Baptized on March 6, 1641/42, Barlow began writing the account of his life in 1673, when his ship the *Experiment* was captured by the Dutch.[5] He is at this time thirty-one years old, and fourteen years into his career as seaman. But he begins his narrative in 1656, when he is around age thirteen, a year before he sets out for London. Thus, the first seventeen years accounted for in the work (constituting about half of the manuscript and the two volumes in which it was published) take the retrospective form of autobiography. After 1673, the account transmutes into something more closely resembling a journal, though even here we are not on firm ground: close inspection of Barlow's manuscript reveals that images of harbors visited early in his voyages include sketches of land views he could not have seen until later. Furthermore, the text has the polished look of having been reworked. As an archivist from the Royal Naval College states, in his "Notes" (dated 1954) accompanying the manuscript where it resides at the National Maritime Museum in Greenwich, London,

> Except for some small differences in the treatment of the pictures, there is little to suggest that the manuscript was produced at intervals during the course of thirty years. There are no obvious breaks in the text, except where the pictures have been fitted in and on page 278 (which was probably left blank for a picture) and there is practically no alteration of anything that has been set down. I think that this indicates that the sections of the manuscript were all based on earlier drafts, even the first hundred and sixty or so pages, which deal with the period before the capture of the *Experiment*. In support of this, one has the remarkably high standard, both in planning and in execution, which supports that Barlow had had a good deal of experience before he started to write and that he knew exactly how he was going to arrange his book.... The latter part of the book may have been produced at sea ... but I think that it is more probable that the record of each voyage was written up during the intervals between voyages.[6]

What, then, is Barlow's work? Is it journal or autobiography? The editor of the published manuscript (and its onetime owner), Basil Lubbock, calls it a journal.

But if so, it is clearly a journal in retrospect. It has the immediacy of the moment combined with the considered retrospection that comes with sometimes a great deal of passed time (in the first half) and sometimes a little (in the second half). It thus has the advantage of giving us a window on Barlow's *reflection* upon everyday experiences. For convenience only, I shall most of the time refer to the account as a journal. But we should at all times remember that, like Barlow, the work is something more difficult to pin down.

We should also be wary of accepting at face value the "facts" that Barlow's remarkable journal-cum-autobiography offers. Though the secular autobiography was a genre in its infancy in the seventeenth century, manifesting a wide variety of forms and styles, its authors shared an awareness of speaking to an audience. They wrote, in Paul Delany's words, a "performance" staged for someone else, even when, like Barlow, they did not publish their work in their lifetime. Such self-conscious performativity shaped the image they presented of themselves.[7] This may explain Barlow's tendency not to admit fault—everyone else, in his telling, is usually to blame. It may also explain why in Barlow's account of his life he never legally broke an indenture, though in fact he appears to have broken his apprenticeship with his uncle; and one cannot but wonder whether his "a-likings," or trial periods, in other apprenticeships were always understood to be trials by his masters as well as by himself.

One thing that is certain is Barlow's economic origins. He came from the ranks of the very poor, and thus he represents one instance of the kind of lower-order subject that has been the focus of this study. His parents' poverty (in addition to his leaving home) is what first comes to Barlow's mind when he begins his retrospective journal. The first sentence reads: "I lived with my father and mother till about twelve or thirteen years of age; my parents were but poor people with six children to provide for (three sons and three daughters) and their living was but small—about 8 or 9 pounds a year." He continues by noting that as a consequence of the family's poverty, his father had little land upon which to employ his children and at the same time could not afford to apprentice all of them in a trade: "My father being a husbandman and for work about the ground, which he could do himself for it was not much, was unable to put us, his children, all to trades by reason the tradesmen would not take us without money or unless we would serve eight or nine years, which is usual with tradesmen in this country." The children were thus forced to resort to makeshift employments in order to supplement the family's income—the emphasis is on "forced" in the case of Edward Barlow, who disliked such local labors: "So we, his children, being grown up, considering his great charge, must provide for ourselves or else want our bread; and I, having no mind to any trade from a child, always having a mind to hear our neighbors and other people tell of their travels and of strange things in other countries, and of their manners, and having always a mind to see fashions, was forced to go to work with our neighbors sometimes when they had need of me as in harvest or making hay and suchlike work, and sometimes going to the coalpits" (15). Barlow adds that the moneys earned from these odd jobs allowed him finally to buy some decent clothes and attend church, "which I never could do before for want of clothes to go handsome in. My father being poor and in debt . . ." (15–16).

Supporting Barlow's statement that his father had little land of his own to work is the fact that on the day Barlow leaves home, he seeks out his father in order to sell him his half share of a fowling gun and finds him not tilling his own land, but rather working the plow for the parish clerk—that is, working as a wage laborer (21–22). Documentary evidence further bolsters Barlow's assessment that his father had but a meager holding and was poor. His father's relative physical settledness, as opposed to the son's mobility, is helpful here. Archival research allows us to patch together a family tree for Edward Barlow (see appendix A), but we know little about the economic conditions of his late-in-life wife and children, not only because of the paucity of existing records, but also because of Barlow's mobility and his reticence about his various residences and relationships (qualities we shall later pursue).[8] However, we can ascertain more about his parents, because they remained most of the time in the same place, at least physically. After apparently moving early in his life from Bury to Prestwich parish (the two parishes were near each other, within Lancashire),[9] George Barlow appears to have remained the rest of his married life within Prestwich—specifically, in the township of Pilkington.

Of the extant Hearth Tax Returns for this area (for the years 1663, 1664, 1666, and 1673), we find that all but those for 1664 list only the names of the people liable to pay the tax, and these do not include Edward Barlow's father, George. The returns for 1664 are more comprehensive, as they also list the names of the people exempt from paying; the township of Pilkington records "Geo. Barlow, 1 hearth" among those not having to pay.[10] Though Hearth Tax Returns have to be taken advisedly as an indication of poverty, since some well-off people received exemption from paying the tax, the law was that only people living in houses worth less than twenty shillings per year were to be exempted. George Barlow was in all likelihood among this group. This is confirmed by his having only one hearth, the typical number of hearths owned by the lowly group of laboring poor, husbandmen, and poor craftsmen.

Those receiving poor relief were also exempt from the Hearth Tax. Unfortunately, the parish records (specifically, the Overseers Accounts) do not mention the names of people who contributed toward the parish rate, merely the names of the overseers and the amounts collected. There is thus no way of knowing whether George Barlow contributed or not. However, we do know that he was in receipt of parish poor relief on three separate occasions: during the years 1660–61 (he received 1s. 6d.), during the next relief period of 1661–62 (he received 4d.), and eight years later, during the years 1669–70 (he received 3s.). This last year there is also an entry for an "Ann Barlow," who could well have been Barlow's wife (her name in documents is variously spelled *Ann* or *Anne*); she received three shillings in poor relief.[11]

Finally, the inventory of George Barlow's possessions, taken upon his death, reflects meager holdings (see appendix B). Though this inventory calls Barlow a "yeoman," it is clearly being overly generous. His goods reflect a small farming enterprise: one sheep, a quantity of hay, some weights and measures, a cheese press, and three stone troughs. The list also shows that George had acquired such comfort items as "quishians" (cushions) and—in addition to the basic chairs, tables, and beds—some quantities of brass, pewter, and copper. But as we have already seen (in our discussion of Harman's "rogue," Nicholas Jennings), even the poor were purchasing such goods in the seventeenth century. It is not a sure sign of being comfortable or economically stable. Indeed, the sum total of George Barlow's possessions at the time of his death came to only nine pounds, ten pence.[12]

In view of all this evidence, then, George Barlow fits the bill of many of the poor lower orders of the period: he is housed, not physically displaced, possesses some creature comforts, but at the same time is close enough to the poverty line that he did not pay the Hearth Tax; he fell into debt, and later in life, in his sixties, he needed occasional parish poor relief; he was forced to work as a wage laborer because his own landholding was too small to support his family; he was unable to pay the fees necessary to place all his children in trades; and he was reliant on other family members' additional earning power to supplement his income. Whether George Barlow felt unsettled due to his fragile economic position, despite his remaining geographically placed in the parish of Prestwich, we cannot know. But we do have the thoughts of his son, Edward Barlow, who was born into this condition of housed or placed poverty and, in reaction, most definitively set upon a course of lifelong itinerancy.

Edward Barlow made several appearances in the previous chapters of this study as we moved toward formulating a theory of unsettled subjectivity: we saw his vision of London as the site of familial and personal fragmentation, and we heard his complaints of abuse by one master and many mistresses in apprenticeships and in other jobs. Despite previously citing him, however, we should resist upholding Barlow as entirely typical. The fact of his account is a worn convention; as noted by the editor of Barlow's journal, there was an established custom in the Stuart period for seamen to keep journals and illustrate them (12). But in other ways, Barlow's account was unusual. Most obviously, his lowly background and his journal's huge volume of pages and illustrations stand out as exceptional. Indeed, though he was born into poverty and left home as a youth, illiterate, with only a few shillings in his pocket, Barlow managed, amazingly, to make a living (if barely) as a seaman, acquire literacy during his seafaring adventures, and—most astonishingly—write some 225,000 words about his life, from age thirteen to sixty-one, in a journal beautifully self-decorated with abundant watercolor and pencil illustrations. Nevertheless, if Barlow's journal gives us his unique version of himself, it also variously reflects (and reflects upon) the common lowly experience of being and feeling unsettled.

The fact that Barlow is a late example of an unsettled subject—though born in the first half of the seventeenth century, he lived through its end— confirms that such a conception of self remained readily available as a part of the lower-order experience throughout the century, despite observations by many historians that economic conditions generally improved and job mobility was more accepted in the second half of the period. Though some prices and wages did rise in the latter half of the seventeenth century, the condition of the very poor may not have improved significantly. The poor maintained themselves above deep poverty through active involvement in domestic by-employments as well as through receipt of extraordinary payments from parish poor relief of the kind George Barlow received. But more of the poor, not fewer, thus remained in shallow poverty. And if itinerancy was more accepted for single male wage laborers in the latter half of the seventeenth century, the settlement laws and their resistance to itinerant women and families expose the continued fear of unsettling displacement. Certainly, as we shall see more fully in the next chapter, seamen and soldiers, and the many who occasionally found themselves serving as such, were actually *more,* not less, involved with unsettledness—in the form of homelessness and itinerant labor—as the seventeenth century progressed. In any case, Barlow, like other seamen, was not much influenced by land-based economic or social states of "settlement" late in the century, since he had already committed, however ambivalently, to a life at sea. Even more significantly, as we shall see in looking at his many charts of harbors and coastlines, Barlow in many ways "belonged"—if such a word can ever be used to describe him—to an earlier age. In sum, if Barlow cannot be held up as entirely typical of poorer subjects in early modern England, he can nevertheless be seen to partake of a common and enduring lower-order experience. To understand fully that unsettling connection, we need to look more closely at Barlow's individualized account of economic, occupational, and personal displacement as represented in his journal.

Barlow's journal, we have noted, is part retrospective. It was begun some fourteen years into his career as a seaman, while he was being held prisoner on a Dutch ship. He explains his reason for writing thus:

> And keeping us in the Straits [off Sumatra] two months, and I having a great deal of spare time, which I thought might be worse spent than in declaring of what I have here in this book, and thus I thought good to describe to my friends and acquaintance and to any which might take the pains to read it over, and here they may understand in part what dangers and troubles poor seamen pass through, and also of the manner and situation of most places which I have been at since I first went to sea. (228)

As we shall see below, Barlow's "friends and acquaintance" are intermittent and shadowy figures in his journal. But his sense of himself as "poor seaman" is extremely strong. On the whole, the journal is heavily factual, and though we learn Barlow's feelings about events and some people, he is not generally given to intense introspection or emotion. On one subject, however, he is passionate: the "dangers and troubles poor seamen pass through." In many long passages, Barlow fervently laments the hardships and abuses suffered by poor seamen, becoming something of an advocate for the entire crew of such impoverished workers. We can safely say that, at least later in his life, Barlow definitely defined himself occupationally as a seaman.

At the same time, however, he was extremely ambivalent about his chosen calling. In addition to frequently lamenting the miserable life of the poor seaman, he often speaks vaguely about being "bound," "compelled" or "forced" to go to sea: "I had bound myself to a hard and miserable calling," he moans, "and there was no way for me but I must endure it" (112). Such bondage would at first seem to refer to his contracted seven-year apprenticeship. The apprenticeship itself—and the fact that Barlow never breaks it—is a testimony to his strong desire for a traditional place in society. Though it was common practice at the time for seamen to sign on as servants, rather than bind themselves in an indenture, Barlow chose the more conservative, "placed" route. Once at sea, he regrets his decision. But, interestingly, he continues to speak of being compelled to go to sea even after his apprenticeship ends. Why? One reason he repeatedly gives is his inability to find other lawful work. He usually attributes this failing to his "having few or no friends to prefer or help me" (425)—a complaint to which we shall return—or to his "uncertain" life, which has prevented him from saving enough money to retire from the sea. Thus, he concludes, "still I must use my endeavor and in a lawful way I must have a livelihood, and get it by sea I must" (263). But another compulsion, prior to such economic need, drives Barlow: his insatiable and almost uncontrollable desire to seek strange sights and to travel. This enduring, deep-rooted "unsettledness"—making him a subject perpetually enacting displacement—defined him as strongly as his "placed" occupation of seaman (to which such unsettledness was suited), especially in his youth.

Barlow's journal, we observed, begins with his youth, describing his family's poverty, which "forced" him to work odd jobs in the fields or in the coal-pits, despite his declared dislike of any trade and his inner wanderlust. At "about twelve or thirteen years of age" (15), Barlow reluctantly goes "a-liking" (that is, on a trial apprenticeship) in the trade of cotton bleacher. During this probationary period, he forms a temporary alliance with a journeyman in his master's employ, and after hearing that worker's accounts of abuse there and making his own assessment of the same, he refuses to stay. He insists to his parents, "I could never like it, and if I did (go back) I was sure I could never stay my time out" (19). Barlow's neighbors, upholding the traditional ideology of stability—even in the face of the widespread fact of unsettledness—reprove him for rejecting his apprenticeship, "saying I would never stay anywhere, for I was given to wandering" (20). Barlow himself often attributes this and later aborted job trials to being "not well settled in my mind" (19). A typical teenager, he clearly sees his "unsettled" mind as a unique character trait. But in fact he is actually repeating, apparently unconsciously, a maxim of the time—as noted by Paul Griffiths—that youth was a "most unsettled age."[13] Soon after returning home from his terminated apprenticeship as bleacher, Barlow does in fact wander off, physically enacting his unsettledness—with no advance warning to his parents. Like so many other poor youths of his time (and half of the secular autobiographers of the period),[14] Barlow strikes out for London, in search of adventure and opportunity. Along the way, he passingly meets up with yet another apprentice fleeing his ex-master (the same cotton bleacher). Such hasty departures from indentures were indeed common.

In London, Barlow first seeks out his sister Anne, who is working there as a servant, and asks her to help him "to any place." He discovers, however, that she "being a servant could not help me with anything," and she convinces him (though he dislikes the idea) to seek out his uncle in Southwark, who owns a post house for Kent (23). At his uncle's inn, Barlow again works odd jobs—helping the ostler to dress the post horses, cleaning the house, drawing beer, and fetching letters from the general post house. When his brother, who was earlier apprenticed to his uncle, asks to return to Prestwich because of illness and a general unhappiness with city life, Barlow agrees to apprentice in his stead as a tapster drawing beer. But he soon finds he dislikes that job, has a falling-out with his suspicious mistress, and refuses to work any more in the tavern, instead tending the horses in the stables and running errands. Barlow's uncle then arranges for him to go "a-liking" in an apprenticeship with a tapster at a tavern in Dartford, Kent. But once again Barlow dislikes the job and leaves. Returning to London, he is confronted by his uncle and aunt, who "set upon me and asked me whether I could stay anywhere or no," for which Barlow has "little answer" (26). During his stay in London, though, Barlow becomes fascinated with the ships on the Thames and desires to go to sea. Finally his uncle, against his better judgment, helps him become apprenticed to the chief master's mate of the naval ship the *Naseby*. Barlow thus becomes indentured to a course of continual unsettledness (which continued even after he completed his formal indenture), traveling the world over until the age of sixty-one, by the journal's accounting, on both merchant ships and men-of-war. His extensive sea wanderings—summarized in appendix C— are interrupted only by the assorted temporary jobs he takes up in London between sailings, recuperative rests between long voyages, and his two-month imprisonment on a Dutch ship off the coast of Sumatra, during which time he starts his journal.

Barlow, then, lived a youth of spatial and occupational mobility, which became an adulthood of relative occupational stability—but one that yet enacted, in his calling, physical displacement, as he moved frequently from place to place and ship to ship. Of course, seamen are by definition itinerant. It is in the nature of their job, as we shall examine more fully in the next chapter (where we will find many an active interchange between landed itinerancy and sea voyaging). But my point here is that Barlow, the land wanderer, did not see himself as a sea wanderer right away. In fact, when he arrived in London, he was puzzled by what those floating things on the Thames actually were. Coming to London Bridge, he says, "I looking below the bridge upon the river, and seeing so many things upon the water with long poles standing up in them and a great deal of ropes about them, it made me wonder what they should be, not knowing that they were ships, for I had never seen any before that time" (23). Only much later, after trying out many different kinds of jobs in several different places, does Barlow settle on becoming a seaman. If he had not settled on such an itinerant calling, I suspect he would have become a perpetual landed wage laborer or job-shifter, given his unsettled mind. Indeed, even as an apprentice seaman, Barlow continued to do odd jobs when in his "home" port; and even after completing his indenture, he at least once between sailings took on the role of peddler, selling Bibles and other goods that he had picked up in Amsterdam (252).

Barlow's history—especially his youth—thus follows a path similar to that of other unsettled subjects of his time whom we pursued in the first part of this book: poverty, multiple and /or serial work, and spatial mobility. This is the case even though Barlow was most of the time "housed" and gainfully employed, and he had a stable and extant parental home to which he could return—although he did so only twice, once twelve years after departing, and the second time twenty years after that. We are fortunate that in the case of Barlow (unlike in the cases of most other such unsettled subjects), we hear the subject's own thoughts about the peripatetic course he follows, which he attributes to being mentally unfixed—or, as he puts it, "not well settled in my mind." If we more closely interrogate Barlow's character as represented in his journal, fuller marks of an unsettled subjectivity become apparent. The final picture of Barlow that emerges—especially when we contextualize his verbal self-representation in terms of the life of seamen generally, as we shall do in chapter 6, and when we add in his pictorial (self)-representations, discussed in chapter 7—is that of a kind of "nowhere" man, detached not only from physical places or occupational jobs, but also from communal, personal, and familial connections. There is good reason why Barlow opens his vision of his life with a picture of himself breaking away from his mother and why it is the only picture of a human relationship among the many charts that "people" his journal: Barlow formed only the most casual relationships along his mobile way.

People come into Barlow's life and then disappear, like the journeyman bleacher with whom he forms a temporary bond. With very rare exceptions, no one is named. Cities, ports, countries, and ships are given names (and in this Barlow differs from the many itinerants who "knew not" where they wandered), but people usually are not. We hear the name of the carrier hired to take him from the country to London upon his momentous departure from home (Thomas Haye); of the surgeon who heals a nasty head wound he suffered his first day aboard ship (Master Turner); and of the man who looked after him while he recuperated (Coke). Some rulers, lords, and admirals are also named—especially if engaged in a major military mobilization—as if Barlow were recording a historical event. Later in the journal, he more often names the masters or captains of the ships on which he serves, and occasionally the merchants' chief factors for foreign lands. But that's about it. Particularly striking is the absence of names for co-workers, friends, and family. With three exceptions—his younger brother, George, his sister Anne (whom he calls "Anna"), and a friend, John Thornbury—none are named. Not the master with whom he was apprenticed for seven years, not the carpenter who twice ships out with him (264), not his father, or mother, or wife, not even himself. The most important of the three exceptions is the naming of his sister Anne, with whom Barlow seemed closest. But, significantly and eerily, she is named only at the time of her announced death (250–51). It is as if personal relationships tend not to endure as nameable identities in Barlow's mind. They exist only in passing.

Even all the friends of Barlow's youth simply fall out of mind when he leaves home: "I did tell my playmates that that would be the last time that I should play with them there," he declares, "for on the next holiday I did intend to be further off" (20). Despite Barlow's conventional statement that he writes his journal for "my friends and acquaintance" (228), and his occasional sending of letters from aboard ship to such "friends" in London, no lasting affective friendship is ever described. In fact, Barlow almost always criticizes or dismisses his unnamed "friends" as inadequate and increasingly nonexistent. Even though in 1677 his one named friend, John Thornbury, helped procure Barlow the position of second mate on the ship *Guannaboe,* bound for Jamaica—the only time in Barlow's life that a friend advances him to a place, and thus perhaps the reason Thornbury gains the unusual honor of being named—Barlow expresses not gratitude but a complaint: "but I had gone long enough to sea to have been a master if I had had the friends some men meet withall, but fortune did not so much befriend me" (308). Indeed, Barlow expects, and even ensures, that he will continue to be disappointed, rather than befriended.

When Barlow sends but "a little money" home to the country, for instance, he adds that it was "yet more than ever all the friends I had as yet would do by me" (139). But when he first returns to his hometown (twelve years after his departure), his main goal is to show that he does not need such friends: in a rare moment of plush solvency, having been at sea nearly continuously for some four and a half years, Barlow spends a good part of his accumulated earnings to buy "brave" attire—"intending," as he puts it, "not to show myself beholding to any of my friends or acquaintance" (175). Though immensely enjoying the admiration and "love" he receives from these persons during his visit, he cynically concludes:

> And so I continued seven or eight weeks in the country, being invited from one neighbor's house to another, everyone striving to show their love when they saw I wanted nothing, it being a common use amongst people to welcome those that can welcome themselves, for had I come down into the country ill-clothed and without money and in need or want, I believe I should have found

as few friends at my coming into it as I had when I went out of it, before I had
come down. (176)

What seems strange about Barlow's attitude here is that he solicits "love" from
his neighbors through superficial "bravery" and loose spending, yet he criti-
cally dismisses such solicited love as insubstantial. It is almost as if he deliberately acts to undermine the idea of an enduring and meaningful bond of
friendship. This is particularly evident when he openly woos the sweethearts
of the local youths, who jealously backbite him for, he says, "going so fine,
and spending of my own moneys." Barlow dismisses the ill affection he
thus creates, saying he has no intention of returning to his hometown again
anyway:

> And many times I would have the company of their sweethearts to go along
> with me to drink or discourse, for if I did but speak but half a word they would
> leave them and go along with me, and I many times did keep their sweethearts
> from them, the more to try their patience and hear what they would say; but
> their good wills and evil wills were all one to me, for I mattered the one as much
> as the other, for I did not think that I should come to live in the country again
> in the manner as they did. (176)

Good will and bad will are both irrelevant to him, says Barlow, because he has
no enduring ties to these people: "for I did not think that I should come to
live in the country again in the manner as they did." And yet, when he returns
to London, he sends home "some small token to some of our neighbors and
acquaintance," as he had spent freely on the villagers while there. Typically,
he is critical of their ingratitude: "but some of them would scarce return me
thanks" (178). What else did he expect? As if he did not in fact expect any
other response, Barlow adds, "yet what I gave I did not matter, for it made me
little poorer, and I gave them more for good will than for recompense, for I
looked not for any" (178). His gift, he suggests, was but a self-glorifying gesture, not intended to solicit reciprocal bonds.

In another gesture seemingly designed to provoke rejection, Barlow, upon
his return to England five years later—after more than three years at sea,
including more than a year of captivity on various Dutch ships—decides to
"try" his friends and relations in the country by requesting ten pounds from
them. He does this even though he doesn't really need the money; he had actually managed, he says, to save some money "by accident and care" while a
prisoner. Considering the jealousies he had earlier created by his dandyish return home, as well as the poverty of his family and most of the other villagers
in his hometown, the outcome of Barlow's request would seem predictable: "I
could find none of them able or willing to supply my wants," he records. He

adds, typically, "and so it would have been if I had been in ever so much need" (251).[15] Barlow seems intent on proving that friends won't be there for him.

Whenever Barlow meets with such ingratitude—which he does almost always, according to his account—he is quick to disparage or break the friendship bond. On an East Indies voyage, for instance, he says, "And I having a small venture for myself and some of my friends and acquaintance, bought some small commodities, and taking care of my friends' goods more than I did of my own, and when I came home I had scarce thanks for all my care and trouble, but it was the first time and it shall be the last that I shall meddle with any in that matter" (194). No wonder that when Barlow embarks for the Canaries on the *Mayflower,* several voyages later, the number of his friends has, in his mind, diminished: "taking leave of those *few friends* I had," he says (281; my emphasis). Subsequently, he will declare that he has only one real friend, though that "only friend" is mentioned only at his death, and never named (351). This lack of significant or enduring friends—a category that has expanded in his thinking to be equivalent to "patrons"—becomes one of the primary reasons Barlow gives for *having* to go to sea: "for to sea I must go," he affirms, since he has "few or no friends and acquaintance that could or would help me" (281). Later, he repeats this complaint almost exactly: "having few or no friends to prefer or help me" (425). But I can't help wondering whether Barlow goes to sea because he has no friends (in the sense of both patrons and close relationships) or whether he has no friends because he goes to sea, or, more generally, because he is forever unsettled and uncommitted to having friends. One thing is clear: though often referred to, Barlow's "friends and acquaintance" are shadowy figures in his journal, present primarily in their absence or lack.

In fact, Barlow's best friend was not a person, but a good wind. Disgusted by the bad provisions doled out on board the Dutch ship, where he worked as a prisoner in 1674, Barlow concludes, "but it was all in vain to wish, for we were forced to endure with patience, praying for a fair wind, for that is a seaman's best friend" (243). In 1675, his ship having set sail alone, without any consort ships (bound for Glasgow to load pickled herrings), Barlow again comments: "but our best friend was the wind, which continued very fair, carrying us along with a quick motion" (267). At another time, finding his ship alone and describing how their companion ship outsailed them, he takes comfort in their "very good wind, which continued with us, which was our friend" (278). Barlow seems to have such good (nonhuman) wind-friends in mind when describing his vain attempts to become master of his own ship. Criticizing his fair-weather human friends, who broke their promises to help him once his "only friend" dies, he imagines "their words being wind which passeth away without any hold to be taken of them" (351). Barlow's comments about good wind-friends, which in contrast to humans are enduring friends, offer a glimpse into why friendship or community would have been especially difficult to maintain at sea. As his remarks suggest, ships at sea—largely because of the differing winds and the ships' different reactions to them—come together and depart from each other loosely, very much like itinerants on land. Given the vagaries of sea travel, no lasting community or friendship between ships could be maintained, even when they tried their best to "keep company" on a voyage. Barlow's detachment from continuous personal bonds is thus very much in accord with life at sea, which could be to various degrees "alienating," as we shall more fully pursue in the next chapter. His sense of alienation is so intense that it extends to exclude even those unnamed and little-described crew members with whom he served aboard ship. Barlow could identify with and speak on behalf of "poor seamen" in a general sort of way, but he could not form meaningful or lasting personal ties with his kindred workers. Barlow's shipping out a second time with the carpenter who had served with him aboard the shipwrecked *Florentine* was a rare occurrence; he usually goes his separate way and, as far as we know, never makes any effort to keep in touch with past crewmates.

Barlow's kinship ties are also extremely loose. Though he has a settled parental home to which he might return, he rarely avails himself of such originary siting. He returns home, we have noted, only twice: the first time is a long twelve years after he left; the second and last time is twenty years after that, and then, not surprisingly, his mother and brother (his father is now dead) "at first did not know me" (412). Very occasionally, he sends some "token" money home to his family or visits with a relative in London. Such an uncommitted attitude characterizes even his relationship with the uncle at whose inn he spends one of his two years in London. Though his uncle clearly attempts to look out for him and set him on a proper course of living, Barlow never expresses any strong feelings of any kind for him (even when the uncle whips him for running off to see the strange sight of a beached whale; p. 25). When Barlow finally leaves the inn for good, his departure provokes no more emotion than the flat comment about his uncle's niggardliness: "My uncle brought me some few necessaries, about ten or a dozen shillings' worth, which was all I had besides an ordinary suit of clothes which was bought of a broker at the second hand before I went to Dartford to live with the vintner: and that was all I had for my service with my uncle and aunt, having lived with them a year" (30).

Even Barlow's relationship with the relative he sees most often—his sister Anne, who works as a servant in London—is intermittent and distanced.

Barlow seems to mourn her death genuinely: "for she loved me very well when she was alive," he says, "as I did her" (251). But as with the reported deaths of other family members—his brother George and his father and mother—Barlow states his love only at the time of their passing. Furthermore, his visits with his sister are very infrequent, and we learn virtually nothing about her other than her poor status as servant and her name (divulged upon her death). I do not mean to deny Barlow's declared love for his sister and other family members who died (or for his dead best friend); but I would nevertheless argue that for Barlow, "love" was expressed primarily in detachment. In the case of his friends, that detachment most often took the form of a felt ingratitude or insufficiency. But even with his family, there was an enduring divide. Thus, when Barlow visualizes a black-hatted connection between himself and his mother (fig. 4), such a unifying bond can be imagined only within the larger picture of radical severance—his leaving home. For Barlow, relational love was intimately connected with separation. It was not emotionally or physically binding in any strong or continuous way.

One gets some sense of the oddly displaced emotion Barlow feels for those "close" to him in his reaction to leaving Prestwich after his first return visit there. He says he expressed great grief on parting—"shedding more tears than I had done in seven years before"[16]—which the villagers interpret to be occasioned by thwarted love for one of the local women. Barlow tells us that the grief was not nearly so localized and nameable:

> But the true cause of my grief I rather think proceeded of a hidden natural cause of some great sorrow or trouble which time would make manifest to me, as the trouble and misery I might afterward fall into. At that time I wholly came down into the country to "recreat"[17] myself in taking my pleasure amongst my friends, little thinking what dangers might afterward befall me, and also taking leave of my father and mother, brother and sister, and other friends and acquaintance, and not knowing whether I should behold the faces of them again, being to be separated many hundred miles from them before I should see them again, for England not being my abode, but many other strange countries which I was to venture my life to, and endure many a hard night's lodging and hungry belly in getting myself a poor livelihood to live by, and so my grief was like them that cry in their dreams, for they cannot tell what nor when. (177–78)

This is typical Barlow. His grief is occasioned by a departure—here a going away, at other times a death—but it is not really the people per se (the relatives or friends) for whom he feels care. It is more a sense of having no enduring connectedness to these people. At this moment, that detachment is imagined as the result of his having taken up an itinerant calling—so that he no longer even has a home country or "abode"—but it is also the result of a more deep-rooted unsettledness of mind that urged him to take up that calling in the first place and prevents him from ever "fixing" on people or places.

Perhaps nowhere is Barlow's lack of investment, or his only temporary investment, in personal relationships more evident than in his various shifting sexual relationships. Though he acts especially lovingly toward one Prestwich village woman during his flirtatious return visit—so that his neighbors assumed he grieved for her in parting and "thought I had fixed my love upon [her]"—Barlow insists that "the love I bear her was for want of other company, taken in by leisure, and I did intend to drive it out by reason" (177). This leisurely attitude toward love does not prevent Barlow from promising to marry the woman after his next sailing to the East Indies. But it does prevent him from holding to his promise, and he doesn't even return home (nor, typically, does he ever tell us her name). Rather, he transfers his "love" to the next passing object: "Yet could I not fix and ground my love so far upon her that I could keep myself from professing the same to some others, which I did the same not long after; which was my great failing in that thing, and I did many times think that God was angry with me for so doing" (286). This is one of those rare moments when Barlow recognizes a failing.

Eventually, at the late age of thirty-six, Barlow does marry a poor servant maid (again, not named in his journal) who worked in the house of a "friend" (otherwise unidentified) in London and for whom he expresses "great love," praising her as an "excellent wife" (309, 310). As testimony to his felt responsibility for his new family, Barlow later states that he gave up a longed-for appointment as master of an East India ship, which was conditional upon his remaining in India, because of his wife and children back in England (361)—though this could also be cited as an instance of his reluctance to remain sited anywhere. Whatever his true motives in this case, it is clear that his family life was continually broken by his many long sea outings; just two days after the marriage ceremony, he sets sail on an estimated seven- to eight-month voyage. Barlow eerily punctuates his many departures and returns with impersonal and brief accounts of the births or deaths of children (only two out of his six children survived to adulthood). Typically, none of these children are named. Only modern archival research has been able to fix their identities (excluding that of the first son, who, Barlow tells us in his journal, was stillborn; p. 311). A search of extant records of christenings finds Hester (1679–86), Mary (1682–84), Edward (1684/85–?), Ann (1688–?), and Martha (1691–95).[18] Barlow's will, made out in 1705 (see appendix D), also reveals the names of his wife (Mary) and his still-living children (Edward and Ann), as well as the persons he appoints as his attorneys: first Mary, and then, in the event of her death, Mr. Bankes, a "land waiter [customs man in charge of landed cargo] at the custom house of London," and Richard Smith, a "wine cooper and merchant living in Devonshire Street without Bishopsgate." But once again, in this last and only other surviving written testimony of Barlow, such naming and interconnectedness occur only under pressure of the ultimate separation, death; Barlow has now reached the relatively old age of sixty-three and is about to ship out on another long East India voyage. "It being a long voyage," he declares, "and many accidents and changes may happen and knowing that all men are mortal and death certain and this time and place uncertain . . . I do now make and order this my last Will and Testament."[19]

Finally, it is also significant that although little can be found out about the everyday economic status and needs of Barlow's wife and children, due to the paucity of surviving records (what little we can gather will be discussed in the next chapter, in the context of poor seamen generally), we do know, from the locations of the children's baptisms, that the family likely moved around a fair bit, skirting the City proper. Hester and Mary were baptized at St. Botolph, Bishopsgate; Edward and Ann were baptized at the Holy Trinity, in the Minories; and Martha was baptized at St. Mary, Whitechapel. Barlow's family, like other poor families of the period, was on the move, though they moved within a roughly circumscribed area—just east of the City and just north of the Tower of London—that was chosen most likely for its proximity to the docks and ports. What anchored this itinerant family, in other words, was Barlow's unsettled occupation.

Did Barlow think of himself as an occasionally unsettled subject, as I have defined it in this book? That is, did he much of the time (if not all of the time) envision himself as displaced spatially, economically, and emotionally? Did he define himself as a subject often only provisionally and casually investing in a series of places, positions, and relationships? I would have to say provisionally yes, even though the primary basis for my judgment—Barlow's journal—was edited by Barlow himself for his imagined audience. Perhaps he in fact saw friends and family as fully developed personalities and at all times felt strong ties to them but also thought that filling in such connections or naming such affections (or the persons themselves) did not belong in a "factual" account of his life. But Edward Coxere, another poor seaman who wrote his life story (a journal-cum-spiritual autobiography, covering the period 1647–85, from age fourteen until age fifty-two), freely names fellow workers, friends, and family. He also forms something of a loose community with his fellow seamen, departing from co-workers but then sometimes reconnecting with them many years later. To the extent that Coxere's seaman community is amorphous, discontinuous, and open-ended, he too is something of an unsettled subject.[20] But Barlow is much more so; he is far more disconnected from such communal or affective ties. Indeed, it is striking how often he speaks of being "unsettled" or "unfixed" in talking about his early job switchings and—even after becoming a seaman—in describing his apparent inability to form a lasting affective/sexual bond.

It should be stressed, however, that in speaking of Barlow's unsettled subjectivity, I do mean subjectivity. For all his unsettledness, Barlow has a very strong sense of himself as an enduring subject. He may not be a unified or consistent "I," but an "I" he is. This is evident in his prolific use in his narrative of the personal pronoun. Though his description of an engagement or port might involve a suppression of such an "I," any accounting that bears specifically on him personally—which is often the case—produces a barrage of personal pronouns, often as many as ten to eighteen on a printed page. This foregrounding of an individual identity, however multividual in its unsettledness, can also be found in Coxere's narrative—though, as befits Coxere's more communal sense of himself, to a noticeably lesser extent. But Barlow's journal is distinct from other narratives by seamen of the Elizabethan period. Focusing on the brief account of shipboard life and captivity written by the seaman Miles Philips (1568–82) as an instance, Richard Helgerson notes that most of the time Philips, like other Elizabethans, shied away in his narrative from a direct highlighting of his distinguishing individual self. Philips's document is thus marked most of the time by an absence of "I's." Philips does not think of himself as an individual but as part of a shipboard community, then as part of a group of captives who submit to their Spanish masters and tormentors, then as a member of a group of youths spared execution and allowed guarded access to Spanish New World life. Only in the last quarter of the narrative, Helgerson argues, when all of Philips's fellow young captives have left him for full absorption into the Spanish New World, does Philips realize he cannot follow suit. And in that moment of aloneness, Helgerson says, Philips discovers his irreducible core of Protestant Englishness, prompting him to seek escape at all costs in order to return "home," as expressed in a barrage of insistent "I's."[21] Perhaps because Barlow was more removed from the period when England and its countrymen were defining themselves as a newly Protestant nation, perhaps because of the intense political and economic unsettledness of the seventeenth century in which he lived, Barlow emerges throughout his account as much more unstable, more difficult to pin down, and at the same time as more prominently, if inconsistently, an "I."

When Barlow does eventually settle upon the calling of seaman, he does so to try to stabilize or make legitimate his strongly felt but unsettled subjectivity (hence his preoccupation with finding a "lawful" livelihood). But at the

same time, he paradoxically—and fearfully, I would add—gives expression
to his unsettled mind. To understand more fully this perplexed identity formation, we need to explore the constitution and character of ships' crews.
What we shall find in pursuing this digressive route is that those going to sea
embarked upon not only a "lawful" occupation, but also a course of displacement—in the sense of voyaging—that in many ways extended (il)legal vagrancy. One and the same person could at various times be an unsettled youth
like Barlow, a seaman, and a legal vagrant. Furthermore, as we saw in previous chapters, such various roles "played" by itinerants could mingle interchangeably with those of a range of unstable but laboring landed poor (again,
like Barlow), who often found themselves literally at sea. Such poor displaced
workers were to become one of the first and largest groups of free subjects
within a new landless proletariat.

Poor Men at Sea
"Never to be worth one groat afore a beggar"

As suggested by Edward Barlow's continued multitasking while he was a seaman—doing odd jobs and peddling books between sailings—the occupation of seaman (or "mariner," as it was more often called in the sixteenth century) was by no means a delimited calling. There was especially much crossover and confusion between the seaman's form of itinerancy, which was considered legitimate in the early modern period, and the suspiciously regarded and often criminalized wanderings of the homeless and nomadic laboring poor. But as we shall see, even housed poor laborers could find themselves unexpectedly unsettled, whether willingly or not, and put to sea. Furthermore, rivaling the numbers of seamen, whatever their origins, was the multitude of wage-laboring landsmen employed in building, repairing, and equipping ships—workers who were at the mercy of fluctuating demands for their labor. Seafaring, then, was crucial to England's unsettled wage-laboring workforce in the seventeenth century and played a crucial part in that workforce's unsettled thinking.

My main concern in this chapter is specifically with the rapidly growing class of poor seamen in the period, as well as with both the easy porousness that characterized their labor—its openness to being cast on and off by differently unsettled types—and the uneasy regard surrounding it. After surveying this emerging proletariat of workers, we can more fully place our unsettled poor seaman, Edward Barlow. We can especially more fully understand his ambivalence toward his calling, which quintessentially expressed both liberty and alienation, both place and displacement. While never entirely a member of this seafaring crew—or any socioeconomic group, for that matter—and while always aspiring to climb the nautical corporate ladder and join "management" aboard ship, Barlow never lost his identification with the subjected, rebellious, and forever adrift wage laborer that was the poor seaman.

Throughout the late sixteenth and seventeenth centuries, we should first note, three peripatetic types—seaman, soldier, and vagrant—were intimately intertwined. Such was especially the case as it became increasingly common practice to press the unemployed and poor into military service. This longstanding policy was eagerly embraced under Elizabeth as a way of ridding the country of its swelling numbers of unplaceable poor (who authorities feared threatened the domestic peace) as well as a way of readily equipping expeditions with disposable forces. Captain Barnaby Rich and other military writers criticized the practice: "In London, when they set forth soldiers," Rich complains in 1578, "either they scour their prisons of thieves or their streets of rogues and vagabonds." But despite complaints about the resulting impoverishment of the forces, which occasionally prompted a temporary cessation of such activities, suspected rogues and vagabonds continued to be targeted for conscription. The Privy Council, for instance, instructed local authorities to round up the homeless for military expeditions to the Low Countries in 1585, to Picardy in 1597, and to Ostend in 1601. Watches were posted where the streets (and street people) ran into the fields, and "perfect searches" were made especially of fairs and alehouses "and such places as those loose persons do lodge."[1]

The sailors who crewed the naval ships transporting soldiers, and who were required to fight in sea battles as well, were as frequently drawn from the same unsettled ranks. Around 1623, though it was a time of peace, we hear a by-then-familiar complaint: that "the navy is for the greatest part manned with aged, impotent, vagrant, lewd and disorderly companions; it is become a ragged regiment of common rogues." The problem intensified during wars, which particularly plagued the latter half of the seventeenth century (England at various times during this period was at war with the Dutch, Danes, French, Spanish, and Algerian Turks). The naval wars against the Dutch (1652–54, 1665–67, and 1672–74), for which Barlow was at times pressed, demanded especially high numbers of seamen; yet it was increasingly difficult to man ships as the wars became decidedly unpopular. The navy expanded throughout the period, however, even under the neglect of James I and Charles I, growing from 24 ships and 6,290 men in 1578, to 41 ships and 8,346 men in 1603, to 156 ships and 19,551 men in 1660, to 173 ships and 41,940 men in 1688, and so on.[2] Since there were no standing naval regiments to speak of, however, naval crews were actually more accordion-like, their numbers deflating in peacetime and inflating in wartime. With the outbreak of war during the late seventeenth century, J. D. Davies notes, "up to 25,000 men had to be brought into the naval service within a matter of weeks."[3] Each flare-up of hostilities thus required a "hot press" to man the growing number of ships—and the streets were the first place press-gangs looked. As a consequence, the quality of the navy continued to deteriorate, and desertion became rampant. So "ragged" was the common seaman, with barely a shirt on his back, that the navy in 1628 had to institute the practice by which the purser peddled clothes and other necessities to the ill-equipped crew aboard ship (the cost was deducted from the poor seaman's pay).[4]

But it was not just the unemployed and homeless who were pressed into service. While the more well-to-do citizens often bought themselves out with bribes, the poorer sorts (wage laborers, mean husbandmen, small craftsmen, petty traders, and the like) were not always able to do so. The spectrum of "low" pressed men is gestured at in Shakespeare's 2 *Henry IV* (1597–98), where Falstaff's corrupt recruiting methods produce a tattered troop of riffraff that includes at least one poor husbandman and a tailor.[5] Christopher Lloyd reports the outrage over such practices in 1597, in the dual complaints about the "destitute" navy on the one hand and, on the other hand, good men getting off with a bribe of one pound, leaving only "men of all occupations, some of whom did not know a rope and were never at sea." As a result of so manning one military expedition in 1625, it was determined that "all the tinkers, tailors, weavers and such like landmen had to be put on shore again" as occupationally unfit. Though they were only supposed to impress men experienced at sea, press-gangs, Lloyd adds, could be especially aggressive in rounding up just such poor landed workers. For example, the Weymouth, Dorset, gang rejected the sickly-looking men who voluntarily turned up for duty and instead "began to raid private houses in search of young tradesmen or whoever was simple enough to accept the press money they proffered." Later in the century, in 1666, Samuel Pepys lamented the necessity of wartime tactics so coercive that the press payment was sometimes even omitted: "To see poor, patient laboring men and housekeepers leaving poor wives and families, taken up on a sudden by strangers, was very hard, and that without press money but forced against all law to be gone."[6] But voluntarily or no, to sea the poor men had to go.

The activities of the press-officers were supplemented by instructions to vice admirals of maritime counties and to mayors of maritime towns to raise a specified quota of men for naval service. As with the press-gangs, however, this system was subject to abuse. Often it was used as an excuse to relieve the local community of undesirables—the unstable poor. In his study of Cromwell's navy, Bernard Capp lists the kinds of poor laborers tagged for service: one group, sent from Sussex, comprised "'a tinker, a Quaker, two glass carriers, a hatter, a chairmaker, and a tanner, with his little boy of seven years old'"; another contained "millers, bakers, butchers, and tailors who 'never saw salt water before'"; and yet another included "a sickly man pressed at the age of seventy."[7] Davies finds the problem continuing in the 1670s: "In one ten-day period of 1673 . . . the navy's new recruits included butchers, cordwainers, ribbon-weavers, bakers, a 'country lad,' 'an old man blind,' and a one-armed apprentice to an innkeeper."[8] Captains would protest to vice admirals about the failure to obtain good men, and vice admirals would in turn protest to constables. But there simply weren't enough experienced and willing seamen to go around.

As late as 1708, the privateer Captain Woodes Rogers, setting out from Bristol on a voyage around the world, laments that "notwithstanding our number [over 150 crewmen], we had not 20 sailors in the ship [the *Duke*], and it's very little better on board the *Dutchess* [his consort ship]; which is a discouragement, only we hope to get some good sailors at Cork."[9] At Cork, they were able to take on some better men, "upon which we clear'd several of those brought from Bristol, and some of 'em run away, being ordinary fellows, and not fit for our employment" (4). What happened to the forty men cleared from the ship we do not know. Of the remaining crew, Rogers complains that they "were continually marrying whilst we staid at Cork, though they expected to sail immediately" (6)—suggesting, as with Barlow, a lack of commitment to either sea or land bonds. Rogers's tally of the final crew for both ships is a list of named officers (double the usual number, he says, to prevent mutinies and replace mortalities) and a complement of 333 sailors, which he calls a "mixed gang": "above one third were foreigners from most nations," and among "several of her Majesty's subjects on board were tinkers, tailors, hay-makers, peddlers, fiddlers, etc., one negro, and about ten boys" (8). Captain George Shelvocke, on his expedition around the world of 1719, further lists among the difficulties facing his ship the fact that among the 101 crewmen, "four fifths . . . were land men."[10]

Given the huge and growing demand for manpower to service the navy, merchant shipping, and privateering expeditions, it is no wonder that seamen were drawn widely from the vast sector of the laboring poor. When privateering or merchant ships returned to home port, or when the navy demobilized, many of the poor crewmen (whether originally vagabond or not) had no craft or trade awaiting them and little alternative except either signing on to another ship or following the landed path of itinerant labor or vagabondage. In his study of masterless men during the first half of the seventeenth century, A. L. Beier found that "no occupational groups increased as much as sailors and soldiers among vagrants from 1560 to 1640." In 1593, 1597, and 1601, statutes were passed aimed at caring for the disabled among these groups and at employing veterans. "It remains to be seen, however," Beier adds, "how effective the system was. Certainly during the civil wars and the Interregnum the demand overwhelmed it, and no evidence has been found that veterans were employed."[11] Efforts to care for injured active seamen appeared in the 1653 Sick and Wounded (or Sick and Hurt) Board, which were not entirely ineffectual (Barlow was twice taken care of when injured, first in an accident in 1659 and then in battle against the Dutch in 1666). Some disabled veterans were also subsidized through allowances from the Chatham Chest, into which each sailor paid; but as Lloyd points out, "that was short of funds after being raided and defrauded." And there was no established naval hospital in the country until the Royal Hospital was founded in 1694; even then, no pensioners were in residence until 1705.[12] Generally, veterans were left to fend for themselves, disabled or not, and most faced unsettling poverty.

Of course, even the employed poor who signed on to ships were generally from among the lowest orders of society—who, as we saw in the first part of this book, were often unsettled, even without ever going to sea (multiply or serially employed, financially unstable, and geographically mobile). Employing a synecdoche of seventeenth-century origin, Pepys succinctly referred to them as "poor illiterate hands," as if they were made up of detachable body parts.[13] Davies provides a longer sampling of the kinds of unstable landed poor who found themselves aboard ship: in addition to the many who came from a long line of seamen, he says, there were "sons of husbandmen, boys left in the care of the parish, . . . children of tradesmen, . . . those who found few opportunities for work in their own areas, or who sought a chance to travel and see something of the world . . . runaway husbands and drunks, . . . escaped prisoners, and failed tradesmen seeking to evade their creditors." "Most seamen," he adds, "had very few possessions," most lived on credit, and "many died in debt" (partly because of the navy's own growing financial troubles, which resulted in long delays of payment to its men upon concluding a deployment).[14]

Some poor, nevertheless, freely signed on to ships out of an urgent need for the up-front conscription payment—usually one shilling—or, even when pressing was not in effect or when they chose a merchant vessel, out of hope of making a better go of it at sea (where wages were higher than on land). Promises of higher pay, together with room and board, "were attractive enough to draw many a weaver from his loom or laborer from his plough."[15] Because naval and merchant ships allowed men to sign on as servants for wages as well as through the more binding apprenticeship system—Barlow ruefully wishes he had taken the former route (29)—the occupation of seaman could easily be taken up and cast off as a form of temporary service. Indeed, for many, "sailoring was normally a casual employment, into and out of which they drifted as they found employment harder to come by on sea or on land."[16] When legal means of termination were not available, there was always the illicit but oft-chosen option of serving notice through desertion.

The men who went to sea thus entered—and in many cases continued— a tradition of a casual, unstable, and porous wage labor. While seamen are the focus of this chapter, many others on land were intimately tied to this kind of labor. The seafaring industry was supported by huge numbers of landed wage laborers who did not go to sea but were nevertheless often conscripted and equally vulnerable to unsettledness. Such workers represent a significant sector of the population. By the 1670s, as Ralph Davis observes, "shipping was one of the three or four largest employers of wage labor in the country"; he adds that "great numbers of people were employed in shipbuilding and repair and the allied occupations (making ropes, sails, blocks, ironware, etc.) and in providing sea stores and victuals." In London, probably more than a quarter of the population depended on the sea for its living.[17]

Among English shipyards, the navy's were the largest, followed by those of the big East India Company (such as Henry Johnson's at Blackwall and Captain William Castle's at Deptford). Though D. C. Coleman has questioned claims that merchant dockyards generally became precursors to nineteenth-century "industries" in the course of the seventeenth century, he does see industrialism afoot in the large naval yards of the period and in a few of the larger private yards, such as Blackwall's and Deptford's, which built big ships and required massive manpower and resources. With respect to the naval yards, he finds that over the course of the seventeenth century, "an average of approximately a quarter of the state expenditure was directed to naval needs, exclusive of naval ordnance," and on average, about half that amount went into the dockyards.[18] Whole towns of workers rapidly grew up around such large dockyards, prospering from their demands for labor. But many also suffered from the irregularities of a boom-and-bust industry, which we have seen in the sailoring sector as well. Coleman sums up the problem: "Periods of vigorous, inflated employment, preceded by the furious recruitment of civilian labor by methods which included impressment, alternated with intervals of depressed conditions, during which labor was laid off, ships rotted and poverty was more noticeable than usual in a region with no other comparable source of employment."[19]

Furthermore, when a hot press was on, these landed wage laborers were liable to the same kinds of displacement suffered by those sent to sea: "labor was sometimes impressed and then dispatched post haste from one yard to another," Coleman notes.[20] The resulting sense of unsettledness was compounded by the failure of naval authorities to pay wages with any sort of regularity. Thus the ropemakers, for instance, calling themselves the Company of Ropemakers and representing impressed men distant from their homes, repeatedly petitioned for "board wages": in November 1665, when they were six weeks in arrears; in March 1666, when they were seventeen weeks in arrears; and yet again in June 1666, when they were now nine months in arrears. As with unpaid seamen, discontent among landed wage laborers employed by the dockyards often broke out into strikes and mutinies—between 1663 and

1665, and again in 1668.[21] It is important to remember this large population of support workers when thinking of seamen, since their labors were in effect interdependent. Certainly, these two groups of wage laborers taken together must have bolstered demand for ballads about seamen in the seventeenth century, which we shall discuss in the concluding chapter. It is not only seamen and their families who would have been interested in these representations of the seaman's condition, but also the large sector of landed wage laborers invested in the seafaring industry, as well as those many others ambivalently watching the combined and growing numbers of such unsettled workers.

But we cannot conclude our discussion of the home front without looking more closely at the home. What we find is that the physical and economic instability of those many men engaged in the seafaring industry could place their families at home in difficult situations. Wives left behind by men shipped to sea faced the most severe financial problems, despite their efforts to make ends meet by taking on makeshift work. A petition in 1667 by the officers and crew of the frigate *Harp*, stationed off the coast of Ireland, is chilling in its account of those left behind at home (the men's wages were fifty-two months in arrears): the petitioners complain that they have "neither money nor credit to buy bread for their wives and children, who are now in a starving condition, being forced to lie in the streets by reason their landlords will trust them no longer, and your petitioners going naked for want of clothes, which together are worse ten thousand times than to die by the hands of the enemy."[22] Peter Kemp points out that conditions improved somewhat during Queen Anne's reign—so that wives and mothers could now be paid a portion of their men's wages when the men were on ships at foreign stations—but it is questionable how well these women could manage on but a portion of a poor seaman's salary.[23] The many women widowed by the deaths of their husbands at sea were especially vulnerable. That such widows often could not support themselves, Michael J. Power observes, "is suggested by a proposal of Secretary [of State] Jenkins in August 1682 for setting up a hospital for housing such families."[24]

The account from the *Harp* crew is somewhat misleading, however. It paints a picture of the seventeenth-century seaman as a dutiful family man. Many surely were. But most sailors of the period were young and single. They were also characteristically reckless and loose with their money (when they had it). Edward Barlow describes sailors "running out so most part of their wages, crying, 'A merry life and a short' [and] 'Longest liver take all'" (160). For these men, a settled life was not on the horizon. As Marcus Rediker records, seamen spoke of themselves as following a "roving course of life," as beset by an "unhappy mind of rambling," and—echoing Barlow—as never "properly settled."[25] When it came to forming family ties, a casual attitude often prevailed, a phenomenon we have previously seen among the families of poor itinerant chapmen and among the very poor generally. Thus, when Barlow's master heard of the death of his wife in 1659, he "laid [it] not very hard to heart," Barlow says, but on his very next leave went seeking for a replacement wife, whom he promptly found (35, 38). Capp observes that "for many sailors the marriage bond was weak and easily broken." We might here recall Captain Rogers's complaint that his sailors "were continually marrying, whilst we staid at Cork, though they expected to sail immediately." Not surprisingly, bigamy was also common among seamen. Capp notes that one captain in 1656 learned that two of his seamen had no fewer than five wives between them! But, Capp adds, wives could be as casual in their attitude to such marriages as their husbands. Susan Cane, for example, "married to a cook's mate, was denied [parish] relief because she had not lived with her husband"; she was described as "a woman of loose life, [who] frequents evil company." Indeed, prostitution was not an uncommon method by which poor seamen's wives, like other poor women, supplemented the family's meager income.[26]

Though we will need to qualify this representation of seamen and their interpersonal disconnectedness in the final chapter, where we will look at ballads about seamen from the seventeenth century, it is clear that the word *unsettled* quintessentially described them. The image of the untethered "free" seaman, as explored by Valerie Burton, came to be worn as a badge of proletarian pride by these wage laborers in the eighteenth century. But seamen began to protest the stereotype in the nineteenth and twentieth centuries, because they recognized that shipowners themselves promulgated the image in an effort to treat seamen's labor as "casual" and thus keep their pay low. In reaction, seamen tried to remake their image into that of stolid breadwinners, steadfastly supporting home and family (the image promoted by the men aboard the *Harp*)—something easier to do with the introduction of the more stable steamship industry in the nineteenth century.[27]

Ideas about seamen, then—even ideas held by seamen about themselves—were not necessarily consistent over time, or even within a given period. With this in mind, we need to interrogate further the perception of seamen as "free" wage laborers in the seventeenth century, not tied down by either property or personal obligations. This characterization of the seaman lies at the heart of the important, if determinedly Marxist, interpretations by Marcus Rediker and Peter Linebaugh of the rise of the seaman proletariat (a reading that has been dubbed the "red Atlantic" version of expansion by

David Armitage and Michael J. Braddick).[28] In *Between the Devil and the Deep Blue Sea*, Rediker traces the origins of the nineteenth-century proletariat to the many landed poor workers who were uprooted and displaced in the course of the late sixteenth and seventeenth centuries. By the early eighteenth century, Rediker argues, seamen emerge from this large, if amorphous, body of displaced workers as one of the largest and first collectives of laborers in England. Their growing numbers, the unique character of their work, and its lonely setting contributed to the formation of a strong laboring identity among seamen—a class identity.[29]

But the road to class identity does not necessarily lead to a unitary or homogenous identity, as Rediker is well aware. Together with Peter Linebaugh, with whom he later coauthored *The Many-Headed Hydra*, Rediker paints a complex and even fractured picture of our emerging seaman proletariat. Such was especially the case in the early, formative stage of its identity in the course of the seventeenth century. Though some seamen, especially in the later seventeenth century, became long-term practitioners of their trade and could thus see themselves as "belonging" to a seaman collective, for most (as we have seen), the "profession" of seaman was casual, intermittent, and porous by nature, mixing uneasily with temporary landed work, and poor landed laborers.[30] Other contradictions in the seaman's shaping identity prevailed as well. In particular, though the seaman often saw himself as proudly (if forcibly) serving the nation's shipping and naval interests, he also often found himself part of a "mixed gang" of nationalities aboard ship, as Captain Rogers put it. Foreigners were legally allowed to constitute about a quarter of the ship's crew (we recall that on Rogers's ship, the *Duke*, "above one third were foreigners from most nations"), which could unmoor the sense of fixed national identity. Indeed, the seaman was in many ways alienated from any landed society, which, as we have also seen, regarded his unsettled labor—and the kinds of men who undertook it—with nervous suspicion.[31]

Part of that alienation and suspicion arose as, over the course of the seventeenth century, seafaring increasingly rejected the apprenticeship and craft system. Some trappings of craft organization remained aboard the merchant ship. As Rediker explains,

> The merchant ship in several ways resembled the traditional workshop. It had a master (the captain), a few journeymen (the mates who aspired, and sometimes managed, to become masters), apprentices (the lesser officers), and day laborers (the common tars). The organizational whole was held together by a corporate collectivism based on principles of hierarchy, paternalistic authority, and deference. Vertical solidarities linked the bottom and the top of the

division of labor. Cultural life at sea expressed these basic principles and relations in a variety of ways.

On the other hand, Rediker continues,

> there were numerous ways in which the ship did not—indeed, could not—resemble a workshop. Sailors, unlike craftsmen, did not own the tools of their trade. They possessed no property in artisanal skills. They depended upon the money wage. They did not labor within a regulated craft; rather, they were fully integrated into an international market economy. They lost and found work according to the violent shifts of war and peace and the anarchic swings of economic cycles. Free of property and skills, unprotected from fluctuating market forces, and living lives shaped by mobility, dispersion, and high mortality, seamen largely failed to develop craft traditions or a craft consciousness.[32]

Merchant captains continued to employ the language of the traditional craft system, referring to themselves variously as "masters (of servants or apprentices), fathers (of children) and kings (of subjects)."[33] But paternal obligations were eroded by the mobile seaman's quick, easy, and regular changes of masters, as well as by the depersonalized nature of the money wage. Linebaugh and Rediker make the acute observation that if anything, the ship was a precursor of the modern-day factory: the deep-sea vessel of the early modern period employed "large numbers of workers [who] cooperated on complex and synchronized tasks, under slavish, hierarchical discipline in which human will was subordinated to mechanical equipment, all for a monetary wage."[34]

As seamen labored aboard their floating factory, inequities between privileged officers and poor seamen—in regard to discipline, wages, work, and especially food—became glaringly obvious and grated upon the lowly workers.[35] This further fostered a sense of class (versus craft) organization. It also sparked a rebelliousness that had its seed in the seaman's first act of severance—his going to sea—and in his subsequent alienation from landed society. Especially in the eighteenth century, this rebelliousness often took the form of spontaneous uprisings on land and at sea.[36] But as the demonstrations of the 1660s illustrate, the seeds of revolution were planted early. An even earlier recognition of the seaman's fractious, and potentially revolutionary, nature was dramatized on the stage of history in the beheading of Charles I: Charles's executioner, most tellingly, emerged on the scaffold disguised as a sailor.[37] Was this (seaman) executioner an insurgent or a nationalist? He was unsettlingly both and neither.

The seaman could also be an unsettling force by virtue of how his "free" labor was conceived and used. Sir William Petty, a key figure in the development

of political arithmetic in England in the later seventeenth century, praised
seamen as "the very pillars" of the English nation not only in their capacity as
naval defenders but also in their function as commodities akin to the cargo
they helped ship: "The labor of seamen, and the freight of ships," Petty explained, "is always of the nature of an exported commodity, the overplus
whereof, above what is imported, brings home money." In Rediker's summa-
tion of Petty's position, "The seaman's labor was a commodity to be sold on
an open market like any other."[38]

Ironically, Petty's optimistic conception of the value of the seaman's labor,
which could be productively capitalized upon, devalued seamen into human
commodities or objects akin to slaves. We can find an early instance of such
dehumanizing thinking in Edward VI's reign, in the government's desperate
attempt to halt homelessness by passing a statute that made arrested vagrants
slaves as well. Not only were they to be assigned owner-masters—to the extent of being branded, beaten, fed "refuse of meat," and shackled—but they
were also made exchangeable or saleable, like "any other of his [the master's]
movable goods or cattels [chattel]." Though enforcing the law proved im-
practical, and it was soon repealed, slavery reappeared in the 1604 statute of
James I, in which judges were given the option to sentence incorrigible rogues
either to a lifetime of banishment or "perpetually to the galleys."[39] The hard-
ened vagrant, in such a ruling, was judged as fit only to serve on ships at sea.

It was not just that seamen and slaves served together at sea; their ties were
closer than that. Two separate commanders in the seventeenth century saw a
kind of identity, or at least a likeness, between seamen and galley slaves. Commenting on the ill treatment of seamen, in notes written in the early seventeenth
century for Prince Henry, Sir Walter Raleigh cites bad victualing as the primary
reason why men "go with great grudging to serve in H.M. ships, as it were to be
slaves in the galleys." Writing early in the reign of Charles I, in 1629, Sir Henry
Mervyn makes the same connection: "Foul winter weather, naked bodies and
empty bellies make the men voice the King's service worse than a galley slavery."[40] In statutes and in contemporary opinion of the time, in other words,
seamen, vagrants, and galley slaves floated interchangeably together "at sea."

In actuality, then, the seamen prized so highly by Petty were as much
captives of their own merchants and captains as the slave cargo they might be
shipping (and they suffered the same mortality rates).[41] This became increasingly the case with the draconian measures of discipline implemented by the
end of the seventeenth century. On one expedition of 1721 to procure a cargo
of slaves, the crew mutinied in protest over the "barbarous and unhumane usage from their commander," which placed them, they protested, in "bondage."[42]
But comparisons to slavery also accompanied protests against the generally

disliked practice of impressment. Throughout the seventeenth and into the eighteenth century, arguments against impressment were voiced in terms of arguments against slavery and for liberty. Thus, Linebaugh and Rediker note, "the 'Humble Petition of the Seamen, belonging to the Ships of the Commonwealth of England,' dated November 4, 1654, complained of disease, poor provisions, bloodshed, wage arrears, and most of all the 'thraldom and bondage' of impressment, which were 'inconsistent with the principles of freedom and liberty.'"[43] It is thus not surprising that revolutionary allegiances in the English colonies developed between seamen and slaves, together with other repressed groups; or that a mob of sailors in Charleston, in 1765, protested another perceived affront to liberty—the Stamp Act—by visiting the home of the wealthy merchant Henry Laurens wearing blackface.[44] By adopting this particular disguise, seamen affirmed their kinship with African slaves. Both seamen and slaves were displaced workers in bondage of the lowest and most unsettling type.

But what could constrain, even enslave, seamen to market forces could also liberate them: seamen could use their commodified labor as a bargaining chip and quite literally mobilize their labor. Not only could they activate protests and strikes (or mutinies), but skilled seamen could hold out for higher wages in times of increased demand for their services. Moreover, dissatisfied workers could spontaneously (and surreptitiously) switch ships and—as often happened in periods of war—jump a naval ship for one of the merchant vessels, which raised their wages in wartime to attract such experienced seamen.[45] Indeed, Rediker comments, "what merchant capitalists and their lackeys saw as 'the natural unsteadiness of seamen' was in fact the use of autonomous mobility to set the conditions of work."[46] In this sense, bondage and freedom went hand in hand.

Displaced but housed, enslaved but free, alienated but communal, objects of capitalism but subjects of resistance, nationalistic but revolutionary— such was the conflicting character of the growing body of seaman wage laborers in the seventeenth century. Such contradictions remained a part of the seaman's collective identity even as it more concretely formed itself into a community and class in the eighteenth century. The seaman's nature was, in a word, unsettled, just as it was unsettling to those many landed Englishmen who depended on "free" wage labor but feared its unsavory and unbound potential. It might well be that the seaman was further unsettled even in his understanding of himself because he found himself part of a difficult-to-fathom, newly emergent breed or class of workers that broke so many of the familiar rules of labor. As such, the seaman's socioeconomic condition adds volumes to our understanding of Edward Barlow.

To use a nautical metaphor, we can employ our survey of the seaman's itinerant and conflicted "calling" as a "quadrant" in order to get a better fix on Barlow's occupational position. What we can establish clearly is that Barlow's settling upon the calling of seaman was not occupationally settling at all. It was anything but. Whether we understand his placement in the position of seaman as being in contradiction to his previous unfocused and shifting labors, or as itself inherently conflicted and unsettled in nature (the two conceptions most likely operated simultaneously in Barlow's thinking), the fact is that instability and unsettledness ruled.

We might return first to the important fact that although some seamen, especially later in the seventeenth century, became long-term practitioners of the trade—as Barlow ambivalently did—the occupation of seaman was often only provisionally (and forcibly) assumed and was also frequently inhabited by the physically unsettled as well as by uncertain poor workers prone to multiple and serial employment. For Barlow, to be a seaman meant rubbing elbows with, and often merging with, such unstable and itinerant poor. It should not be surprising, then, that Barlow often thinks about his calling specifically in terms of illicit placelessness and even beggary.

Such thoughts, as we have seen, were often projected onto the young landed Barlow from without, as neighbors and family repeatedly accused him of being shiftless for not settling on a trade, "saying I would never stay anywhere, for I was given to wandering" (20). Even strangers pegged Barlow for an out-of-place wanderer. For instance, while still in his landed youth—shifting from job to job and place to place—Barlow stands idly looking upon the river at London Bridge and is approached by a sailor who automatically assumes he is a recent immigrant to London and "out of place." Barlow's uncle later guesses that the man was "a spirit or kidnapper":

> one of those who used to entice any who they think are country people or strangers and do not know their fashion and custom, or any who they think are out of place and cannot get work, and are walking idly about the streets [Barlow's situation when approached]: then they, (the kidnappers) watching their opportunities, come to such persons, both men and women, and inquiring of them whether they are out of place, or want work, or are minded to go to sea, promise them great wages and good fortune at such places as they will help them to: and many times they give them money and entice them along with them to their houses. (27)

Once lured onto a ship, Barlow continues, such would-be workers/seamen are then forcibly kept aboard until sold into service for four years in the New

World. Some two hundred thousand workers were sent to the New World as indentured servants in the seventeenth century, many kidnapped in this fashion or otherwise pressed.[47] Interestingly, Barlow does not see such a fate as all that bad, since many of the women, he says, end up marrying well overseas; and the men also, once terminating their bondage, often do better for themselves than had they lived at home (28). The lure of the displaced Other for Barlow is strong.

Not only is Barlow as a landed youth taken for one who is "out of place"— and he is indeed at that time between odd jobs, "walking idly about the streets"—but also, while still an apprentice seaman, he experiences firsthand what it is like to be treated as a vagrant seaman, that is, one of the many displaced and out-of-work mariners who wandered the towns and roadways of England in the period. When he visits his master's ship in port, Barlow tells us, his own ship unexpectedly sets sail without him, heading from Portsmouth for Falmouth. Desperate to reconnect with it (and all of his belongings on board), he catches a ship to Plymouth; then, fearing being pressed into service on a man-of-war and lamenting the "uncertainty" of the seaman's life, he hurriedly travels the rest of the way to Falmouth overland—a wintry, forty-mile journey—with only a shilling in his pocket. Along the way he is treated sometimes well, sometimes indifferently. Once, lost in the dead of night, he approaches a house: "and at last I desired them to let me have a lodging anywhere for that night, for I was in a strange place where I never was before, and did not know the way and had little or no money to bear my charges." At first the inhabitants "denied me a lodging in their barn and told me they did not know what I might be." Finally, however, he successfully "begged" lodging and was even given some food. The next couple of days, he was forced to beg food along the way, though he saved enough money to buy lodging at night. Finally, he arrived in Falmouth and reconnected with his ship (94–97).

Despite being treated like a beggar and being told by people that "they did not know what I might be," Barlow does not this time internalize his firsthand vagabond experience; he does not speak of himself as feeling inwardly or psychically displaced during this adventure. But at many other times, the various external assessments of him as hopelessly "unsettled" do seem to strike an inner chord. Not only does Barlow frequently refer to himself as being "not well settled in my mind," but he also often compares himself to rogues and beggars. The first time he returns home, for instance, he says he spent fifteen pounds on a good suit of clothes, thus impressing his former neighbors. Despite his evident pride in their admiration, however, he knows, even if they don't, that the money was an unusual windfall, the result of having been paid for an exceedingly long voyage. Tellingly, he adds that "if they had seen me many times before and since on such condition as I was many times in, they would sooner have asked what beggar or what jail-bird I had been" (175).

Even more significantly, Barlow, in times of hardship at sea, often compares his life, not simply his clothes, to that of a beggar—except, he says, the life of the poor seaman is worse. On one trip aboard the *Augustine*, within a long general lament (provoked by short victuals and stinking drink) about the hard life of the seaman, Barlow declares,

> And I was always thinking that beggars had a far better life of it and lived better than I did, for they seldom missed of their bellies full of better victuals than we could get: and also at night to lie quiet and out of danger in a good barn full of straw, nobody disturbing them, and might lie as long as they pleased: but it was quite contrary with us, for we seldom in a month got our bellyful of victuals, and that of such salt as many beggars would think scorn to eat; and at night when we went to take our rest, we were not to lie still above four hours. (60)

Barlow's lament continues for another fifty-three lines; he concludes by declaring "but I had always a mind to see strange countries and fashions, which made me bear these extremities with the more patience" (61). But again, decrying his poor Christmas fare aboard the *Martin Galley*, he recalls that "the poorest people in all England would have a bit of something that was good on such a day," and that "many beggars would fare much better than we did" (68). Aboard the *Yarmouth*, facing yet another Christmas dinner of "but a bit of old rusty beef" (161), Barlow launches into an attack on the abuse of the ship's "poor men" by the officers, who seize the best victuals. He then expresses a hope to save enough money "to leave off the sea as soon as I could," because he feared that in old age, he would be treated like a beggarly slave or rogue: "For I saw by daily experience that if I went to sea when I should be grown in years, that then I should be little better than a slave, being always in need, and enduring all manner of misery and hardship, going with many a hungry belly and wet back, and being always called 'old dog,' and 'old rogue,' and 'son of a whore,' and suchlike terms, which is a common use amongst seamen" (162). He adds, "I think I was born under a threepenny planet, and as the old proverb is, 'Never to be worth one groat afore a beggar'" (163).

In actuality, however Barlow might have been treated at sea, he appears not to have ended up "a beggarly slave or rogue"; nor did he leave his family destitute, as so many seamen did. Though extant poor-relief records for the period are very sparse for the parishes in which we know his family resided—St. Botolph, Bishopsgate; Holy Trinity, the Minories; and St. Mary, Whitechapel— and though in fact for some of the parishes such records are nonexistent, we do know from the Land Tax returns for St. Mary's, 1693/94, when Barlow resided there, that he rented a house for seven pounds (probably a yearly rent).[48] Whitechapel was a notorious "black spot" of impoverished and overcrowded housing,[49] with annual rents ranging from one to twenty pounds but most being in the region of five to twenty pounds. So at least among these very poor, Barlow placed in the lower end of average.[50] Furthermore, evidence from Barlow's will (made in 1705 and proved in 1708) indicates, surprisingly, a certain amount of accumulated wealth: he divides his estate into three parts (with equal divisions to his wife, his surviving son, and his surviving daughter when she reaches the age of twenty-one). In addition to the mention of general household goods, Barlow itemizes a number of silver items: a silver tankard, a silver salver (tray), two silver cups, a silver sugar dish, several silver spoons, and a small silver dram cup (see appendix D). How Barlow came by these valuable items is unclear. We know that they were not inherited from his impoverished father, whose meager goods were inventoried (see appendix B). Most likely he either bought them on his travels or acquired them as his portion of the prize money upon capturing an enemy ship when he was in the employ of the navy (in accordance with the custom of the time of dividing up such booty among the crew). Significantly, the items had dwindled to just the one silver tankard by the time Barlow's widow, Mary, made her will in 1713 (proved in 1715), suggesting her need to sell off the valuables to support herself and her children.[51]

Even more significant, however, is the fact that on the basis of his journal, one would never suspect that Barlow had accumulated any lasting wealth. He insistently refers to himself, even later in life, as a "poor seaman": "he that is poor shall be poor still," he declares in 1674 (242); thus "a poor man" is denied advancement, he laments in 1682 (351); "thus a poor man is abused with proud and ambitious masters, finding no recompense, having no money to try the law," he sighs in 1683 (358). In his repeated criticisms of the injustices done to all "poor seamen," including himself, by the East India Company (laments usually occasioned by the company's rules against seamen making personal investments when on company business), Barlow drips irony—"the Company showing such kindness to poor seamen" (1684; p. 365)—and voices protests: "many poor and sensible people suffering that never had any thought of wronging the Company in the least" (1685; p. 370); "it being a very unreasonable thing that a poor man cannot have liberty to dispose of what is his own without giving them [the Company] what they please . . . they will not pity their poor servants" (1695; p. 455); "all poor seamen are forced to take what the Company are pleased to give them" (1701; p. 528); and finally, "in this manner are poor seamen abused in [the Company] taking such small matter from them that buy it only for their own sustenance and use in their voyage" (1702; p. 531). Whatever his actual accumulated wealth (and whenever and however he accumulated it), Barlow perceived himself to be one of those poor seamen, "never to be worth one groat afore a beggar," often blaming his abusive masters (in navy and merchant ships) and especially his capitalist merchant employers. But at the same time, he concludes almost every tirade against his impoverishing profession with the affirmation "but my desire was, from my youth, to see strange countries and fashions, and I must, with hunger and cold, pay for it" (163).

Given Barlow's actual spatial and occupational shiftings as a youth, which provoked observations by others that he "could not stay"; given his own assessment of himself as unsettled in his mind, which prevented him from forming lasting social and affective bonds; and given his eventually settling upon a most unsettling calling, a calling he intersperses with odd jobs and which was often provisionally assumed by landed vagabonds and itinerant laboring poor as well as by poor householders liable to economic and spatial mobility and even homelessness—poor men with whom he cohabited on ship and with whom he likewise identified as beggarly "poor"—one cannot simply dismiss Barlow's frequent comparisons (and contrasts) of himself to beggars as incidental or just the expression of feeling decidedly "low." Barlow's thinking of himself as like, or not like, a beggar is in this context more profoundly telling than that: it bespeaks a kindred with many other poor seamen, who—deep within, some of the time, if not all the time—would have thought of themselves as profoundly unsettled subjects.

As confirmation of a more deeply sensed connectivity with the unsettled poor at sea, consider Barlow's fear that, should he continue to go to sea, he would in his old age "be little better than a slave." During another lament over "what great extremities poor seamen must endure," provoked by his telling about short rations aboard the *Cadiz Merchant* as it sailed from Jamaica to England, Barlow once again compares sailors to slaves—"all the men in the ship except the master," he concludes, "being little better than slaves" (339). As we have seen, Barlow often talks about the seaman's life as a kind of bondage or compulsion, and I have suggested that his sense of himself as being bound or forced to go to sea was in part an expression of an almost uncontrollable inner drive to wander. That he associates this binding force also with slavery further reflects, I would argue, an inner fear that the calling to which he is driven is something worse: a kind of internally driven enslavement to unsettledness. And, of course, it is a slavery with long chains of connection to the bondage that seamen suffered under impressment, as commodities of capitalism, and as co-workers of galley slaves. Barlow himself most likely worked alongside galley slaves when, in order to stay out longer at sea, he agreed to change berths from the *Augustine* to the *Martin Galley* (67; this latter ship's poor provisions provoked one of Barlow's many comparisons between himself and beggars).

Moreover, the class distinction we observed aboard ship—between upper and lower decks—was the source of much unsettled constraint for Barlow. Even those lowly seamen who steadfastly held to the sea, we have seen, more often than not found themselves in the maritime equivalent of landed itinerancy: willy-nilly committed to a lifetime of wandering in uncertain poverty. Routes to advancement on ships became ever more tightly closed off in the latter half of the seventeenth century, especially in the navy.[52] In his journal, Barlow speaks of trying and trying again to raise his position so far as to attain the title of master or captain of a ship. After completing his apprenticeship, he was able to attain the lower officer positions of gunner, boatswain, midshipman (a newly instituted naval position), and mate. But despite over forty years of experience at sea, he records, he was always thwarted in his efforts to become a master. Later in life, he focuses his ambition on merchant ships, especially those of the East India Company, because he sees absolutely no hope for advancement in His Majesty's service, where patronage ruled and thus so did unskilled "gentlemen officers" (whose "fear and unskilfulness" Barlow disdains; p. 463).[53] But the East India Company also thwarts him. In the long narrative that is his journal, Barlow could never get beyond the forever lower and unsure position of journeyman. He thus joined the many other lower-order seamen who became the maritime counterpart to the growing numbers of landed apprentices who completed their indentures only to find themselves denied the position of master and forced to travel a road of perpetually unplaced labor. Like such land journeymen, the sea journeyman Barlow was bound to be physically, socially, and economically unsettled. In more ways than one, then, Barlow lived most of his poor life "at sea."

I say "most of his life" because Barlow *did* temporarily master the East India ship the *Scepter* for the remainder of its voyage when its commander died in the Red Sea in 1697.[54] Also, though in his journal he records that he was never appointed to the command of a ship, Barlow *did* eventually gain the command position aboard an East India vessel after his journal ends (it stops abruptly with the Great Storm of 1703, when Barlow is sixty-one years old). Barlow documents in his will of November 18, 1705, that he is about to set sail as "commander" of the East India ship the *Liampo* on "a voyage to Mocha in the Red Sea." Sadly, the *Liampo* was lost at sea off the coast of Mozambique in 1706.[55] We do not know for sure whether Barlow went down with the ship. His will was proved in 1708, which meant either that he died in 1708 or that news of his death only reached his family at that time (not unlikely, given the long travel time of East India ships). The one piece of evidence that suggests Barlow may have survived the shipwreck is that his journal survived it. We know that Barlow at least some of the time brought his journal with him on his sailings, as he mentions saving it from the *Florentine* when that ship went down after hitting Goodwin Sands in a storm (260). Of course, he may have simply left his journal behind on his last voyage. One cannot be sure.

Certainly, however, it is tragically fitting that at the moment of achieving the professional place to which he had always aspired, Barlow lost it. Despite his undeniable sailing expertise, Barlow seems more suited to the unsettled position of poor seaman than that of company master. This is the case in spite of the fact that he does occasionally adopt the stance of management. When sued by the wife of a seaman for allegedly killing her husband through blows to the head, for instance, Barlow admits that he inflicted punishments on the man (and the crew generally) while he was chief mate on the *Sampson*, on a trip to the East Indies in 1692–94. But he was just doing his job, he protests. Then—quite out of character, and as if parroting the view of company officers—he argues that "many seamen are of that lazy, idle temper, and let them alone and they never care for doing anything they should do, and when they do anything it is with a grumbling unwilling mind, so that they must be forced and drove to it, which is a great trouble and vexation to those men that overlook them, and many times are forced to strike them against their will when fair means will not do it." (Barlow and the dead seaman's wife eventually agree on a cash settlement; p. 452). More often than not, however, Barlow sees himself on the other side, as one of the poor seamen abused by those with power—as when the captain of the misnamed *Delight*, he tells us, "offered to strike me and took up a carpenter's adze, offering to cut me over the head" (357). It is also the poor seaman's voice we hear when Barlow complains, as he frequently does, against the injustice of impressment; in one long tirade on the subject, he five times uses the expressions "poor man," "poor men," or "poor seaman" (146). The same "poor seaman" repeatedly protests in his journal against inferior food aboard ship, against delayed wages in His Majesty's service, against docked pay for damaged goods on merchant ships, against being unfairly kept down from advancement in both His Majesty's service and merchant service, and against the East India Company's unjust rule forbidding seamen to make personal investments in goods while in the company's service (a policy Barlow frequently breaches and for which he often pays penalties).

On three occasions, Barlow also adopts the revolutionary stance of the insurgent poor seaman more actively protesting injustices by the privileged men above him. The first time is in 1675 aboard a ship bound for Scotland to load pickled herring. The master refuses to harbor the vessel, which is leaking badly; Barlow protests, "which made our master and I to fall very much out about it, as many times we did afterward, for she proved so leaky all the voyage, and I speaking for all our good, and a little more than the rest of our men did, by reason they were fearful and durst not well speak, so that I got myself most anger about it" (267). On two later occasions (in 1683 and 1702), when he confronts the captain of the ship on which he is serving and protests abuse, he is put off the ship as punishment. In the incident on the *Delight,* mentioned above, Barlow physically restrains the captain from striking him on the head and is abandoned onshore in Achin, Sumatra—"and thus a poor man is abused with proud and ambitious masters" (358). In the other case, he is transferred by an irate East India captain to one of His Majesty's men-of-war (546). No wonder that Barlow's journal ends with a last, bitter jab against upper-deck power: he interprets the Great Storm of 1703, with which his journal concludes, as a warning against a wicked generation that includes "all commanders and masters [that] are grown up with pride and oppression and tyranny" (553).

And yet, for all his rebelliousness and criticism of seafaring management— especially the privileging of inexperienced commanders who bought their positions in the navy and in merchant ships—Barlow, like other poor seamen, was a simple patriot who took pride in his fellow seamen's courage in defense of their nation. In expressing his anger at the traitors who rumored that the French fleet was coming to aid the Dutch in a sea engagement of 1666, thus causing the English fleet to split up and weaken its forces, Barlow echoes the seaman's simple patriotism. Seamen, he affirms, are "true-hearted subjects," "spending our dearest blood for our King and country's honor, not thinking it too much to spend our lives for the advance and liberty of our native country, whilst our traitorous countrymen lay at home eating and drinking the fat of the land, and rejoicing at our overthrow" (119). On the topic of the same battle, he again lauds the courage and skill of the English seamen, affirming that if the numbers had been equal, "we should have had them [the Dutch] to have showed us their butter-box arses and run from us the first day, for they are nothing if they have no more ships than we have, but we may thank our own traitors-born countrymen or else we had not come to this" (122). Barlow was a rebel, but a patriotic one.

Barlow also presents something of a paradox in his attitude to his labor. Though he saw himself as a constrained, even enslaved, worker, abused by the impersonal mechanisms of the sailing "factory" in which he was incarcerated as well as by the injustice of those in charge of his factory-like conditions, Barlow learned to use the fact that his labor was a commodity to his advantage, thus attaining a modicum of freedom. As his sailing experience became more "valuable," he frequently resisted shipping out as a form of protest or negotiation, holding back because he was angered that he did not get proper recompense from a previous voyage, or because he was denied the position of master that he so desperately craved, or because the wages offered were not satisfactory. For instance, when Barlow thinks his master cheated him of his wages upon completion of a voyage to Jamaica in 1679—the "poor men" being forced to pay for damages to the cargo of sugar, "which caused me to fall out with him"—Barlow vows never again to ship out with that master: "I never would sail with him again" (326). After a similar instance of docked pay following another trip to Jamaica in 1681, Barlow "stayed at home a long time, hoping to have got a ship myself to have gone master of" (341). In the end, because of uncertainty created by the turbulent political times (the struggle between Charles II and Parliament over the disinheriting of Charles's brother, the Duke of York), Barlow acquiesces and ships out again for Jamaica on the same ship with the same master (341–42). He did, however, successfully negotiate a raise in position: from second mate to chief mate. But yet again, the crew is docked pay for damaged goods—"depriving the poor man of his lawful hire" (350)—and yet again, Barlow reacts by refusing to ship out, "staying at home some time, having a great hope of getting a ship that I might go master myself" (351). The cycle keeps repeating. Disappointed with false promises of a command position—so "it proves many times with a poor man, when he most depends upon the fair words and slippery performances of many men, their words being wind which passeth away without any hold to be taken of them" (351)—he is forced again to take employment as chief mate (on a ship bound for the East Indies). But at the same time, by withdrawing his labor for a time, Barlow negotiated a better wage, "agreeing by the month with the commander for six pound five shillings, which I thought to be good wages and better to go for that than to stay at home and to have fair promises and no performances" (351–52). (This turns out not to be such a good deal after all, since it is on this voyage that Barlow, affirming his free agency in resisting being struck by the ship's captain, is cast ashore in Sumatra.) In another instance of asserting "free" wage labor, in 1691, Barlow evaded enlistment in the navy—hot pressing was afoot in order to man the war with France—by instead revisiting his hometown of Prestwich, twenty years after his last visit. On returning to London, Barlow refuses to set sail in an East India ship because "the commander and I could not agree about wages or hire," so he volunteers as midshipman on a naval vessel (413). What we see reenacted repeatedly, in other words, is the struggle of a man thwarted by merchant capitalists in his efforts to advance himself who at the same uses his labor as a valuable commodity in order to bargain with those very capitalist powers and assert free will.

One particular figure of merchant capitalism whom Barlow considered "one of my worst enemies" (502) was Sir Henry Johnson, a shipbuilding magnate for the East India Company. Barlow blamed Johnson for blocking his appointment in 1699 as commander of the East India ship the *Scepter*. Barlow had competently commanded the vessel when its captain died on its previous East India voyage, and he had expected the promotion as recompense. But according to Barlow, Johnson stood in his way—and to make matters worse, held off on paying him moneys owed from the previous voyage. In retaliation, Barlow refused his labor for nearly a year, noting in his journal that there were "several commanders of East India ships desiring me to go their chief mate as I was before, and likewise Sir Henry Johnson proffered me forty shillings the month more than I had before if I would go chief mate in the *Scepter* again, which I refused, knowing as many of the rest of the owners did, that I was far more fitting and qualified to have gone commander than he that did" (503). In the end, Barlow ships out as chief mate on another Johnson-built ship because he is persuaded to do so by Johnson's brother, who will go as chief supercargo of the ship ("pretending what kindness he would do me"; p. 503)— but also because Barlow recognizes that agreeing to take the job would be the best way to recoup the moneys Sir Henry owes him, which he successfully does before shipping out (503–4).[56] For all the felt injustice done to him, then, Barlow used himself as a desirable commodity to withhold labor from Johnson until he was able to negotiate a satisfactory compensation and wage. Barlow's conflict with the shipping magnate demonstrates especially well how Barlow, like many other seamen, was bound to his masters and the factory-like engines of capitalism that were their ships, but how he was also a "free" wage laborer who could effectively enact resistance.

Like seamen generally, then, Barlow is a complicated and even contradictory figure: unplaced but employed, enslaved but free, commodified object but active subject, patriotic but rebellious, and—as we saw in the last chapter—family man but affectively unattached. That Barlow so frequently thinks of such unsavory types as beggars and rogues (made slaves) when he contemplates his calling signals a contradiction within him that we have seen within the space of unsettled landed labor as well: on the one hand, liberty to travel freely; on the other hand, subjection to the compulsion to travel as well as to the hardships occasioned by the indeterminate conditions of such travel (whether in serving a fluctuating market or a nomadic ship). That Barlow as often contrasts as compares himself to beggars also points to his dual or alternating subjectivity: in part or sometimes he is occupationally defined as a seaman (and *not* unplaced); in part or sometimes he is psychologically, economically, and spatially defined as "no man" or as entirely "unsettled."

The irony is that such a feeling of unsettledness is inherent in the condition of being a seaman. That is, feeling placed and feeling unsettled are distinct senses of "self" for Barlow, but they can at the same time be seen to complement each other: unsettledness is the dark side of his seaman's calling.

Barlow adopts two other, more minor modes of self-definition in the course of his journal:

1. *A God-sanctioned "I."* This devotional self can be glimpsed when Barlow retrospectively invokes God's dissatisfaction with his sexual looseness, as we have seen (286). The defining presence of God for Barlow seems to have been triggered by his deliverance from a terrible storm off the Cape of Good Hope in 1671. Following this life-threatening incident, Barlow cites Psalm 93, verse 5, and then composes his own "song": a ballad detailing the distressing event, which concludes with the conventional moral that poor seamen should put their trust in God (196–97). References to God's will, mercy, and anger more often enter the journal from this point on. But even then, such God-defining moments appear only occasionally, and usually at conventional moments for prayers: at the beginning and end of sailings, for instance, or in the face of adversity. God, in other words, is a present but intermittent—not dominant— medium of self-identification for Barlow. Like most seamen, Barlow had a mostly, if not consistently, secular mind.[57]

2. *A gentleman "I."* This elite persona is adopted by Barlow, as we have seen, on his first return to his Prestwich country home. Preparing for the visit, Barlow shells out money he can ill afford to spend in order to buy rich and fancy clothes far above his station. As he himself admits, these showy clothes were "too high for my calling to wear" (174). Arriving in such elevated splendor, with an additional sixteen pounds in his pocket—no doubt his net worth—he then performs for his hometown the role of well-to-do "gentleman." He proceeds not only to sport his expensive attire but also to spend money generously on the townspeople. To the extent that his guise is a trick, donned to fool his ex-neighbors into thinking him well-off and to "stick it to" his former peers by making himself more attractive to their sweethearts, it is reminiscent of trickery practiced by the unsettled in rogue pamphlets of the period. Such fictional rogues also often disguised themselves as gentlemen (or were gentlemen fallen on seedier times) in order to pull off some fraudulent scheme.[58] Barlow may well have been inspired by this literature, which was so popular earlier in his century. Certainly he would have heard such rogue stories in his youth, perhaps orally recounted in the local alehouse, even if he could not yet read them himself. Whatever Barlow's inspiration, however, the gentleman/rogue persona was but an experimental identity for Barlow.

Though he dons it for several months, it is but a one-time investment. Barlow does not take up that role again, nor could he afford to sustain it.

Barlow thus occasionally adopts other roles (such as a God-sanctioned "I" or a roguishly gentleman "I"), but the two selves that he predominantly manifests—sometimes in a kind of Manichean struggle with each other—are fixed seaman and unsettled "nowhere man."

Nowhere do we more vividly see Barlow picturing himself as seaman and as unsettled subject than in his many color and pencil drawings interspersed within his text. Here Barlow's extraordinariness as well as his commonality appear especially clearly. As we shall see, his sketches place him firmly within maritime chartmaking conventions of his time and thus further contribute to his efforts to stabilize himself in his occupational "calling" of seaman. But at the same time, Barlow's drawings are highly unusual in their lowly origins (sketched as they were by a poor seaman) and in their sheer numbers (no fewer than 147 pages). Furthermore, as we shall see, Barlow's numerous drawings inhabit the early modern tradition of chartmaking in singular ways that especially highlight not a stable but an unsettled viewing eye/I.

Charting Barlow

With few exceptions, every one of Barlow's 147 pages of illustrations in the 279-page manuscript of his journal pictures either a close-up "emblem" of a single, isolated ship that Barlow sailed in (for example, figs. 5 and 6), strange land or sea creatures (for example, figs. 7 and 8), silhouettes of land masses spotted from specific positions at sea (as seen in figs. 8 and 9), or—by far the most frequent, totaling some 111 pages of illustrations—a number of ships arriving at, anchored in, and/or departing from a harbor or port (exemplified by figs. 10–19).[1] There is port scene after port scene after port scene. The insistent, repeated depiction of such coastal scenes seems almost compulsive. In each of these sketches, many ships are depicted, and often individually detailed; but the inland area is usually not represented or only marginally outlined. Barlow might at times hatch the immediate shoreline with different shades of color in an effort to give an impressionistic three-dimensional sense of the lay of the land, and he might also sketch in along the shore a few trees, a castle, and/or some undistinguished, blocklike houses of a town. But his focus is primarily on the variable ways that sea meets land in an instance of siting or harboring. Only the contour of the harboring coastline or port is fully imagined as distinct from picture to picture.

What are we to make of these many coastal drawings? In order to answer this question, we need to place Barlow's sketches in relation to other drawings in sea journals of the time and especially in relation to navigational charts and treatises of the sixteenth and seventeenth centuries. This tack will contribute a new, sea-based focus to the work of the recent army of scholars interested in cartography, led by Richard Helgerson with his study of English chorography in his 1992 *Forms of Nationhood*.[2] At the same time, our approach will allow us once again to see that Barlow was not an entirely isolated subject. Just as he shared many of the conflicted experiences of other unsettled poor seamen of his time, so his concern with, and his style of, depicting relatively uncontextualized coastlines, ports, and harbors can be understood to participate within a general struggle to "place" shifting shores. In important ways, as we shall see, Barlow's coastal depictions—drawn as they are from a lowly, unsettled perspective—stand isolated and apart from other such efforts; but at the same time, we can discern a strong influence from certain charting conventions.

Specifically, Barlow was influenced by two related strains of maritime pictorial convention of the period:

1. *Individual sketches of harbors, islands, or views of land by established land dwellers or by officers at sea in their journals.* Henry VIII made a significant contribution to this tradition, as Edward Lynam notes, by commissioning many manuscript views of the important harbors and estuaries of southern and eastern England (for example, the anonymous chart of the coast between Exmouth and Tor; fig. 20). Elizabeth I also employed surveyors and engineers in this work. Richard Popinjay, for instance, charted the ports of the south coast and the Channel Islands between 1562 and 1587.[3] Such sea maps, of course, were but the coastal complement to the growing demand in England for estate maps, town plans, and county surveys, a demand filled by such surveyors and cartographers as Christopher Saxton, John Norden, John Speed, and John Ogilby.[4] Saxton's careful rendering of the Hampshire coastline (1575) in his atlas of England and Wales (fig. 21), replete with sailing ships and sea monsters, and Norden's series of sketches of Orford Ness in 1601, such as his detail of Orford Haven (fig. 22)—which shows ships sailing from the sea toward Orford harbor, ships at anchor within the harbor, and yet other ships heading further up the river—reflect a period when cartography and hydrography often merged. But the seacoast was to claim its own area of expertise. Though coastal-charting projects limped along under the general neglect of things maritime under James I and Charles I, they were renewed with fervor by Charles II; finally, in 1795, a Hydrographers Department was established in the British Admiralty to draw, print, and sell charts of not only Britain but, in J. B. Hewson's words, "almost the entire world."[5]

Individual seamen (usually officers) participated in these charting endeavors. Officers would often draw, or employ draftsmen and painters to draw, sketches of harbors, coastlines, islands, and other points of interest on their trips. These were increasingly published together with a narrative of the voyage, in what became a downright fashion for sea journals in the late sixteenth and seventeenth centuries—from the manuscript sketchbook, in color, of coastlines and views of the West Indies that Sir Francis Drake had recorded on his last voyage of 1595–96 (for example, fig. 23), to the Earl of Sandwich's personal manuscript drawings of harbors near the Straits of Gibraltar (1657–58), to the many published views of islands, coastlines, and harbors of William Dampier's various trips round the world in 1679–91 (for example, fig. 24). Charts, sketches, and sea narratives sailed together in the same boat.[6]

2. *Illustrated rutters.* Rutters (from the French *routier,* meaning "route book") were originally narrative sailing directions in manuscript compiled by

masters and pilots for navigating along the seacoasts of northern Europe. Their southern predecessors for Mediterranean waters were called *portolani.* Both *portolani* and rutters might record such information as the magnetic compass courses and the distances between ports and capes; the distance at which coastlines could normally be discerned, as well as descriptions of the coast and of significant landmarks; and the flow of tidal streams, as well as high-water marks at new or full moon in important ports and channels. As J. H. Parry explains, however, "Northern rutters differed from southern *portolani* in ways which reflected the different methods of pilotage in shallow and deep seas. Their information on bearings and courses is less full and less precise; their estimates of distance—when given at all—are usually very rough. . . . On the other hand, most rutters gave remarkably full and detailed accounts of soundings, both depths and bottoms, not only in the immediate approaches to harbors, but along whole stretches of coast. They also devoted a good deal of space to information about tides."[7] I would add that whereas *portolani* emphasized direction finding, sometimes even including instructions for long-distance crossings between recognizable places, rutters remained primarily focused on coastlines.[8] The first printed rutter was Pierre Garcie's *Le Routier de la Mer,* which was printed at Rouen sometime in the first decade of the sixteenth century and was both translated and published in English by Robert Copland as *The Rutter of the Sea* (1528). This work provides directions for sailing around the coasts of southern England and Wales and along the coasts of France, Portugal, and Spain, from Flanders to the Strait of Gibraltar. (In 1541, Garcie's text was published together with Richard Proude's *The Rutter of the North,* which added sailing directions for the circumnavigation of Scotland.) In the course of the sixteenth century, the French and Dutch published many such rutters together with "drawings or crude woodcuts of headlands and strips of the coast to assist in identification."[9]

The first such illustrated rutter published in English, *The Safeguard of Sailors* (1587), was translated from the Dutch by Robert Norman.[10] In addition to sailing directions for areas of northwestern Europe, the book contains many views of landmarks and elevations of land as seen from sea (for example, fig. 25). The coastal elevations shown here closely resemble those in the 1595–96 manuscript notebook made by Drake's painter on his West Indies voyage (fig. 23). Indeed, as D. W. Waters notes, the Drake drawings "not only identified coastal elevations sketched as the ship made her landfall or stretched past the shore but also information on tidal streams, on the depth of water and nature of the sea bed, and on harbors." In other words, the Drake notebook—especially when combined with the daily navigational journal of the voyage, also discussed by Waters—formed, in essence, a rutter.[11] So, at times, did Dampier's abundantly sketched journals of his voyages. Illustrated journals and rutters could sometimes be one and the same thing.

All such manuscript and printed illustrations and narratives, as well as pilots' notebooks and oral reports by seamen, were soon compiled into atlases of coastlines, which were still accompanied by verbal sailing instructions and pictures of coastal elevations, as well as by information about courses and distances between ports, latitudes of various places, tides, soundings, and so on. These atlases usually included the added attractions of instructions on how to trace a chart and a practical manual on navigation. The first of these compilations for popular use at sea was Lucas Janszoon Waghenaer's two-part folio, which was translated into English by Sir Anthony Ashley under the title *The Mariner's Mirror* (1588).[12] This book of sea charts was so influential that it became known simply as the "Waggoner," which further became the generic term for all subsequent nautical chart books well into the eighteenth century. Waghenaer's two atlases together cover the waters of northwestern Europe, providing forty-six plane charts (drawn by compass bearing and distance, without latitude or longitude scales) arranged systematically following the coast and showing the river mouths and harbors disproportionately enlarged (see fig. 26). Fathoms of water or soundings were indicated, especially for ports; views of the coastline in silhouette with accompanying notes were inlaid in the land masses of the charts; symbols were added indicating different kinds of buoys and beacons, landmarks, safe anchorages, hidden rocks, and so on (instructions on interpreting the symbols were included in another part of the book); and three scales of leagues to a degree were provided—for English leagues (the same as French), Spanish leagues, and Dutch leagues. Each chart was followed by a description of the particular area of coastline and directions for sailing along it. Such directions also often included notes about inland products and the commerce of ports. Emphasizing their practical nature, the guides concluded with a list of geographical names in Dutch, French, Spanish, and English, and a table of the sun's declination.[13]

The Mariner's Mirror was superseded by the English translation of Willem Janszoon Blaeu's *The Light of Navigation* (Amsterdam, 1612; reissued in English in 1620 and 1622), which was in turn displaced by the Dutch and then English printing of Blaeu's *The Sea Mirror* (Amsterdam, 1625; reissued in 1635 and by Joan Blaeu under the new title *The Sea Beacon* in 1643 and 1653).[14] In these books of sea charts, Blaeu says, he amended and expanded Waghenaer's earlier work. The manual on navigation and the sailing directions were updated and made fuller. And in the atlas part of the books, Blaeu added more compass rhumb lines and increased the number of sea charts—which reached 108 in his *Sea Mirror*—as well as expanded their size so that the estuaries and harbors could be correctly delineated on the same scale as the rest of the chart. "As touching the cards," Blaeu explains in his *Light of Navigation,* "I have especially much bettered them with the reaching of their compasses very necessary to be used, and also enlarged them, and according to the examples of the best cards so corrected them that therein you not only see how you may sail into and come out of all havens and channels but also how far they reach and are in wideness and length distant from each other: which never heretofore (be it spoken without boasting) was so perfectly and so beneficially done for the good of seafaring men." Blaeu also increasingly included in his charts more symbols as well as more buoys and beacons (because there were in fact more of them when he published).[15]

We might compare Waghenaer's chart of the southwest coast of England in his *Mariner's Mirror* (fig. 26) with Blaeu's detail of the same area in his *Sea Mirror* (fig. 27), showing on the left Falmouth harbor ("Vaelmuyen" in the chart) and on the right Plymouth harbor ("Pleimuyen"). Blaeu's enlarged close-up of the harbors, we see, allows for a more accurate rendering than does Waghenaer's. Consider, for instance, Falmouth harbor. On the east side of the entrance to the harbor, the area of rocks submerged and awash (marked by triangular shapes interspersed with *x*'s) has been expanded in Blaeu's chart, the sands within the harbor have been more finely delineated, the contours of the harbor more precisely rendered, and safe anchorages (marked by the symbol of an anchor) more fully noted. Other, more pictorial details of sea and land, however, disappear: gone are Waghenaer's sea monsters and most of his ships, as well as his decorative inland sketches of mountains, trees, estates, and animals. Gone also are Waghenaer's inset views of coastal elevations as seen from different positions at sea, which further made his charts seem ornate and distractively "busy" (Blaeu transferred the coastal elevations to the narrative section on sailing directions). Such coastal views remain in Blaeu's chart only in trace: as the traverse line drawn in Falmouth road from the thirty-two-fathom mark to the three trees that mark "a little wood" on the inner northwestern shore of Falmouth harbor, or as the two traverse lines to trees in Helford haven (to the west of Falmouth). Blaeu says in his sailing directions that one must keep these, together with other landmarks, in one's sights on entering the harbors (hence the traverse line is both the line of the viewing eye from aboard ship and the line of the ship's course).[16] Excepting as well the occasional town, castle, and church marker, other details extraneous to the contour of the coastline are absent in Blaeu's chart. Even the decorative cartouches, which are very elaborate in Ashley's renderings of Waghenaer's charts, are relatively plain in Blaeu—as is his more restrained hatching of the coastline (intended, in Waghenaer, to gesture at cliff lines in a more pictorial way).[17] The overall effect in Blaeu's chart is of a more clear, linear, and exact coastal focus.

With Blaeu's further addition of a denser number of rhumb lines for determining ships' courses, as well as of a latitude scale in some charts, his maps resemble southern *portolan* charts (which emphasized direction finding) as much as northern rutters (which focused more singularly on seacoasts).[18] It is the latter tradition that we are pursuing here, however, and we might conclude our survey of such coastal charting with mention of its fullest fruition in the seventeenth century, *Great Britain's Coasting Pilot* (London, 1693) by Greenvile Collins (exemplified by his map of Falmouth harbor, fig. 28).[19] Commissioned by Charles II, this large folio of charts was the first original engraved sea atlas by an Englishman published in English.[20] It covered the whole of the English coast, as well as parts of Scotland and Ireland. Though Collins occasionally includes rhumb lines and a latitude scale in his charts and sometimes also images coastal elevations (as in fig. 28), his focus in his charts is intently on the shoreline. The coastal views that appear in his map of Falmouth are thus relegated to their own separate box (as is his charting of Helford sound).[21] Collins has room for such insets because his maps are even larger in size than Blaeu's. By so amplifying the proportions of his charts, Collins is also able to trace the river inland more fully than had previous chartmakers. He further adds yet more guiding details: more fathoms; more symbols of safe anchorages, shoals, sands, and so on; and more markers. Thus, Falmouth Rock is marked on Collins's chart by the pole now fixed on it ("to show where it is overflowed") as well as by a half-moon to its right, which indicates, says Collins, that "such a rock or sand is to be seen at the half-tide; that is, from half ebb to half flood."[22] In addition, Collins includes in his charts more signs of churches, houses, castles, and woods that were important for ship positioning. But most details peripheral or ornamental to the shoreline itself are relegated to his cartouches (such as in fig. 29), which extravagantly announce not only the harbor being portrayed but also his dedication of each individual map to a specific patron. (In this sense alone, the maps look back to the more decorative and personal style of manuscript drawings for royalty and other persons of privilege.) Even larger in size, more detailed, and more exact than Blaeu's charts, Collins's maps, in sum, offer the seaman the most accurate renderings of coastlines and harbors of the time.

Printed chart books of more distant coastlines were less accessible to Englishmen in the seventeenth century. For sailing the Mediterranean, the only printed source at first was William Barentz's Dutch waggoner of 1595, which was translated into French in 1609; it was superseded by book 3 of Blaeu's *Light of Navigation* on the Mediterranean, which was published in

Dutch in 1618 (this chart book went through four Dutch editions between 1618 and 1646 but was never translated into English).[23] Coastlines further afield were even less well charted in print, such work being thwarted largely by the obsessive control and secrecy with which the Spanish and Portuguese guarded their manuscript rutters and charts of the West and East Indies, respectively—hence the frequent need for the English sailing into those seas to hire or abduct Spanish or Portuguese pilots. Masters and pilots might, however, turn to the illustrated accounts (though not sailing directions in the strict sense) of the navigations of Van Speilbergen and Jacobe Le Maire, printed in Holland under the title *The East and West Indian Mirror* (1619). And much later in the century, they could also access John Seller's *The English Pilot* (London, 1671, with subsequent volumes in the next few years), which charts not only the British Isles, the North and Baltic seas, Greenland, and the Mediterranean, but also the coasts of Africa, India, and Japan. Finally, those of high status would further have had access to William Hack's South Sea waggoner (ca. 1684), a manuscript of 135 watercolor drawings, with annotations about the coast and hinterland, charting the west side of South America (see fig. 30)—but Hack's work was not published and therefore not widely available.[24]

Our focus on illustrated rutters or atlases of northwestern Europe, then, follows the majority of printed waggoners of the sixteenth and seventeenth centuries. I have further chosen to focus primarily on atlases printed in English because those would have been the chart books most accessible to Barlow (who had minimal learning and only haphazardly acquired literacy). We have so far noticed several developments in such chart books, which we viewed together with the related genre of individual charts or sketches of coastlines made by English surveyors and seamen in their journals. To summarize: the *coast line* becomes increasingly a *single line* in later charts, with only perhaps some hatching to indicate elevation; the coastlines are increasingly enlarged to allow for more details; the harbors, sands, shoals, and fathoms are more exactly drawn (often with symbols and keys); the hinterland and symbols thereof, such as farmsteads or horses and sheep, increasingly fall out of the representations; and ships and sea creatures fade away (the latter reproduced as separate "specimens" on their own in sea journals of the period, as in fig. 31). In the later productions, such as Collins's *Great Britain's Coasting Pilot*, we have a full "scientific" siting of the place of a harbor and river, such as Falmouth, from which the seeing/seafaring "I" (represented by the sailing ship)—the eye/I that produced such a map—has been excised.

We could thus say that Collins's charts mark the moment of an achieved "state" of hydrographical knowledge. Michel de Certeau uses this term in commenting on the erasure of ships from navigational maps in the course of the early modern period. "The sailing ship painted on the sea," says de Certeau, "indicates the maritime expedition that made it possible to represent the coastlines." Such a sailing ship, he continues,

> is equivalent to a describer of the "tour" type. But the map gradually wins out over these figures; it colonizes space; it eliminates little by little the pictural figurations of the practices that produce it. . . . The map [is] a totalizing stage on which elements of diverse origin are brought together to form the tableau of a "state" of geographical knowledge. [It] pushes away into its prehistory or into its posterity, as if into the wings, the operations of which it is the result or the necessary condition. It remains alone on the stage. The tour describers have disappeared.[25]

Both ship and describer on board are represented by the viewing lines drawn from ships in the sketches by Drake's painter in 1595–96 (fig. 23). The bare trace of such a describer can be seen in the traverse lines *sans* ship in Blaeu's charts of the first half of the seventeenth century (fig. 27) and in the dotted lines marking Dampier's routes in sketches of his voyages in the late seventeenth century (fig. 24). But the practice of viewing/sailing is mostly absent from the late seventeenth-century charts of Collins and entirely absent from the contemporaneous drawings of William Hack (fig. 30).[26]

We can now see that when Barlow sketched and painted his many harbors and ports, as well as occasional coastal elevations, he was participating in a lively and developing tradition of coastal charting. Indeed, one might claim that if shipbuilding was becoming an industry in the course of the seventeenth century, so was chartmaking. The sheer number of Barlow's drawings, together with his lowly status, makes his charts remarkable, but the chartmaking itself was not. In fact, chartmakers and writers on navigation called upon seamen to draw such maps so as to "practice" piloting and accurately record the coastline for future reference. Waghenaer thus prefaced *The Mariner's Mirror* with "An Exhortation to the Apprentices of the Art of Navigation" (of which Barlow was one, being apprenticed to a chief master's mate) "diligently to mark" the landmarks upon departing from a river or haven, "all of which, or many of them, let him portray with his pen."[27] Waghenaer's further advice that the seaman should check his observations on approaching land against the extant charts leads Ashley, in his rendering of Waghenaer's charts, to leave the sea blank (as opposed to the Dutch tradition of drawing in the sea with wavy lines), so that the seaman could correct errors and draw in new information about risings of land, rocks, sands, and so on: "The sea is purposely left in blank," Ashley declares, "because the traveler, finding perchance some point of the compass, risings of lands, depths, soundings, or ought else mistaken; or some rock, sand, or other danger left out, or not rightly expressed (for nothing so perfect but hath his fault) may as he traveleth set down and correct the same with his own hand, as it shall best like him self: which doubtless will be no small furtherance and contentment even to the best doctors in this science."[28] Blaeu also, in his *Light of Navigation,* repeatedly urges "young" seamen or pilots to draw pictures of sea- and landmarks, coastal views, and harbors: "When you are within and at an anchor, then visit all the points of the haven, and note them down with a pen cardwise [in a chart], how they reach outward and inward, that when you come thither again, you might enter into the same place again, and know the situation thereof."[29]

The emphasis that Waghenaer, Ashley, Blaeu, and others give to drawing harbors and other landmarks underscores the need at the time not only to train young pilots, but also—as evidenced by the paucity of charts of faraway coasts—to record recently discovered lands. As Norman J. W. Thrower observes, "A place is not really discovered until it has been mapped so that it can be reached again."[30] Accuracy was crucial. John Smith, for instance, in 1614 laments that he had bought six or seven charts of the "New England" coast (from Cape Cod to Pembroke's Bay), but the charts were "so unlike each to other, or resemblance of the country, as they did me no more good than so much waste paper, though they cost me more." He thus drew his own chart "to direct any that shall go that way to safe harbors and the savages' habitations."[31] An accurate picture of a harbor, which Smith evidently believed his chart to be, *places* that harbor within a stable "state" of hydrographical information readily accessible to all.

To the extent that Barlow occupationally defined himself as a good (if poor) seaman, he appears eagerly to have answered the call to draw (and thus place) coastlines, landmarks, and harbors. This was the case even though he twice states in his journal that he wasn't interested as a young apprentice in learning "the mariner's art" from his master because he was happy enough to have learned to write: "having learned to write I thought that enough" (49; see also 29–30). Barlow appears to be referring here specifically to what Blaeu terms "great navigation," or oceanic course setting and position finding using astronomy and instruments. Despite his disinclination for this art, Barlow does come to acquire oceanic navigational skills in the course of his long career. As chief mate on his later voyages, part of his duties would have been to take readings of the ship's course and keep a logbook (an example of which he proudly reproduces for us on pp. 334–37).[32] But Barlow's passion was for the art of Blaeu's "common navigation," or pilotage—marking routes along coasts as well as into and out of harbors, using only a compass and sounding

lead.[33] As Barlow's numerous drawings of coastlines, harbors, and ports testify, the art of pilotage was his special calling. On his last recorded voyage,
Barlow was even hired by the captain to pilot the ship from Batavia, Java, to
China (530). During this last leg of the voyage, Barlow's journal at moments
reads very much like a rutter, with more details than usual about land masses,
latitudes, and fathoms of water, as well as illustrations of ports—including
one that is his most professional sketch of all.

This is the sketch of the island of Pulo Condore, in the South China Sea
(fig. 10). It is Barlow's most professional sketch in that it is the most detailed
and "scientific" chart in his collection. Unlike most of his other drawings, this
chart is complete with compass rhumb lines for direction finding as well as
fathom markings for pilotage (anchorages here, as in his other charts, are further indicated by his drawing not anchors but ships with sails furled). The
chart is also unusually professional in its perspective: Barlow adopts an
objective viewing position far outside and above his own personal frame of
reference, his ship. This chart, in sum, comes closest of all Barlow's charts to
projecting an impersonal "state" of hydrographical knowledge that vies with
Dampier's own precise and objective sketch of the same island (fig. 24).

Two aspects of Barlow's drawing, however—the second in particular—
make his chart a throwback to an earlier seeing/seafaring age. The first is the
aesthetic quality of the drawing: like his contemporary in manuscript charts,
William Hack (see fig. 30), Barlow hatches his penciling in a pictorial way to
suggest cliff lines and mountains. Furthermore, though the hinterland is otherwise unrepresented, it is not, strictly speaking, bare; it is washed with color.
The second aspect is the presence of many ships surrounding the island and
going into and out of its main harbor. It is as if Barlow were as much interested in sketching the activity that gave shape or place to Pulo Condore as
in depicting the island itself. The ships in Barlow's chart in effect actualize the
island.

In drawing after drawing, we find, Barlow pictures the seafaring act—
carefully delineating individual ships as if they were individual persons—that
meaningfully and subjectively locates the many harbors and shores he illustrates. In this sense, Barlow is more interested in the *practice* than in the state
of hydrographical knowledge. Compare for instance, Barlow's chart of
Falmouth harbor (fig. 11) with the charts of the same harbor that we have
studied by Waghenaer, Blaeu, and Collins (figs. 26, 27, and 28). We have noted
that in the course of improving the "science" of representing harbors such
as Falmouth, the seafaring eye/I gradually falls out of the picture: from
Waghenaer's chart brimming with seafaring ships and the monstrous dangers
sailors feared at sea, we move to Collins's neutral and rational template of the

harbor devoid of all such colorful personae.[34] Whatever its evident deficien-
cies, Barlow's chart aspires to such "scientific" exactitude as well, and thus to
be a practical aid to navigation. The two castles that signpost either side of the
mouth of Falmouth harbor are helpfully represented in his chart, as is the
town of Falmouth itself (on the upper left). Barlow also sketches in the "little
wood" (at the center top of his chart) that Blaeu says the seaman must keep
in his sights when entering the harbor east of Falmouth Rock, and he hatches
in the coastline at points where cliffs would be. He further situates the harbor
verbally within the chart, writing a caption on the protruding land mass at the
left foreground that is capped by Pendennis castle: here, as he usually does in
his charts, Barlow gives both the local area where the harbor lies (the County
of Cornwall) and the country (England), and he then cites its latitude (which
he forgot to fill in here) as well as—for those harbors in western Europe—its
bearing and distance from London. (When in foreign ports, he also usually
includes in his narrative a description of the products, town, and inhabitants
of the port, as was common in sea journals and rutters of the time.) Barlow
evidently wanted very much to *place* Falmouth harbor, as well as the many
other foreign harbors he sketched on his travels, and thus to answer the call
for seamen to situate lands through drawings and charts.

But unlike Collins or Blaeu—or even Waghenaer, for that matter—
Barlow "peoples" his harbor with sailing ships. Ships in the background stand
at anchor before the town of Falmouth and at the upper east side of the
harbor, and ships in the foreground sail into and out of the harbor. Always,
Barlow charts the *act* of entering and departing from harbors. In this way, his
charts most closely resemble much earlier pictorial manuscript charts, such
as that made in the reign of Henry VIII of the Exeter and Devon coast, or
Norden's early seventeenth-century chart of Orford Ness, both of which also
image ships at anchor and entering or leaving harbors (figs. 20 and 22).
Barlow's sailing ships even more intently transmit the process of sailing, so
that the course each ship takes usefully conveys to the seaman where to tack
on entering or leaving Falmouth. He even shows the ships firing their cannons as they salute the castle (and are saluted back) on arriving and departing from the port.

This routine activity of cannon firing is often imaged in Barlow's drawings; see also, for example, figures 12 and 13. The act smacks of aggression,
however ritualized, suggesting that the sailing event is a strenuous (and even
dangerous) process of finding out and maintaining harbors. Such a sugges-
tion is reinforced by Barlow's long narratives of struggles against cross winds,
foul weather, miscalculated courses, poor rations, deadly diseases, and hostile
nations. On a return voyage from the East Indies in 1671, for instance, Barlow's

merchant ship the *Experiment* is nearly destroyed by a vicious storm east of the Cape of Good Hope, near the island of Mauritius (fig. 6). On his next venture in the same ship, this time to China, Barlow and his crew suffer sorely (and many die) from the bloody flux—"and many are the miseries that poor seamen endure at sea when they are sick" (213). Furthermore, on its return voyage, while passing through the calm Strait of Banka, the ship is suddenly ambushed by the Dutch and captured (224–26). The incident reveals clearly how easily and unexpectedly "friendly" communicative salutes could turn into aggressive salvos. Such was also the case when, during a parley between the English and the Turks at the Turkish port of Algiers, the Turks angrily opened fire on the English fleet (55–56). One might say that the threat of unexpected attack at all times lay behind the predictable salute of cannon firing, a threat that the ritual greeting hoped to dispel.

The real or implied violence inherent in the vicissitudes of the sailing act and quintessentially represented by the cannon firing that marks so many of Barlow's harbor scenes further reinforces another nagging sense that emerges as one looks through Barlow's many charts: that there is something offensively *unsettling* about Barlow's insistent, repeated depiction of ships arriving at and departing from harbors, in port scene after port scene after port scene. Unlike other chartmakers, moreover, who sketch general areas of the coast as well as local close-ups of those areas, Barlow in his charts moves discontinuously from port to port. With the exception of the initial sequence of depictions tracing the river Thames and its Medway tributary—pictured as if Barlow were representing the umbilical cord of his link to London, which is severed once his ship gains open water—there is no reassuring visual connector between the depicted harbors. Even in the case of the Thames sequence, Barlow later inserted disjunctive views onto the river banks—in no particular order—of such far-flung places as Cuba, Florida, Hispaniola, Grand Canary, Cape of Good Hope, and Jamaica. "Place" in Barlow, one might say, is imagined as a disturbed or disconnected process that never stays. There are endless variations on the harboring process, but no connecting visual line within that process, and no privileged or assured, settled harbor.

Of course, Barlow's charting of harbors as an ongoing, strenuous process of visualizing or actualizing them is more representative than I or his contemporaries' charts have so far let on. Those chartmakers who appear to have attained a stasis, or "state," of official hydrographical knowledge were really engaged in making the illusion of such stability. They themselves were very well aware that the subject of their art was in fact disturbingly "movable." They recognized that time and especially storms continually worked to change the positions and features of harbors, sands, and shoals—especially of the English Channel, Holland, and other northern shores—which is why they encouraged their readers to make changes in the charts when new discoveries were made or errors found, and to attend carefully to newly issued charts. Thus Waghenaer's "Admonition to the Reader" in *The Mariner's Mirror* begins by pointing out at length that "certain of the sandy coasts and shores, as also diverse mouths and entries of rivers . . . are *movable,* and have not always their being in one self place." After citing many examples of such changes wrought by storms, he concludes that "many havens are decayed, and many are altered"; he cautions the reader that despite careful updating in his charts, "upon the like causes, the like changes may happen . . . seeing that things to come, and uncertain, can by no means possible, be perfectly described."

Blaeu has similar thoughts about uncertain variations of coastlines in his introductory address, "To the Reader," in his *Light of Navigation*—which is why he says it is necessary to replace Waghenaer's now-outdated work:

> It is also well known to every seafaring man how much some havens and channels in the seas are and have been in process of time clean altered and changed, specially in these countries of Holland, Zealand and Friesland, which also for the most part are so much altered since they were described by the said authors [Waghenaer and others] that some of them have now no likeness nor similitude thereof, some are almost spoiled, and some wholly abolished and clean stopped up . . . whereby such descriptions at this time are not only unfit but very hurtful, if a man should rule himself by them.

Collins, in his prefatory letter titled "To the Master, Wardens and Assistants of the Trinity-House of Deptford-Strond," also recognizes the changeableness of coastlines and potential for variation from his charts. He says that "if at any time there should be made new discoveries of any rocks or shelves, that are not yet known; or that sands shall change their situation (as often they do) I shall be ready by your advice and commands (by God's blessing) to make a further progress in this survey." His plan for correcting charts, however, follows more centralized lines than does Waghenaer's or Blaeu's, as befits the official status that his own charts were given at the time. The Trinity Corporation, Collins advises, should order all masters to bring in their journals of home and foreign voyages, which should then be inspected and the information compiled so that "in a few years, we might have much more exact sea-charts and maps." He also wishes that "those persons that make and sell sea-charts and maps, were not allowed to alter them upon the single report of mariners"— reflecting the current haphazard practice of keeping up with coastal variations—"but with your approbation, by which means our sea-charts would be more correct, and the common scandal of their badness removed." But whether their charting was institutionalized or not, seacoasts continued to be troublesomely "movable," so that as late as 1848 a report to Parliament by the Hydrographers Department found that among those coastlines still needing surveying was the greater part of the south coast of England.[35]

Rutters, it should be noted, were subject to similar changefulness, not only in shorelines but also across seasons. Indeed, they could become downright dangerous when they were written in a different season than when they were used. This was the problem Barlow himself faced on one voyage when, after the death of his captain, he found himself commanding the *Scepter* in unknown waters at the mouth of the Red Sea. Though he had a journal aboard made by Sir John Gayer, governor of Bombay, who had been at Mocha eleven years before, Barlow says the rutter was made at a different time of the year and was thus dangerously misleading (477).

Finally, the problem of keeping up with unsettling variations in coastlines was but a local aspect of a general problem with variability in navigation in the period. Despite the proliferation of new, improved instruments for determining latitude, for instance, readings were often contradictory or wide of the mark. When the Earl of Sandwich calculated his latitude by observation of the stars and then compared his findings with those of his captain and others in his fleet, he regularly found discrepancies, usually of twenty to forty minutes (which translates into a difference of twenty to forty nautical miles).[36] Most vexing to contemporaries was the seemingly unfathomable "variation of the compass": the fact that the magnetic compass needle varied from true north irregularly (versus proportionately) as one traveled eastward or westward. Such inconsistent variations, Edward Wright declares in his second dedication to his translation of *The Haven-Finding Art* (1599), has caused "much deformity and confusion in many parts of the chart."[37] Faced with such perplexing irregularities of the compass, many contemporaries despaired of finding a set rule of longitude. Thus, Blaeu dismissed any discussion of longitude as "unnecessary" and "not only unprofitable, but also (if a man should trust thereunto) both hurtful and deceitful."[38] (For more on the nature of this problem and efforts to discover some "order," "method," or "rule" to magnetic variations, see appendix E.) In sum, even as chartmakers aspired to scientific exactitude and increasingly left out sea monsters and sailing ships that represented the seaman's uncertain labor of sailing, the art of navigation was by no means an exact science.

The coastal chart book, for all its aspirations to establishing accurate, objective, and official representations of shorelines, at the same time shows such unstable tenuousness. "Place" in these books moves around not only from book to book—reflecting the changeability over time of shorelines, landmarks, channels, and harbors—but also within individual books. I am referring here to the way the land in chart books changes appearance according to the different methods by which it is shown: described verbally in the narrative of sailing directions; sited mathematically by bearing, latitude, and some version of longitude; depicted visually, as seen from different distances and courses at sea; charted as part of a general map of the contours of a coastline; and sketched up close so as to reveal new details of its harboring features. All of these descriptive methods further the efforts to place the land. But at the same time, they testify to its shifting variability that requires different envisionings to grasp it. The coastline, in particular—the representational form Barlow favored—by definition images tenuousness in imaging liminality. The cartouche to Collins's chart of the section of the south coast of England that includes Falmouth harbor vividly pronounces such a state of being on the edge (fig. 29). The drawing depicts the point at which opposites make contact: Plenty above (figured by fruits and flowers) is brought together with War below (imaged by pikes, flags, cannons, and drums); and Landsmen on the left (working mines and reaping bread) stand on the same plane with Seamen on the right (netting fish and handling casks of goods). The sense of these opposites meeting or coming together is underscored by the central visual line of the picture signposted by the two-headed phoenix above, the doubling of fish below, and the single shell. Along that central pictorial line—broken only by the words declaring the place of "Falmouth," which allows for a similar coming together (the presentation of the chart of Falmouth by the client, Collins, to his patron, Sir Peter Killegrew)—opposites become alike and, in the shell, even approach singleness. Such a singular moment suggests the unitary linearity of the seacoast as imaged in Collins's charts, where land and sea also meet in a kind of calculated Rorschach image (I'm thinking here of the famous picture of vase/face) expressive of oneness, but oneness as unstable liminality.

Recognition of—as well as deep sympathy with—such unsettledness, as much as the search for a settled place, may explain Barlow's specific fascination with coastal chartmaking. Barlow, I have argued, lived such a liminal or perpetually "on-edge" position as a poor youth who, like so many others of his age and socioeconomic station, felt compelled to leave home, family, and community and set upon a course of "movability" from place to place, job to job, relationship to relationship. This continual enactment of displacement by the youthful Barlow was an especially intense expression of a kind of lower-order experience that was available in varying degrees to some, if not all, of the wage-laboring poor of early modern England. We have termed such a lower-order experience "unsettled subjectivity." But, interestingly and even paradoxically—given what we know of seamen—Barlow sought to resolve such unsettledness at the same time that he expressed it by eventually going to sea. As "poor seaman," he lived the rest of his life relatively settled occupationally but forever itinerant (shifting from ship to ship and place to place, and never entering into any recognizable shipman's community), forever unsettled with respect to occupational security (always an insecure journeyman, at least until his last, uncompleted voyage), and forever mingled with other poor laborers and actual vagabonds who also, willingly or not, found themselves "at sea." Seen within the context of his journal, Barlow's many charts of local coastlines and harbors can be read as furthering his desire for place: situating the lands and ports he visited aboard ship as well as situating Barlow himself within a recognized genre of chartmaking. But the uncertain variation inherent in all such arts of navigation, quintessentially represented by variable land sitings as well as by the sheer liminality of shorelines in coastal charts, would have touched Barlow deeply as a continuing unsettled subject perhaps even more than as an occupationally stable seaman or pilot (for whom unsettledness was, as we have seen, in any case part of the job).

Thus, Barlow in his own coastal charts emphasizes the image of unsettledness that is an inherent (if suppressed) feature of all such charts. Looking at the sheer number of his sketches, filled with ships coming and going, one might say that such unsettled liminality, or the act of being always on the edge of place, is what really endures. What we see over and over again are images of provisionality, disconnection, and dislocation. The mind doing the seeing/seafaring here will not or cannot stay. Thus, the convention of drawing but the contours of coastlines, as well as other developments toward an impersonal state of hydrographical knowledge in the chartmaking of the time, served Barlow's personal turn. Barlow will not or cannot "fill in" or fully occupy the land and make it a *place* any more than he can form tight personal or communal ties. He favors coastal scenes that remain unsited or only casually and impersonally occupied.

Barlow's alliance with his harboring sites, in this sense, is not predicated on place but on *space*. As we have previously defined these terms, "place" is by nature stable and predictable, like one's home or office (however vulnerable to destabilization such places might be). "Space," on the other hand, is inherently unstable and unpredictable, more open to different ways of being occupied, like a train station. It is precisely the unsettled openness of Barlow's charts, then, that makes them spacious. Barlow's inclination to a spatial rendering of place might further explain his compulsion—in addition to any artistic needs he had—to draw harbors rather than simply to describe them (such charts are always presented to us in his narrative, I would add, at the moment of departure—as with his expressions of attachments to family and friends). We might in this context recall Barlow's statement that in his youth, at least, he substituted learning to read and write for learning navigation. Understood in light of this comment, Barlow's journal can be seen to be a substitute kind of navigation, by which he narratively charts his way through his life story of unsettled jobs, unsettled relationships, and unsettled places. In this sense, Barlow's spacious charts are a complement to his written narrative. But at the same time the charts, in their spaciousness, resist the settled connectivity of the written word. Indeed, the charts often literally break up the narrative line on the page (as in figs. 4–7 and 15), thus reinforcing our impression within the charts of ongoing dislocation.

Even Barlow's part-time home of London—that great place of leave-taking in his narrative—is represented by Barlow more as a waterway through which people (or, more accurately, ships) travel than as a town with any habitational depth to it (fig. 15). The city here is compressed into a flat fringe that follows the curve of the Thames. This sketch by Barlow is very different from other drawings of London on the Thames, such as that published by Norden in *Speculum Britanniae* (fig. 32), which more fully embodies the city along the shore. Significantly, whereas Norden gives prominence to the settled area west of London Bridge, Barlow is more interested in the waterway to the east of the bridge, above which the great ships could not travel. Consider by contrast also Barlow's sketch of another stretch of the Thames even further down the river (fig. 16). Here Gravesend and a few other sparse habitations are shown. But the land within on either side of the river is not allowed to be fully settled. Rather, the idea of sitedness is put to sea, as Barlow sketches on the land different views of western British isles as seen from different bearings and distances at sea. Here again Barlow invests a charting convention—we saw a similar technique of using coastal views as insets within the land masses in Waghenaer's charts—with his own personal, unsettled vision. This is not to say, it should be stressed, that Barlow ignores locality. Like other seamen, as we have seen, he almost always carefully sites a port by giving the country within which it lies as well as its latitude and its distance and bearing from London (if it is in Britain or Europe). But such localities exist for Barlow more as assembly points than destinations—hence the traveling distance to and from London is so crucial. The ports, harbors, and coastlines are sites from which to come and go, as is London itself—not settled places in which to reside.

This compulsively "unsited" character to Barlow's drawings gives more resonance to another convention in his sketches: the relative absence of people. As in drawings of ships by other seamen, such as Edward Coxere, either Barlow's ships look empty or the seamen on board are drawn so minuscule and anonymous (like all his unnamed friends and family in his narrative) as to appear to be part of the ship. See, for example, Barlow's sketch of the *Augustine* in figure 5. The impression of anonymity in this colored sketch is reinforced by Barlow's painting all the men on board in red clothing (with some touches of blue). Barlow here anticipates the donning of uniforms by regiments of marines in 1664 and by naval crews in general much later, in 1857 (though the adopted colors would then be blue and white; red tended to be the favored color given to land-based soldiers).[39] The motif of red coloring in the picture not only makes the men dressed in red all alike; it also makes them visually akin to parts of the ship similarly colored: the gun ports painted red (as was the tradition of the time), the red in the flags, and the decorative border in red laced with white that encircles, and hence isolates, the ship. As viewed through the coloring of Barlow's painting, then, men at sea exist only within and as a complement to, or as an extension of, their itinerant ships. There are no singular seaman "I's" as seen through Barlow's eyes.

The main exceptions to scene after scene of harbors and coastlines or the occasional ship emblem are yet another kind of conventional drawing in maritime journals and logs: Barlow's few sketches of strange creatures (whale, rhinoceros, flying fish, etc.), sometimes standing inland of the coastal scene but more often appearing alone, like the ports, without any contextualization. These drawings, such as Barlow's picture of a ravenous shark and accompanying pilot fish (fig. 7), are the biological equivalent to coastline liminality; they image animal life on the margins of the familiar, of the "at home." The connection between the liminal shore and the liminal creature is underscored in figure 8, where images of strange sea creatures are interspersed with views of foreign coasts. Once again, then, sea convention figures Barlow's unsettled mind—or, more exactly, Barlow specifically brings out the unsettling nuances in the conventions of sea drawings of his time. Particularly striking is Barlow's tendency to set in action the creatures he depicts. As opposed to Dampier's sketch of a shark (fig. 31), which presents us with an inert scientific specimen, Barlow's sketch in figure 7 shows the shark in the act of attacking a man. The other of his drawings of strange sea creatures reproduced here (fig. 8) depicts them in action as well, swooping down or leaping up to catch flying fish, or hungrily eyeing such activities from below (as does the shovel-nose shark). That such strange, unfamiliar, or *unhomely* practices are imagined as voracious, and thus able to devour the self (as the "ravenous" shark devours the man), suggests Barlow's unease with his perpetual liminality occasioned by an "unsettled mind" that compelled him to seek the unfamiliar and live "at sea." The unsettled life, one might say, threatens to devour any hope Barlow has of a stable or fixed identity.

But it could also be argued that it is the harboring coastline that threatens Barlow. We might recall, thinking along these lines, that it was in the sheltered waters of the Strait of Banka that Barlow's ship was ambushed. Nervousness about such apparently secure places—not only about whether they are in fact secure but about the fact of security itself—could be another way of reading how Barlow intersperses views of approaching coasts with images of devouring creatures in figure 8: that is, as if shore and devourer were of one kind. The harbor, in particular, seems a highly ambivalent place for Barlow. Imagined often as a kind of womb (see especially figs. 11, 13, 14, and 17–19), the port shelters and rests the roving mind; but it also threatens to destroy such a self by staying unsettledness—hence the need for Barlow to be always on the move in his charts from port scene to port scene to port scene. It is unclear to me, in other words, what is more threatening to Barlow: being unsettled or being settled.

With such unresolved, perplexing thoughts in mind, we might in conclusion revisit the one very unconventional picture among Barlow's drawings, the one that also stands at the forefront of his journal: the picture of himself as a youth turning his back on his beckoning mother and leaving home (fig. 4). As we have seen, this is the single drawing in Barlow's journal that foregrounds a human relationship; it thus demands unusual attention. Dramatizing detachment, displacement, and liminality—Barlow stands at the very edge, or "shoreline," of the picture—the drawing serves, one might say, as a kind of sea beacon, pointing our way through the illustrated rutter of Barlow's itinerant life that is his journal. I earlier suggested that the wheatfield here, drawn as it was in retrospect (the account began fourteen years after Barlow left home), may well have been intentionally refigured by Barlow to suggest a road or highway, upon which he has intently set. Revisited once again, now that we have traversed Barlow's narrative of displacement illustrated by his "movable" charts, the wheatfield/road resembles something of a waterway before a harbor. Such waterways in Barlow's time (as today) were called "roads." In this refiguring, Barlow's mother becomes a kind of beckoning harbor, inviting him to stay. Barlow's attraction to such nurturing stability is strong enough to make him partially turn his head back toward his harboring mother; but the rest of his body steadfastly embarks upon the water road leading to open seas, just as ships in the foreground of Barlow's charts of harbors are always on the move. The unsettled seeing/seafaring "I" of Edward Barlow could never stay.

In this regard, the unique Barlow joined the many other lower-order subjects who, in their own unique ways, in varying degrees and at varying times, were vulnerable to the experience of unsettledness. Not every lower-order subject would have experienced such unsettledness to the degree that Barlow did, but many surely would have done so at least some, if not all, of the time. So far we have explored such unsettled subjects as wage laborers in historical accounts of the early modern period and in the self-representation of the "historical" journal that was Barlow's. But to the extent that Barlow's journal is also an aesthetic artifact—a *representation*—he points us in another direction. His journal asks us to pursue even further the representational road upon which he has partially embarked. I thus propose that, in order to follow this path further, we turn to more public and general aesthetic representations of seamen in the early modern period—specifically, to the plethora of ballads about seamen that flooded the streets of seventeenth-century London (and were carried to all reaches of the realm). Such ballads were aimed not only at "poor seamen" like Barlow and their relations; they would also have targeted those many landed laboring poor engaged in supporting the seafaring industry, as well as the equally large sector of the population that was nervously attentive to the growing importance of wage laborers—especially seamen—as a large and vocal proletariat. Interestingly, we shall find, in ballads of the period the unsettled wage laborer that was the seaman can undoubtedly be heard, but at the same time his voice is converted into the more respectable and comforting expression of, and desire for, stability and home. Settledness, we shall find, sells, even to the unsettled laboring poor. But so does the repressed fact of unsettledness—which, though repressed, continues to find a voice in the street ballads about seventeenth-century seamen.

⌒ PART THREE ⌒

Toward a Lowly Aesthetics of Unsettledness

The Ballad's Seaman
A Constant Parting

In May 1660, Edward Barlow, serving as apprentice seaman aboard the naval ship the *Naseby* (later renamed the *Royal Charles*), sailed to Holland on orders to fetch back England's soon-to-be-restored king, Charles II (41–48). The ship was commanded by no less than the distinguished General Lord Montagu (later to become the Earl of Sandwich). And accompanying Lord Montagu, acting as his secretary aboard the ship, was Samuel Pepys. Barlow and Pepys—an odd couple, to be sure. There is no evidence that either knew of the other's presence on the *Naseby*. Why would they? Barlow was but a common poor seaman, with little hope of significant advancement; Pepys was a relative of Montagu, already well on course for an important position in naval administration.[1] The two would have inhabited entirely different social and physical spaces (or decks) aboard the ship. But history offers telling stories of strange bedfellows, and such is this tale. For Barlow and Pepys, despite the socioeconomic divide, actually shared several interests: they both lamented the poor condition of the navy (including the ill effects of corruption, gentlemen officers, impressment, and long-delayed wages); they both kept journals of sorts (Pepys's diary becoming legendary, Barlow's journal-cum-autobiography dropping, until now, into obscurity); and they both showed a taste for a particularly "low" aesthetic form about seamen in their period: the broadside street ballad. Indeed, if it were not for Pepys, many of the abundant ballads about seamen published in the seventeenth century—ephemeral as the form was—would never have survived for our study today.

Barlow's journal at various times points tellingly to the kind of representational forms that shared the streets with ballads, and even to the ballad form specifically. His illustrations of exotic creatures, for instance—the man-eating shark, "the most ravenous fish that swims in the sea" (fig. 7); or the "strange wonder" of "a great whale" killed at Greenwich (25); or the "monster" born to a female passenger on a Dutch ship ("having several shapes, which made the beholders afraid, so that they presently drowned it in a tub of water"; p. 240)—could easily have found their way onto the streets of London as cheap broadsides peddled alongside the many other images of strange marvels that were eagerly consumed in the period. As often as not, these illustrations were accompanied by a ballad song, as in Martin Parker's "A Description of a Strange (and Miraculous) Fish"—another beached whale—or the anonymous "Pride's Fall," where the extended title prefaces a woodcut of a humanoid "strange monster" followed by a printed song.[2] Significantly, Barlow at one point in his journal provides the basic ingredients (image and text) of a broadside ballad, specifically about an encountered danger at sea: not only does he draw a picture of his ship the *Experiment* in distress off the Cape of Good Hope in 1671 (fig. 6), but he accompanies that picture with a poem describing the harrowing ordeal (196–97). Just such a broadside describing a near loss at sea was published around 1670–83/84 under the title "The *Benjamin's* Lamentation for Their Sad Loss at Sea, by Storms and Tempests" (it can be found in both the Pepys and Roxburghe ballad collections). The poem—a more catchy song than Barlow's plodding verse—was accompanied by two woodcuts, one of a sailing vessel and the other of a man swimming with a fleet of embattled ships in the background.[3]

Barlow, then, though not a publishing artist or balladeer, definitely showed affinity for the published broadside. And given the large number of extant early modern sea ballads, which represent a significant fraction of those actually published in the period, it would seem that Barlow's contemporaries had an affinity for—or at least a strong interest in—seamen as well. They had good reason. As we saw in chapter 6, as many as twenty-five thousand men might be mobilized in the navy's service in times of war, and similarly large numbers were impressed as wage laborers on land to work in the naval dockyards or in other support work. Multitudes of wage laborers were also involved in fishing and merchanting ventures; the East India Company, especially, mobilized such workers in large numbers. To the extent that seafaring was one of the largest developing, if unstable, areas of wage labor in the seventeenth century, other contemporaries kept a watchful eye on its activities. No wonder that ballads about seamen proliferated. And yet the most recent book on fictional representations of seamen, Harold Francis Watson's *The Sailor in English Fiction and Drama* (1931), looks extensively at literary forms of the period 1550–1800 but makes only a nodding gesture to sea chanteys, and nowhere acknowledges the important body of ballads in the seventeenth century that were specifically about seamen.[4] This chapter hopes to fill that void.

To embark upon a study of ballads about seamen, however, is to encounter up front a problematic crosswind: the vexed question of ballad audience. The problem is exemplified by the (apparently unconscious) contradiction in Natascha Wurzbach's description of ballad buyers. "The mass of the ballad public," she declares in *The Rise of the English Street Ballad, 1550–1650,* "belonged to the urban bourgeoisie—merchants and craftsmen and the servants of their

household—and secondly to the urban and agricultural working classes."
Further down on the same page, however, she asserts, "The ballad catered for
a mainly lower-class, relatively uncultured, practically minded public with
simple needs in the way of entertainment."[5] With a more consistent and clear-
sighted embrace, Tessa Watt, in her groundbreaking book *Cheap Print and
Popular Piety, 1550–1640*, argues that the ballad reached all classes and thus
disseminated a "shared culture." This would explain why, beyond the indul-
gence of a mere antiquarian interest, such middling to upper sorts as Pepys
and Roxburghe enthusiastically engaged in assembling the two largest collections of ballads of the period. But Watt also acknowledges that "publishers did
increasingly 'target' humbler readers."[6] Certainly, most erudite contemporaries in the seventeenth century (however much they may have eagerly
bought, collected, or copied out ballads) scathingly denigrated such art as
"low."[7] Of course, as Garrett Sullivan and Linda Woodbridge argue, the elite
actively constructed such a notion of the popular in opposition to "high" culture. Drawing on the work of Leslie Shepherd, these authors trace the process
by which the street ballad of the sixteenth century, "once aligned with courtiers
and clergymen . . . gradually became linked with, in Thomas Nashe's terms,
'every rednose fiddler' and 'ignorant ale knight.'"[8] Indeed, the formal features
of seventeenth-century ballads—simple language, uncomplicated narrative
lines, crude and plentiful woodcuts, common tunes, and black-letter print
(the print type used by the government for proclamations intended for the
widest dissemination to the public)—all suggest that these ballads were aimed
especially, if not exclusively, at the lower orders. The reiterated address at the
beginning of many ballads to "lusty lads" or "all youth" reinforces this sense:
youths, as we have seen, made up the majority of the poorer sorts. And while
the mode of circulating ballads—singing and peddling them on city streets, in
public houses, and in the countryside—may have made them universally accessible, such a "multimedia" dissemination, combining as it did the textual
with the visual and oral, especially made ballads available to the semiliterate
or illiterate (as well as to those who could afford to hear but not buy a ballad).
Finally, the price of broadside ballads itself is telling. Costing only one penny
at the end of the sixteenth century and dropping to half a penny by the end of
the seventeenth,[9] ballads were affordable to the very lowest sectors of early
modern society, excluding only the destitute. All in all, it seems clear that ballad makers and promoters adjusted the form and circulation of ballads to tap
into the large, if poor, lower-order market. The question then is, did ballad
content, as well as form, speak in special ways to lower-order interests?

Scrutiny of broadside ballads about poor seamen—a group representative, as we have seen, of the large and growing class of wage laborers in the

seventeenth century—allows us to begin to answer that question.[10] We might specifically think about the representation of seamen in such ballads in relation to the expression of "low" unsettled subjectivity that we found in the journal of the poor seaman Edward Barlow. What we shall here discover will once again reveal Barlow's uniqueness. But it will also show his shared sensibilities with other lower-order subjects of his time as expressed in ballads. Finally, it will demonstrate the difference between the relatively private aesthetic of unsettled subjectivity that is Barlow's journal and the definitely public one that is the ballad—an art form deliberately marketed for the many.

Barlow's journal and self-drawn charts, we have suggested, though never published, have already pointed us down the road of public aesthetics. Barlow's manuscript was intended, as I have noted, for an audience (even if his targeted audience was really, as I suspect, only himself) and was everywhere imbued with his own unsettled vision. His verbal and visual images of unsettled subjectivity thus carry us away from the "fact" of a mobile domestic economy and subject as explored in part 1 of this book to their imaginative "representation." Thus, we are now poised to entertain literary and artistic representations of unsettledness in the early modern period, and all the knotty interpretative questions of authorship, audience, and metaphoricity (versus literalness) that such representations pose. Such a shift in material is not, however, by any means absolute. As I argued in part 1, and further demonstrated in part 2 (in the case of Edward Barlow), the historical fact of unsettledness was itself actually metaphorical or metonymic. Like the aesthetic, it had the power of virtuality. That is, the unsettled experience, and by implication unsettled subjectivity, could have been felt, if only occasionally and ambivalently, by those not physically vagabond but *associated* with an unstable mobility: by a poor seaman like Barlow, for instance, as well as by other itinerant laborers and even poor householders (including multiply tasked women) who held many jobs, needed occasional poor relief, and moved often. For such persons vulnerable to physical and psychical displacement, the possibility of "reading" oneself into the unsettled experience might well have become greater the more that experience was rendered not literally (which requires either identification or denial) but at one remove—that is, metaphorically or aesthetically (allowing for a more negotiable and discontinuous association). Indeed, as we shall see, though the ballad offers a more couched and at times even suppressed version of unsettled subjectivity, its voice is also finally more dispersed and multiple.

What varieties of narratives about seamen do we find among the extant ballads from the early modern period? Interestingly, though images of ships often decorate the broadside page, stories about ships weathering storms, such as Barlow's poem about the *Experiment* or the anonymous ballad about the *Benjamin*, are not the most common. Sea ballads typically fall into one of four types, the last two being the most numerous: general praise for seamen; tales about infamous privateers, such as Captain Ward; nationalistic celebrations of naval victories (most common in the second half of the seventeenth century); and love songs, usually written in the form of a dialogue between a seaman and his lover spoken at the moment of parting. As with Barlow's journal, all these ballad types are mostly secular, with only nods to the "heavens" or "God" in the context of a maid praying for her seaman's safety, seamen facing possible shipwreck at sea, or celebrations of a victory against an enemy fleet. These ballads thus follow the secular outlook of seamen, which we noted in chapter 6, as well as the general shift in ballads—observed by Wurzbach—from more religious topics in the sixteenth century to more secular ones in the seventeenth.[11] Seamen in these largely secular poems are presented as enduring great hardships, but they are also given the un-Barlow-like descriptors "bonny," "gallant," and "lusty"; and in addition to being described as courageous (with which Barlow would certainly agree), they are typically referred to as "faithful," "loyal," and—most noteworthy for our study of unsettledness—"constant." Of course, the topic of love and constancy is a literary staple of the period, treated in varying ways in a range of genres—from sonnet sequences, such as Philip Sidney's *Astrophil and Stella*, to plays, such as William Shakespeare's *Troilus and Cressida*, to romances, such as Mary Wroth's *Urania*. Sea ballads do not stand alone in addressing this topic. But they do voice their own uniquely "low" perspective. Specifically, sea ballads about love speak the value for the lower orders of representing constancy *together with* unsettledness—or, as I have termed it, "a constant parting."

The numerous sea ballads about love, in particular, are obsessed with the subject of constancy. Perhaps the most idealizing of these, which particularly begs comparison with Barlow's aesthetics, is the anonymous "The Seaman's Sorrowful Bride" in the Pepys collection.[12] The greater part of the ballad is spoken by the seaman's "constant mournful bride" and expresses her unrelenting love for her new husband ("The floating sea shall dried be, / before I will repent" my choice, she says) as well as her "troubled mind" over being so soon separated from her husband and her fears over his endangerment at sea. She blames their untimely separation alternately on Holland, "the cruel wind," and—most often—"cruel fate." Each offender, her refrain reiterates, "parts my love and me." She begs Neptune, fate, rocks, and winds to be kind to her lover, and she sets her mind on their reunion: "For I will never be at rest, till I my love do see." As if in kind response, the song ends with "The Seaman's Answer," whereby the seaman announces his safe return and enduring love for his bride in the face of absence and adversity at sea. He concludes by bidding "adieu" to the seas and embracing a land-locked love:

> Now we will revel day and night,
> within each other's arms,
> In thee shall be my chief delight,
> I'll shield thee from all harms:
> Kindly thy body I'll embrace,
> and ever constant be,
> No other joys shall e're take place,
> I'll live and die with thee.

The seaman, as the ballad celebrates, is as "constant" in his love as is his bride. Indeed, he finds his defining "place" in her arms.

Two of the four woodcuts to this ballad especially confirm the "placed" or settled love of the seaman and his bride: the emblem of a lover's knot and the large picture of a port town (fig. 33). The lover's knot is a traditional sign for constancy in emblem books. As if such constant love gives shape to the very place in which the bride resides, awaiting the return of her seaman husband, the harbor forms itself into the figure of a heart. Significantly, the port's dwellings are foregrounded and no ships are present—stressing the future settledness of the newlyweds in this loving harbor. One might go so far as to say that the heart-shaped harbor, open as it is at the bottom, is a physical extension of the bride who awaits the seaman in readiness to embrace him.[13] Other ballads metaphorically echo this thought. In "The Seaman's Return to His Sweetheart," for instance, the seaman's lover (not wife) welcomes him home after an eighteen-month absence and offers her arms as safe harbor: "You may cast anchor for a while, / In my arms is safe harbor all sorrow to beguile."[14] Echoing this thought in yet another ballad, "A Dainty New Ditty of a Sailor and His Love," the lady invites the seaman to cast anchor more provocatively within her:

> Cast anchor here, this harbor shall be thine,
> In hymen's bands we will together join.
> So shall I shelter thee from all annoy,
> The tides love shall be thy safe convoy.[15]

But it is not only the bride who offers herself as safe harbor. If we consider the poetry together with the image of the harbor in "The Seaman's Sorrowful Bride," we realize that the seaman himself seeks to be a harboring presence.

Bride and groom, he projects, will revel "within each other's arms," and the seaman promises his bride that his "embrace" will "shield [her] from all harms."

The contrast with Barlow's images of harbors, as we have analyzed them, is striking. Although Barlow also often imagines the harbor (and by association his mother) as a sheltering, womblike place, he at the same time expresses great ambivalence about that idea, to the point of equating shorelines with something threateningly alien, like a ravenous shark. We have also seen that on further reflection, Barlow actually resists sited place, stressing the ongoing practice rather than the achieved state of finding out sheltering harbors, focusing on the activity of ships coming and going from ports, and only barely sketching in buildings or the interior land. To invoke the defining terms of this study, if the harbor of "The Seaman's Sorrowful Bride" or other such metaphorical harbors in ballads would seem to image settled *place*, Barlow pictures unsettling *space*.

How are we to explain this seemingly radical difference between Barlow's aesthetic and that of ballads such as "The Seaman's Sorrowful Bride"? The obvious answer is that place sells; space does not. That is, whatever the "realities" of their situation, seamen and their ladies, and other such lower-order subjects susceptible to displacement, who were the major purchasers of ballads, wanted to think of themselves (as Barlow himself often wanted to think of himself) as settled and secure. They wanted to be comforted by images of place even in—perhaps because of—the realities of an all-too-pressing placelessness. But this answer needs qualification. Other evidence suggests that not all buyers of ballads wanted to think of themselves as securely placed—or, perhaps more accurately, that buyers of ballads did not always want to so think of themselves.

For all their celebration of "constancy," that is, ballads of seamen and their lovers also picture the dark side of placed love, imaged as unsettledness. This can be felt in the insistent depiction from ballad to ballad of partings between seamen and their lovers (who are more often, significantly, maids, not wives). While some ballads may begin with a seaman's return or have a conclusion or second part that celebrates his return (or, tragically, laments his death at sea), the majority of the ballads begin with and stay focused on a parting. In this respect, we are reminded of what largely makes Barlow's harbors feel unsettled: his own almost obsessive depiction of port scene after port scene after port scene, imaging ships leaving as often as arriving in port. Reminiscent of Barlow, furthermore, is the seaman's insistent reiteration in the ballads, as he approaches his lover to tell of his departure, that he is "forced to go" or "must go" to sea. Often the source of coercion is specifically attributed to the seaman's having been impressed, or "pressed."[16] But equally often, what impels the departure is left unexplained, as when in "The Seaman's Sorrowful Bride" the new bride abstractly blames their separation on "cruel fate." In yet other ballads, though the seaman says he "must" go to sea, the motivation clearly comes as well from within, as appeared to be the case with Barlow. The seaman of "The Unfeigned Lover" may approach his lady lamenting, "I here *must* bid thee now adieu," but the caption to the ballad asserts, "He to the seas *resolved* to sail, / And bid his dear adieu" (my emphases). Furthermore, while declaring his love and insisting he will prove constant, this seaman—again sounding very much like Barlow—as avidly asserts that "through those pathless waves o're Neptune's throbbing breast, / from my very youth I took delight." The maid knows which way the wind blows: she resignedly prays for him, "if thou *needst must* go, / seeing thou in this *must have thy will*" (my emphases).[17]

In yet other ballads, the seaman becomes testy when his lover questions the necessity of departure and tries to persuade him to stay. In "The Faithful Lover's Farewell," when the seaman, John, declares to his betrothed, Betty, that he must go to sea, since "I cannot now well support thee, and live like other men," she begs him, "Some other way study to live with me here on shore." John's irritable response: "Prithee leave thy dreaming, and be an obedient wife."[18] Almost never do the two lovers marry before departure. On the contrary, such thoughts of marriage are often impatiently dismissed by the sailor because, he says, he has no time. In "The Seaman's Leave Taken of his Sweetest Margery," when the seaman promises to marry his love—"if I ever marry a wife, / it shall be my sweet Margery"—the maid urges him to do so before he goes: "I prithee do that before we part, / that joyful day I might but see." His answer:

> Be not so hasty, rather stay,
>   for at this time it cannot be;
> I must aboard this present day,
>   and leave my sweetest Margery.[19]

Timing is everything: a hasty departure provokes hasty thoughts of marriage, which can then be dismissed by the seaman as too hasty. His command that Margery instead "stay"—in the sense of both remaining behind and desisting from rash thoughts of marriage—follows directly upon his own urgent need to leave. For all the professions of faithful love and constancy, then, these ballads mostly tell tales of unknotted or unencumbered love and, finally, of "resolved" separation.

Thus, it would seem that if place sells, so does placelessness. Or, rather, ballads about constant or faithful love between a seaman and his lover allow the audience to see (or not to see) both commitment and unsettledness, stability and displacement. Such a twinned and conflicted experience, as we noted in chapter 6, would have in fact been the position of many poor wage laborers at sea. But the ballads allow for an either/or as well as a both/and viewpoint. Sometimes ballads overtly play with these two possible interpretations, as in "A Dainty New Ditty of a Sailor and His Love." This ballad begins with a maid welcoming her seaman home after a long absence at sea and insisting he must now stay settled on shore with her:

> Thy absence long shall grieve my heart no more,
> Since thou art come thou must with me remain,
> And not as yet go to the seas again.

The seaman, however, says he wants no such encumbering ties:

> I am resolved to lead a single life,
> I have a voyage for to take in hand,
> Which fits my humor better than the land.

In the exchange that ensues, "Maid" and "Man" alternate stanzas, the maid arguing for why the seaman should "cast anchor" with her, the seaman countering each argument with one favoring a return to his "lusty ship." In every way, he declares,

> My love is fixed upon the sounding main,
> .   .   .   .
> I mean to have
> The sea my wife, and therein make my grave.

When a settlement of marriage between the two seems hopeless, the maid finally resolves to die. At this point, in the penultimate stanza of the ballad, the man declares, "Nay stay." Everything he had spoken, he assures her,

> 'twas only for to try
> Thy love to me and faithful constancy:
> And now I find thou dost both say and hold,
> I will not leave thee for rich Croesus gold.

The maid concludes the ballad with rejoicing at the prospect of a settled union between the two lovers: "That our hearts may be no longer t'wain, / But linked in love, and so for aye remain."[20] In this ballad, the maid is constant throughout, but the man gets to play freely with inconstancy and the unsettled life before finally casting anchor in wedlock.

It is significant in this respect, if we return to "The Seaman's Sorrowful Bride," that the two other woodcuts to that ballad are of two very different-looking ladies. Despite the images of the love knot and of the settled harbor promising to embrace the newlyweds, the two ladies give one pause. How constant is the seaman's love if two ladies, not one, await him? Or, to invoke a cliché active in the period, exactly how many wives does this seaman have in port? The question is not as frivolous as it seems, since a number of ballads overtly ignore the party line and warn about the inconstant love of seamen. In "The Mother's Kindness," the mother warns her daughter to avoid seamen because "of such there is not one in ten, / But what are careless roving men"; and in "The Cruel Lover," a seaman persistently woos a maid, but "so soon as her heart she resigned, / he changed like the wavering wind."[21] Indeed, the title to one ballad is "The Mariner's Delight; or, The Seaman's Seven Wives" (the caption further adds "all alive at that time")—this a maid discovers only after the seaman determinedly wins her love and, upon going to sea, prays "thee be constant to me, as I shall prove real and true."[22] Other ballads also tragically or jokingly tell of sailors ruthlessly ditching maids after winning them over with their professions of constancy.[23]

It should be added that the maids of ballads, like many a real-life maid, sometimes serve the seaman in kind, marrying or dallying with another while he is away on his twelve-month, or eighteen-month, or seven-year voyage. A late example of such a turnaround by the lady is the comic ballad "Jack Robinson," by Thomas Hudson. In this song, we hear how Jack jumps ship on a return to Portsmouth after three years at sea and goes in search of his lady love, Polly Gray. When he can't find her, he goes for a drink to a public house (a latter-day alehouse) and is shocked to see that the landlady of the place is Polly. She at first doesn't recognize him and has to be convinced of his identity by his showing a handkerchief she had given him "three years ago, before I went to sea." Jack dotingly says, "Every day I looked at it, and thought of thee." But though Jack has remained fixed on his love, Polly has moved on. Her comically presented change of heart is a realistic response to the uncertainty of her lowly life as expressed through the indeterminacy of itinerant news:

> Says the lady, says she, I've changed my state,
> Why you don't mean, says Jack, that you've got a mate,
> You know you promised me—says she, I couldn't wait,
> For no tidings could I gain of you Jack Robinson;
> And somebody one day came to me, and said,
> That somebody else had somewhere read,
> In some newspaper as how you was dead;
> I've not been dead at all says Jack Robinson.

Raised from the "some"-time dead, Jack promptly takes off, himself now embracing itinerant uncertainty—life at sea.

> I'll get a ship, and go to Holland, France and Spain,
>   No matter where, to Portsmouth I'll ne'er come back again,
>   And he was off before they could say Jack Robinson.[24]

It is not, then, simply that ballads that apparently extol the faithfulness or constancy of seamen and maids suppress within them a "forced" unsettledness of variable and sometimes uncertain origin. It is also the case that, as one reads from ballad to ballad, the very idea of constancy changes, sometimes playfully toyed with, at other times ruthlessly mocked or undermined by seaman or maid. Indeed, broadside ballads appear to delight in holding up different positions or roles for seamen and like-minded buyers of ballads to try out and experiment with. In this sense, such ballads quintessentially exploit the absence of "wholeness" that Alexandra Halasz attributes to the "marketplace of print": "a proliferation of texts and discourses that cannot be controlled from any single position, nor can its multiplicity be contained within a unified representation."[25] The extent to which ballads deliberately market multiple perspectives can be seen in the frequent clustering around a central subject of songs promoting different subject positions. A good example of such a multivalent cluster of sea ballads appears in the appendix to volume 6 of the published *Roxburghe Ballads.*

The five ballads gathered together in this appendix do not appear to share the same author (all are anonymous); nor, with the exception of the first two, the same printer; nor do they all belong to the Roxburghe collection.[26] In fact, they are grouped together in the loosest of ways: they simply follow each other sequentially within the list of many ballads added to volume 6 in the appendix. But there is a logic to their appearing together. An array of common strains does run through them: the first four ballads have the same approximate date (1686); the first two give the maid and seaman the same names (Nelly and Henry); the third also calls the maid Nelly, and the fourth calls her by the shortened version of that name, Nell; the fourth is clearly an "answer" to the third; the fifth (ca. 1692–93) claims to have been written aboard the same ship, the *Britannia,* on which the seaman of the fourth ballad says he sails; and finally, the third, fourth, and fifth ballads are all sung to the same tune, "The Languishing Swain" (also identified, in the fourth ballad, as "I Loved You Dearly" and in the fifth ballad as "The False-Hearted Young Man").

We might begin to get a handle on this loose cluster of ballads by starting with the first one, "A New Song of Nelly's Sorrow at the Parting with Her Well-Beloved Henry, That Was Just Ready to Set Sail to Sea"—though it should be noted that it is the *Roxburghe* editor, not early modern contemporaries, who decided on the order in which the ballads are presented here.

"A New Song of Nelly's Sorrow" and its second part, the second ballad in the appendix, appeared together in a published collection titled *Neptune's Fair Garland* (1686). For all its touting of "new," the ballad offers a very conventional dialogue between a seaman and his maid upon her hearing that, in the narrator's words, "Alas! He [the seaman] was compelled to go, with her he could no longer stay." The unidentified compulsion driving the seaman Henry is so strong that the word "must" appears four times in the short ballad's fifty-two lines. There is only the slightest hint in the ballad that such compulsion might come from within. We get just a glimpse of a potentially competing love—a wanderlust—that might spur Henry, in his reference to having to cross Neptune's "throbbing breast" (a sexualization of sea voyaging that we have seen in other ballads, in their references also to "Neptune's throbbing breast" as well as to the "lusty ship" and to "the sea my wife"). As is typical in such ballads, the maid Nelly is launched upon her own voyage of sorrow upon hearing that Henry must depart, and she "almost drowned in despair." Just as typically, the seaman nevertheless reiterates that he must go, in this case doubtfully reassuring her with the fact that "there's many more as well as I, with me must sail the ocean main." In the end, like so many other such maids left behind, Nelly acknowledges defeat and prays that heaven will guide him safely: " 'Well Love,' said she, 'since thou must go, the Heavens be thy careful guide.' " And so, the narrator concludes, "these loyal lovers parted were."[27]

If "A New Song of Nelly's Sorrow" rivals "The Seaman's Sorrowful Bride" in its depiction of a loyal love "compelled" into severance, its second part, "A New Song of Henry Setting Forth to Sea," though more of a narrative cliffhanger, concludes by aligning itself with "The Seaman's Answer" to his sorrowful bride. When Henry's ship departs, we are told in this second ballad, the crew's "hearts was filled with sweet content." But a storm soon brews, the ship is wrecked, and all but eleven of its crew drowned. Henry is among the survivors picked up by a ship heading for Yarmouth, and he returns safely to Nelly to tell his harrowing tale. She responds by declaring an end to all such risky roaming, and he willingly agrees:

> "My dear," said she, "thou shalt not roam, nor run the hazards of the sea,
> Thou shalt in safety stay at home, I'm glad thou art alive with me."
>
> Her friends and his were all agreed, and he himself did give consent,
> That they should married be with speed, and live at home in sweet content.[28]

Henry is not as passionate or vocal a spokesman for settled love as is the seaman of "The Seaman's Answer." Indeed, he is noticeably silent in the ballad: only the narrator and the maid—who forcefully advocates staying at home—speak. However passively, though, Henry "himself did give consent," and the ballad's two parts thus join the many other such ballads that promote secure and unchanging place.

But that is not the final word on the stories of Henry and Nelly. In yet another ballad published about the same year (third in the *Roxburghe* gathering), Nelly speaks of her own constancy but bewails betrayal by her seaman lover. The full title to the ballad is "An Excellent New Song, Called Nelly's Constancy; or, Her Unkind Lover. Who, after Contract of Marriage Leaves His First Mistress, for the Sake of a Better Fortune." Oddly, if rather charmingly, Joseph Woodfall Ebsworth, the editor of this *Roxburghe* volume (and volumes 4–9), introduces this piece with a disclaimer: "We refuse to believe," he asserts, "the faithful Henry of the *Neptune's Fair Garland*, 1686, to be the same person as the un-named 'Unkind Lover' of the next-following song, 'Nelly's Constancy,' and its Answer. Two different Nellies, perhaps, but either one deserving a toast as the Lass that loves a Sailor."[29] Actually, the character of Nelly has not changed all that much. But the seaman she loves (never named) does seem to be a different person or, equally likely, to have adopted a different self-identity.

Reaffirming her constant love in "Nelly's Constancy," even in the face of betrayal—"My heart you have, go where you will"—this Nelly asks, "What makes young men be thus unkind, / To gain maids' loves, then change their mind?" Her posited answer is money:

> You love another, I'll tell you why,
> Because she has more means than I,
>
> . . . .
>
> 'Tis money is your chiefest aim,
> All women else would be the same.

She concludes with a warning for all maids:

> Be careful lest your heart's betrayed:
> Believe not all young men do say,
> They'll vow they'll love, yet go their way.
>
> Like my dear love that courted me,
> Who's wed another, and gone to sea.[30]

It would seem that the "other woman" in this ballad doesn't achieve a settled love either, since the seaman does not stay put: he has "wed another, and gone to sea." This is one inconstant seaman. As if triggering a zest for such inconstancy, the ballad then ends with a collective carpe diem call by seamen to come ashore while in port and—in one interpretation, at least—merrily breed:

> "Then call a boat, boys, unto the ferry,
> For we are come, boys, to be merry;
> It shall n'ere be said, boys, when we are dead,
> But the Jolly Sailors are rarely bred."[31]

What looks to be the seaman's answer to Nelly's complaint (though it was published by a different printer) appears next in the *Roxburghe* appendix as "The Seaman's Answer to His Unkind Lover" (also ca. 1686 and to the same tune, "The Languishing Swain"). Here the seaman's identity transmutes yet again: instead of a constant lover or faithless money-grubber, he becomes a roguish pragmatist facing the likely inconstancy, he says, of her—not his—unwedded love:

> 'Twas not for money that I wed, I never asked her what she had,
> You said you would not married be, till I returned again from sea.
>
> That was the reason, pretty Dove, which made me seek for another love,
> I thought when I to sea was gone, you'd wed before I could return.[32]

Given the frequency of sea ballads in which the maid urges marriage at the moment of parting and the seaman refuses, asking her to wait until his return, the seaman's answer here is a surprising and suspicious turnabout. But even if it's just a lame excuse, it raises the possibility—supported by other ballads and the evidence of history—that maids as well as men change. The sense that the seaman is in fact roguishly mocking the maid is reinforced by his outrageous proposal that, since she says she will only marry a seaman, she should marry his look-alike brother, who is sailing on the same ship with him, the *Britannia*, in the straits near Turkey:

> I am glad you do impart "A seaman still shall have thy heart."
>
> I have a brother with me here, who's younger than I by one year,
> He is a seaman truly bred, my dearest Nell, let him thee wed.
>
> You cry "Stop Thief," your heart I have, my brother he the same do[es] crave,
> And begs that I would write to you, to give thy free consent thereto.
>
> If you but saw us both together, you could not tell one from the other;
> Then prithee, Nell, do not deny, though I am wed, let him enjoy.[33]

Since he has heard that Nelly is "ranging o'er the sea" in search of him, the seaman even gives her his address ("We're both in the *Britannia* bold, i' th' Straights where strangers much behold, / . . . near the Turkish shore") and invites her to come see his brother for herself: "Then come, my fair one, come away! My brother longs to see the day / That you will be his happy bride. Then waft her hither, wind and tide!"[34] What a cocky fellow! It is as if the seaman here feeds on the irresponsible jollity of the seamen's call to port that ends the previous ballad. But even this is not the end of the various voicings of seamen in this cluster of ballads.

The final ballad that belongs to this gathering, "The Faithful Mariner," returns us more seriously to the notion of constancy. Although it is sung to the same tune ("The Languishing Swain," alternatively titled "The False-Hearted Young Man") as the previous mocking ballad, and though its author claims to write from aboard the same ship, the *Britannia*, this ballad writer sounds completely different from the previous seaman: his is an earnest love letter written to a maid identified as "fair Isabel, his loyal love" who is firmly situated in "the city of London." Even so, a competing desire can be detected in this letter. The seaman, that is, elaborates the "sweet" pleasures of sailing with the British fleet in the Spanish straits. He opens, "Fair Isabel, of beauty bright, / To thee in love these lines I write" but immediately moves to focus upon sensual sea delights: "the sweet delightsome banks of Spain," the British fleet "with swelling sails, with swelling sails, and streamers sweet," as well as the "beautified" seas and "pleasant breathing gentle-gales."[35] Desire for the sea, however, is suppressed within the poem; it lurks within metaphor. The ballad is foremost a simple descriptive letter from a seaman about his voyage, a letter that remains anchored at its beginning and end on his placed love "in the city of London." Despite the lure of the sea, then, this ballad mostly returns us to the secure constancy of a faithful love.

Or so Ebsworth, the editor of the *Roxburghe* appendix, has made it seem. After all, this is, as we've noted, *his* ordering of the ballads, not any early modern ordering. The first two ballads and the second two ballads clearly form pairs, but the very fact that the ballads in the second pair have been individually preserved in separate collections is telling (see note 26). They may have been read or heard independently. Indeed, there is no knowing which of the collected ballads would have been encountered by a contemporary as he or she walked along the streets or sipped beer in an alehouse or browsed the book stalls at Paul's. Nor is there any knowing which ballads would have caught someone's ear, encouraging them to sing along (voicing the parts of seaman or maid or both), nor which would have been bought as especially worthy artifacts to possess. One thing that we *do* know is that the ballads, taken together, offer a full platter of different roles from which hearers and potential buyers could have sampled at will. In this sense, it is beside the point whether any one maid or seaman is the same as or different from another as one moves between ballads (and this may be part of the point of the seaman's offering his look-alike brother to his ex-lover as "compensation").[36] They are all the same and all different, because they allow the audience provisionally to play out—through their very variability—multiple and dispersed identities. And of course the singing of ballads encourages such experimentation, allowing the audience to sing along in the voice of man, maid, mother, captain—or even, in one ballad, ship.[37]

In the final analysis, this may be the most significant difference between Barlow's private aesthetic and the marketed aesthetic of broadside ballads. Written from the perspective of a single man and primarily for himself, Barlow's journal enacts speculation in a limited number of roles (however fractured), mostly playing out the almost Manichean struggle within Barlow between a settled and an unsettled mind (with respect to place, job, relationship, etc.). Ballads, on the other hand, written from the perspective of the many for the many, project a myriad of different roles or identities that may be promiscuously picked up and discarded by its audience upon hearing or viewing them, quite literally with a mere turn of the head. In effect, "freedom" and "variety" of identity are what broadside ballads market. Whether the audience pays for the ballads or not, the songs make available diverse subjectivities on a psychologically "no-cost," provisional basis. A new role lies just around the corner, on the very next broadside page, and often even between the lines of the same page. Such multivarious role speculation would have been available, it should be stressed, not only to seamen or seamen's maids, but to all the ballad's audience. The itinerant seaman, so often about to embark upon a new voyage, thus functions in ballads as a metaphor or trope for an unsettled subjectivity that was truly spacious—as has, in a more limited, realistic way, our seaman Barlow in his journal. Nevertheless, such an aesthetic representation of the unsettled experience appears to have been aimed especially at lower-order subjects, who most intensely lived out indeterminacy and dispersal, holding multiple jobs just to get by and at any time subject to displacement (from job to job, place to place, relationship to relationship). What the aesthetics of the ballad offers such subjects is an unthreatening, pleasant version of unsettled subjectivity—one that could be imaginatively and freely experienced, as it could not be in real life—at *no cost*.

But it should never be forgotten that cost or the market is in fact what propels—and is propelled by—the ballad, as well as the unsettled subject. "Multividual" subjectivity, we have seen, was rooted in a mobile economy—of which seafaring is but an intense example—in which the lower orders were fully invested. An unsettled market, one might say, is the fluid ground that connects seamen and landsmen. As if to reinforce this connection, the sea ballads often stress that seamen are workers. Her husband at sea is "*at work for gold and treasure,*" says a seaman's wife as she cavorts with a landed itinerant in "A Job for a Journeyman-Shoemaker" (my emphasis).[38] "We'll ply our *business* nimbly / where e're we come or go," the seamen say of themselves in "Neptune's Raging Fury" (my emphasis).[39] Ballads in praise of seamen, such as "Neptune's Raging Fury" or "The Seaman's Compass" by Laurence Price (1655–80), depict seamen as suffering hardships not only to defend the nation, but also to supply it with goods. These commodities include costly consumables (jewels, spices, fruits, rich fabrics, and the like) for the comfortable middling and upper sorts to purchase. But they also include raw materials upon which the seamen's land-based look-alikes, the unstable laboring poor, could themselves work:

> To comfort poor people,
>   The seamen do strive,
> And brings in maintenance
>   to keep them alive,
> As raw silk and cotton wool
>   to card and to spin
> And so by their labors
>   their livings comes in.[40]

Such goods, we have seen, were the raw materials of the bustling new domestic trade in the early modern period that fostered multiple employment among the men and women of the lower orders as well as landed itinerancy (in the form of peddlers and chapmen distributing the finished products). Finally, maids singing in ballads of their intent to marry a seaman also envisage the seaman as foremost a tradesman. In "The Seaman's Compass," the maid praising seamen announces,

> Come tradesmen or merchant,
>   whoever he be,
> There's none but a seaman
>   shall marry with me.[41]

The maid of "The Fair Maid's Choice" methodically rejects various mostly lower-order occupations—miller, tailor, carpenter, shoemaker, blacksmith, brewer—while echoing the same preference in her refrain: "of all sorts of tradesmen a seaman for me."[42] Whatever or whoever else these seamen are in ballads, they are heavily invested in an *economy* of mobility that makes all such workers exchangeable, despite the voiced preferences of the maids. They stand for a growing proletariat of unsettled wage laborers who might at any point, though in various ways, identify with them in song.

This may well explain what at first seems a rather puzzling inclusion in a cheap little three-ballad volume titled *The Midshipman's Garland* (printed between 1692 and 1703 and sold for a penny).[43] The first of the three ballads in this volume offers a familiar naval song welcoming a seaman home. The third ballad is also a common naval type of the time—a narrative about a sea battle. But the second ballad, sandwiched between these two, seems an odd choice. It is a ballad of street cries voiced by peddlers of mostly homegrown, domestic stuffs, titled "The Traders' Medley; or, The Cries of London." What is this ballad about street trafficking doing in a midshipman's garland? Itinerant seamen and itinerant hawkers, the *Midshipman's Garland* would seem to answer, are of a kind. They are part of the same mobile economy heard daily on the streets of London (or any other city, for that matter). Indeed, we might recall that Barlow, the unsettled seaman, had also been a displaced land worker and, between voyages, a onetime peddler of books.

We will not wander off the course of sea ballads, then, if we conclude our discussion with consideration of two broadsides specifically about street peddlers. By so redirecting our focus to what we might call "market" broadsides, we shall gain a threefold advantage: (1) reason to revisit, with new perspective, the onshore economy of itinerancy that initially generated this study's theory of unsettled subjectivity; (2) an opportunity to examine the most overt aesthetic representation of the lowly subject occupying the space of transient wage labor; and (3) occasion to open up further the dicey question of audience that is always at issue when dealing with marketed representations. As we have seen in discussing the cheapness of broadside ballads, price determines the viable audience and therefore possible interpretations of the "wares" sold. Thus, in the first market broadside discussed below, which was more expensive than a ballad, the wealthier middle class steps into the picture and demands consideration.

I refer to one of the early Cries of London. Beginning in England in the 1590s, the early Cries, such as *The Town Crier* (fig. 34), are crude engravings that typically picture hawkers set off one from the other in colonnades but gathered together on a single broadsheet. Each peddler sells a particular commodity: shrimp, haddock, figs, buttons, points, pins, and like items (many of them products of by-employments typical of the unsettled domestic economy engaged in by poor men and especially women of the period). As Sean Shesgreen argues, what is being pictured here is a new kind of getting and spending, which swept across London and extended into a web of distribution and exchange linking rural and urban consumers.[44] These wandering street sellers, like their fellow peddlers and chapmen (as we have seen), were victims

of legal attacks in the late sixteenth and seventeenth centuries—with abuse
increasing up to the nineteenth century—even as the hawkers clearly fulfilled
a real need within London and the countryside for mobile trade.[45] Interestingly
(and this is a feature to which we will return), the vendors are portrayed the-
atrically and almost heroically—posed between stalwart pillars—at the same
time that they are seen as alien and isolated specimens of "outcast" men and
women. Underscoring their displaced status, a street beggar lurks among
them (at the bottom left), soliciting alms ("bread and meat") and thus risk-
ing arrest as a vagrant. Indeed, taken together, the pictures display the ambiguously "free" role speculation that we have associated with unsettled labor;
and in fact, as Shesgreen notes, though Cries show sellers peddling only one
type of ware, hawkers historically shifted wares and sold more than one type
at once.[46] As if to acknowledge the potential for multiple or serial job-shifting
on the part of any one such worker, the water bearer's staff intrudes upon the
space of the prune seller. The montage of vendors pictured on a single broadsheet, then, is a dispersion across space of a potentially single identity, now
imaged as "free"-floating and multiple.

Giving more immediate and realistic expression to the unsettled subjectivity imaged in this broadside engraving (*The Town Crier*), the speaker, or
"presenter," of the broadside ballad "Turner's Dish of Lenten Stuff; or, A Gallimaufry" (1612) opens with the declaration, "I will tell you what they cry, / In
London all the year." What follow are serial characterizations of street sellers
and vocalizations of the hawkers' cries: the fishwife's

> nye mussels lily white:
> Herrings, sprats, or place,
>   or cockles for delight.
> Nye welflet [well-fed?] oysters

and the broom man's

> Old shoes for new brooms,
> . . . .
> For hats or caps or buskins,
>   or any old pooch [rare] rings

and the costermonger's

> Ripe cherry ripe,
> . . . . . .
> Pippins fine, or pears

and the collier's

> Buy small coals, or great coals,
> I have them on my back

and the mouser's

> Buy a trap a mouse trap,
> a tormentor for the fleas

and so on.[47] Each hawker is given the space of a stanza or two, the textual equivalent to the partitioned visual spaces in *The Town Crier*. And as in *The Town Crier*, the multiple hawkers become as if serial representations of a single subject that is a multiple "I." Indeed, as the presenter voices the separate cries, he at times inhabits the persona, as if the crier were the presenter himself. For instance, from the stanza space devoted to peddlers, the speaker abruptly shifts voices in the opening of the next stanza: "Buy small coals, or great coals, / I have them on my back." Here the distance between presenter and collier collapses; the "I" of the presenter and the "I" of the collier have become one, with one pack. What this and other such inhabiting moments underscore is that all these hawkers speak through the single voice of the presenter, allowing him—or any singer or owner of the ballad—casually to take on and cast off street identities at will. This is no removed, nostalgic, or romantic vision of unsettled economics. The presenter makes many a biting critical comment on the roguish cheating by the hawkers, so that to take on the persona/voice of the collier, for instance, is also to take on the tricks of his trade. The presenter also occasionally roams farther afield in the second part of the ballad, intermixing hawkers proper with players, roaring boys, lawyers, usurers, and rack-renting landlords (all, by implication, with their own hawking interests). Nevertheless, the song for the most part offers as its own ware serial street personae that a single speaker can voice with the sheer delight of a conspicuously unsettled "I."

It is this possibility for active and interactive engagement in its song that makes the representation of Turner's broadside ballad different from the more disengaged broadside engraving of *The Town Crier*. Certainly, both are aesthetic artifacts, ones that could be pasted up on a wall and admired from a distance. But the ballad is also an engaging oral song. It invites, at times even demands, participation in ways that the solely visual aesthetic of the Cries broadside does not and cannot. As they sing along, the ballad's audience provisionally voice all or part of the ballad's various serial identities (adding more as they switch between ballads) and thus momentarily inhabit those roles, provisionally making them their own—but at no cost. The audience can freely take or leave the offered voices, speculating wholeheartedly or intermittently in the ballad's multiple and dispersed identities. Such an audience quite literally expresses unsettled subjectivity.

In this respect, the other difference between the engraved Cries and the ballad becomes especially significant: the fact that the two forms targeted different economic sorts. For all their apparent complementarity, *The Town Crier* broadside was in a different socioeconomic class from the broadside ballad. The former cost a relatively expensive six pence, about the same price as a pamphlet. The latter, as we have seen, cost a mere penny (and at the end of the seventeenth century only half a penny). Servants and apprentices had more disposable income than has in the past been supposed, as Paul Griffiths's study shows.[48] Even so, six pence—though still relatively cheap by print standards—would have been a big expense and probably beyond the economic means of most such workers. This includes poor laborers and householders as well as (much of the time) poor seamen, such as Barlow.

If the audience of *The Town Crier* consisted primarily of the more wealthy middling sort, as Shesgreen also contends,[49] then the increased "distance" inherent in the engraving (in comparison to the engaging oral ballad) becomes more explainable. One might consider such distancing as a kind of aesthetic safety net, allowing identification at a remove. The wealthier sort may well have delighted in envisaging the multiply dispersed economic subject, seeing in those serial snapshots aspects of their own diversified economic interests—hence the "heroic" quality Shesgreen sees in the hawkers' stances. Certainly, in the early modern period the middling sort of all kinds were also heavily involved in the new market processes that we have identified as unsettled. Middle-class entrepreneurs, for instance, proliferated in the sixteenth and seventeenth centuries in order to service the expanding marketing network. Established tradesmen (including well-to-do chapmen, who maintained market stalls) sold to eager consumers of all degrees the diverse new domestic wares that were produced by the poor. And large investors capitalized on the liquid flow of money and paper exchange to reap huge profits. By virtue of their personal investment in a mobile market—and all its unpredictable vagaries—such businessmen conceivably could have recognized themselves, however partially or fleetingly, in unsettled poor laborers. But recognition does not necessarily mean full acknowledgment or acceptance. However much they profited from and participated in a fluid economy—and increasingly came to admit reliance upon transient wage labor in the course of the seventeenth century, as we have seen in the more liberal settlement laws of 1662 and especially 1697—the middling sort also feared unsettledness as alien and even threatening to their desired socioeconomic place. The idea of such a threat is spelled out in the central cry of the watchman's warning: "Maids in your smocks, look well to your lock." If wealthy merchants heeded the call of a fluid market grounded on mobile wage labor, they at the same time didn't want such labor entering their homes (or becoming intimate with their daughters). Indeed, as we have seen, shop owners encouraged the persecution of street hawkers, since they competed with them for profits.

Thus, just as Thomas Harman, in his *Caveat for Common Cursitors,* translates the disturbing realities of multiple and serial jobs by poor wage laborers (as we witnessed in chapter 3), so do the Cries—but in the opposite direction. Harman represses the mobile work of poor laborers further downward, reimagining it as roguish disguising; the Cries repress job diversity upward, converting it into stable frames of ennobling poses. In the process, the Cries keep any self-mirroring aesthetic safely at a distance, compartmentalized, and "on the wall." They contain (in the sense of "enclose" or "check") unsettled and unsettling wage labor. Only in this way could the middling sort have taken aesthetic delight in such economics. In other words, there was a limit to the amount of identification with the mobile working poor that the middling sort could entertain.

In the end, then, of the two versions of Cries broadsides—engraving on the one hand and ballad on the other—it is the more lowly street ballad that most fully (and again, quite literally) *voices* lower-order, unsettled subjectivity. As we have seen in looking at ballads about seamen, and further realized in examining the market ballad of street cries, "Turner's Dish of Lenten Stuff," broadside ballads give voice to a myriad of possible roles, which they invite the singer or buyer to try on freely and discard at will. Barlow would undoubtedly have found full and varied expression of his "unsettled" mind in voicing such ballads. So would have many other seamen and their families, as well as the large numbers of unstable and displaced landed laborers dependent upon the seafaring industry or simply engaged in multiple or serial employment, such as was typical of women's labors. The unsettled experience represented through the voicings of ballads would have been, whether fully, partially, or intermittently, most "available" to such working poor in early modern England. It is to the broadside street ballad in particular, then, that we must look if we wish to explore in more detail the virtual or representational spaces of the unsettled "I." That is a subject deserving further study.

Epilogue:
Unsettling the New Global Economy

I cannot repeal the laws of change. In every State in every area of this country the average 18-year-old will change the nature of work seven or eight times in a lifetime now, in a global economy.

PRESIDENT CLINTON, "Remarks Concluding the First Roundtable Discussion of the Forest Conference in Portland," April 2, 1993[1]

We want to be able to say that anybody who works 40 hours a week and has children in a home will not be in poverty after this plan passes [the Welfare Reform Act], that we're going to reward work, we're going to encourage people to get off welfare. And the way it starts is by saying if you do work 40 hours a week, if you have a child in the house, you won't be in poverty. Let me give you an idea of why that's so significant. Eighteen percent of the American people in the work force today are living below the Federal poverty line.

PRESIDENT CLINTON, interview with the New York and New Jersey press, July 22, 1993[2]

Two news-making "revelations" about the American economy by the Clinton administration in the early 1990s were (1) that there was a new, "global" economy afoot that demanded an increasingly mobile workforce (thus undermining traditional expectations of lifelong employment with a single employer); and (2) that this workforce included the poor—mostly hardworking people who nevertheless were unable or only barely able to get by (thus undermining traditional notions of the poor as typically unemployed or lazy).

Clinton's oft-quoted prophecy of frequent job-switching has since proved to be, if anything, conservative. The massive downsizing of the blue-collar workforce in the 1970s and 1980s, to which Clinton was responding, was swiftly followed by corporate restructuring in the late 1980s and 1990s, which further unmoored hordes of middle-management workers. The 1992 groundbreaking book *Workplace 2000* more accurately predicted that "in the next decade . . . the average American will most likely work in ten or more different types of jobs and at least five different companies before he or she retires."[3]

This prediction is now a reality, and it includes the working poor as well as the working non-poor. The *Los Angeles Times* gives examples from both ends of the work spectrum in its report "A Rising Force of Mercenaries" (November 6, 2000): "'Dot-com' manager Bill Garnsey earns more than $130,000 annually, plus stock options. San Jose mail clerk Rachel Salinas is a single mother who for years has made about $10 per hour with no benefits. They appear to share little in common. Yet each is essential to the 'new economy,' and each finds a new job at the rate of one per year."[4] The difference, of course, is that Rachel Salinas's job-shifting has not been upwardly mobile, as has that of Garnsey, who has capitalized on the "new" mobile market. Rather, Salinas, who had only just secured a permanent position at the time the article was written, had been living a hand-to-mouth existence, working temporary jobs without benefits. "Nationwide," notes the same report, "about 30% of U.S. workers already fall into the 'contingent' categories—temps, part-timers, contractors and on-call employees—according to the U.S. General Accounting Office."[5] Many of these temporary workers work full-time as "permanent temps," though not for long in the same job. Many are in the ranks of the working poor, and many work below Clinton's magic forty-hour week. More realistically redefining the hours and wages of the working poor, an article in *The Urban Institute*, "Playing by the Rules but Losing the Game: America's Working Poor" (May 2000), concludes that "one in six non-elderly Americans live in families with incomes below twice the federal poverty line and in which all adults work, on average, at least 1,000 hours a year [half-time]: these individuals comprise the working poor."[6] The economy has taken a roller-coaster ride since Bill Clinton spoke in 1993, moving up, then down, then slowly up again in the current phase of limping recovery (as of mid-2005). During these uncertain times, some improvements *have* reached the poor, including a higher minimum wage and legislation increasing medical and tax benefits for low-income families. Nevertheless, the working poor, according to the *Urban Institute* report, still constitute some 17 percent of the non-elderly population.[7] As with all roller-coaster rides, we don't really go anywhere—especially true, it would seem, for the laboring poor on board. "I think that our citizens should never forget that the largest number of poor people in America are the working poor," the president reminded us in his "Remarks on the Welfare to Work Initiative" in January 1999.[8]

We have jumped forward four hundred years and crossed an ocean, and we seem to be, oddly, back in the same place with a familiar feeling of the "new" about uncannily similar happenings. Americans in the late twentieth into the twenty-first century can be surprised by an emergent economy characterized by mobility, instability, and job diversity, and find "news" in the fact that most of the poor within that economy actually work. But so could the English in the late sixteenth into the seventeenth century.

Surprised by its own "new," mobile workforce, early modern England, as we have seen, focused not so much on the poor as on the unsettled. Authorities first and foremost struggled to define who was and was not vagrant. Part-time workers and those who shifted from job to job—despite their essential role in the changing economy—did not make the grade. Thus our Wiltshire man was arrested in 1605 for vagrancy because he was "sometimes a weaver, sometimes a surgeon, sometimes a minstrel, sometimes a dyer, and now a bullard." "Sometimes" did not a legitimate worker make. This laboring man, declared the official entry on his arrest, had "no trade to live by."[9] That this transient worker was part of a growing body of multitasked householders (male and female) as well as itinerant laborers in the period—what we today call "permanent temps"—could not yet be fully acknowledged. Similarly new, and not quite acceptable, was the recognition that most people in need of parish relief were in fact working poor. A census taken in the city of Norwich in 1570–71 revealed this clearly. More than four hundred years before the *Urban Institute* survey cited above, Norwich could be surprised to discover so many of its own citizens "playing by the rules but losing the game." The Norwich census listed about 25 percent of the city's nonforeign population as poor. It further revealed that more than 66 percent of the male adults and 85 percent of the female adults were nevertheless engaged in some form of employment.[10] Like today's working poor, many of Norwich's poor workers had switched jobs or were holding down more than one job at the same time. John Yonges is listed in the census as a "cordwainer, journeyman, and now a waterman"; William Cocker as "a worsted weaver" who also "goeth about with aqua vitae"; William Richeson as "worsted weaver now in laboring work"; and Edmund Smyth as "barber and porter." With couples, by-employments multiplied: John Force was listed as "worsted weaver but [also] uses lace weaving" together with Elizabeth, his wife, "that fills pipes and weaves lace."[11] Like the Clinton administration, Norwich authorities took action to increase benefits—and punishments—to its poor: more of the impotent were given parish support; stocks of material were provided for the unemployed to work on; and the local Bridewell awaited the work-shy, where they were forcibly put to work.[12] One might say that this was an Elizabethan version of a "welfare-to-work" program. But authorities found it difficult fully to acknowledge the "new" category of deserving working poor. If the poor were designated "able," the city seldom subsidized them. Only about one-third of the poor families were deemed worthy of relief.[13] In sum, however much Norwich tried to adjust its relief according to its "new" findings (just as the Clinton administration tried to adjust its treatment of the "newly discovered" working poor), benefits in Norwich expanded only minimally, and most of the working poor remained just that—as they do in America today.[14]

If history repeats itself, so do historians. How often have we heard that in a given period "the middle class is rising," or that "subjectivity is being discovered," or that "a new economy is emerging," or that "vagrancy is on the increase"? The fact that such assertions recur in assessments by different scholars of different historical periods does not make them incorrect, however. For history does indeed repeat itself—not exactly, not entirely, but in ways that may seem "new" to those living the moment and even to those interpreting it. Such a sense of newness may be a response not so much to actually new phenomena as to an intensifying of already existing institutions and events. But the events could still be felt to be "new." Thus, I really should not have been left agape, as I have to admit I was, when just as I embarked on this book project, press releases broke about our "new," global economy that demanded mobility and job diversity and was grounded on a shifting mass of working poor. I had just been reading about how the same realities were discovered as news—and felt to be just as unsettling—in late sixteenth-century England! This in no way denies the "fact" that something new is afoot in modern America. But it does suggest that our economic happenings may not be as revolutionary as they at first seem. Indeed, in crucial ways, the global economy reworks forces in America that were already active in the "new," market economy of early modern England. More specifically, our explosive networking of information and exchange, which both produces a mobile workforce and is reliant on it, repeats and extends in important ways the expanding dissemination of goods and currency as well as of the itinerant workers (laborers, chapmen, entrepreneurs) who networked early modern England, and beyond.[15]

I do not mean to claim that the emergent twenty-first-century American workforce is identical to that which evolved in late sixteenth- and seventeenth-century England. But the similarities are striking enough to provoke thought about the nature of American identity in this "newly" felt moment of intense economic change. It may very well be that the "multividual" subjectivity that was available, even if only partially or intermittently, to the large numbers of laboring poor among early modern subjects—a subjectivity that was fragmented, dispersed, multiple, and always changing—is a sensibility available as well to, especially, the American working poor in the twenty-first century. To conclude where I began, the notion of unsettled subjectivity has potentially a very wide reach indeed: beyond the arrested vagrant of early modern England, to the itinerant or multitasked lowly laborers of the period (both on land and at sea), and, finally—with all the admitted disjunctions and remove of history—to the lowly modern subject of our "new," global economy today.

Appendix A

Edward Barlow's Family Tree

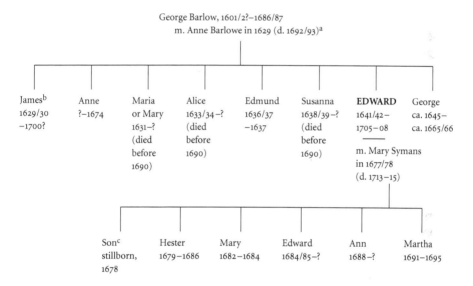

George Barlow, 1601/2?–1686/87
m. Anne Barlowe in 1629 (d. 1692/93)[a]

| James[b] 1629/30 –1700? | Anne ?–1674 | Maria or Mary 1631–? (died before 1690) | Alice 1633/34–? (died before 1690) | Edmund 1636/37 –1637 | Susanna 1638/39–? (died before 1690) | **EDWARD** 1641/42– 1705–08 | George ca. 1645– ca. 1665/66 |

EDWARD m. Mary Symans in 1677/78 (d. 1713–15)

| Son[c] stillborn, 1678 | Hester 1679–1686 | Mary 1682–1684 | Edward 1684/85–? | Ann 1688–? | Martha 1691–1695 |

This chart is based on Edward Barlow's journal, supplemented by searches of the registers of Prestwich and the surrounding parishes of Radcliffe, Middleton, Bury, and Blackley (unfortunately, the Blackley registers do not start until well into the seventeenth century, and though the Prestwich registers begin in 1599, there is then a gap until 1603). Other important sources of information include the *International Genealogical Index* and the London parish registers of St. Botolph, Bishopsgate; Holy Trinity, Minories; and St. Mary, Whitechapel.

Dates with a slash indicate that the birth or death occurred between January 1 and March 24, before the change in the calendar in 1752 (the old-style date appears before the slash, the new-style date after the slash).

a. George Barlow was probably born an illegitimate child to George Fletcher and Anne Barlowe in Bury and, as was the custom of the time in such cases, took his mother's surname; we cannot be sure of the circumstances of his birth, however, because of the gap in the Prestwich records. There is no more trace of him (or of a George Fletcher) in Bury after his birth. It is thus likely that at some time he moved from Bury

---

to Prestwich. Oddly, if this is the case, he married a woman with the same name as his mother (and the same surname as his). *The Registers of the Parish Church of Bury in the County of Lancaster; Christenings, Burials, and Weddings, 1590–1616,* transcribed and edited by Rev. W. J. Lowenberg and Henry Brierley (Rochdale: Lancashire Parish Register Society, 1898), 1:32. For George's death, see the inventory of his goods (appendix B). For his marriage to Anne Barlowe, see *The Registers of the Parish Church of Prestwich; Baptisms, Burials, and Weddings, 1603–1688,* transcribed by Henry Brierley (Cambridge: Cambridge University Press; printed for the Lancashire Parish Register Society, 1909), 34:169; for Anne's death, see *The Registers of the Parish Church of Prestwich in the County of Lancaster; Baptisms and Burials, 1689–1711, Weddings to 1712,* transcribed by Henry Brierley (Cambridge: Cambridge University Press for the Lancashire Parish Register Society, 1913), 49:41.

b. For the baptism of James, see *Registers of the Parish Church of Prestwich, 1603–1688,* 34:27. The date of James's death is conjectural, based on the record of the death of a James Barlow of Whitfield, in Pilkington, within Prestwich parish (*Registers of the Parish Church of Prestwich, 1689–1711,* 49:48). No baptism can be found for his sister Anne; interestingly, though Edward Barlow speaks of Anne as living and working in London as of 1656/57, her death is registered in Prestwich (*Registers of the Parish Church of Prestwich, 1603–1688,* 34:143). Names were registered in Latin—hence the uncertainty over whether "Maria" was Englished as "Maria" or "Mary." For the baptisms of Maria/Mary, Alice (Alizia), Edmund, Susanna, and Edward, see *Registers of the Parish Church of Prestwich, 1603–1688,* 34:28, 31, 34, 36, 40. No burials have been found for Maria/Mary, Alice, or Susanna, possibly because they moved away or were married and their deaths were registered in their married names (though no records of marriages for them have been found). In any case, in 1690 Barlow records that, of his whole family, only he, his mother, and a brother (James) were still alive. Edmund lived only a few months (ibid., p. 110). No baptism or burial for George has been found; his dates are conjectured from Barlow's journal entries (pp. 16 and 112, respectively). Barlow records his marriage to Mary Symans in his journal (p. 309). The exact date of Mary's death is uncertain, but we know her will was made in 1713 and proved in 1715 (Will of Mary Barlow).

c. For the births and deaths of Barlow's children, as well as his own death, see chap. 5, nn. 18–19.

Appendix B

Inventory of George Barlow, 1686

A true and perfect inventory of the goods and chattels of George Barlow in Pilkington in the Parish of Prestwich and County of Lancaster, yeoman, deceased, the twenty-first day of January in the year of our Lord one thousand six hundred and eighty-six. Followeth:

Imprimis:	Two tables	00 15 00
	In chairs, stools and quishians [cushions]	00 12 06
	Seeling [seating?] in the house	00 12 00
	Four trests [trestles?]	00 04 06
	Fire iron tongs with other iron ware	00 06 06
	In shelves and boards and other loose timbers	00 15 06
	In brass and pewter	00 17 08
	Two beds	01 03 04
	Seven arks [chests] and one garner	01 02 10
	In copper ware and earthen pots	00 09 06
	Three stone troughs	00 03 10
	One sheep	00 04 00
	Weights and measures and one cheese press	00 06 00
	In hay	00 10 00
	In apparel and huselmont [hustlement? i.e., household goods]	00 17 08
	TOTAL	09 00 10

The whole content is nine pounds ten pence total as hath been prised upon the twenty-eighth day of January in the year of our Lord before said.

Prised by us

Robert Willson [signed]
Abraham Mather [signed]
Edmund Ramsbottom [signed]

19th February 1686

Source: Infra Wills and Probate, Lancashire County Record Office, WCW1686.

Appendix C

Record of Edward Barlow's Mobility (On Land and Sea)

Dates	Travel (major places)	Employment	Journal illustrations
Youth, up to 1656 (age 14)	Within area local to Prestwich parish, Lancashire	Harvest work, making hay, and other wage labor on neighbors' farms; also, hauling coal from coalpits (earned ½ penny per day plus victuals)	None
Dec. 1656 (for two weeks)	To Manchester	Trial apprentice to "whitester" (bleacher)	Town of Manchester
Mar. 1657	To London (visits sister Anne at Snow Hill, then to Southwark)	Tapster for uncle's post house ("Dog and Bear") in Southwark	Barlow leaving his mother and home
ca. Sept. 1658	In Southwark; day trip to Greenwich to see dead whale	After argument with aunt, refuses tapster work; becomes stable helper and errand boy at post house	None

Note: Some illustrations, especially those of landmasses, may have been added by Barlow after the time period in the narrative where they appear. The information given here about Barlow's voyages draws in part upon an appendix to Lubbock's edition of Barlow's journal, which includes more details about the specific ships, fewer about places and dates, and none about land travel or Barlow's illustrations; see "Appendix I, Barlow's Ships," in Barlow, *Journal,* 554–59. My compilation of Barlow's illustrations has been aided by the handwritten "Analysis" by an archivist of the Royal Naval College, Greenwich, which is collected together with Barlow's manuscript at the National Maritime Museum in Greenwich, London. Dates follow the new calendar (i.e., Jan. 1 marks a new year).

Dates	Travel (major places)	Employment	Journal illustrations
1658 (for two weeks)	To Dartford, Kent	Trial apprentice to vintner	Beached whale and town of Dartford, Kent
1658	To Southwark	Rides post for uncle, to Kingston-upon-Thames, Chipstow, Dartford, Gravesend, etc.; other odd jobs	None
Mar. 1659	Voyage on *Naseby* (Admiral ship under Lord Montagu) with fleet to Elsinore, then to Copenhagen	Apprentice to chief master's mate; suffers bad head injury 8th or 9th day aboard ship	25 consecutive pages of illustrations, with inset views of land-masses at sea, follow-ing the river Thames from London Bridge to the Buoy of the Nore, then up the Medway to Chatham and Rochester, and concluding with Sole Bay (Suffolk coast); Elsinore and the Sound; Copenhagen and the Sound
Winter 1659 – Mar. 1660	Recuperates from head wound at Chatham; to master's lodging in London at Whitehouse Street, Ratcliff; to master's new wife's cookshop (sign of the "White Hart"), Whitechapel	Draws beer, then refuses that work; scrapes trenchers, winds up the jack, draws water, sweeps, cleans stables and ken-nel, makes mustard, and does other odd jobs; head wound dressed twice daily at Bedlam	None
Mar. 1660 – Mar. 1661	Voyage on *Naseby* (commanded by Lord Montagu) with fleet to Holland to bring back Charles II at the Restoration; ship renamed *Royal Charles;* winters aboard ship at Gillingham, awaiting pay	Seaman-apprentice; paid Mar. 1661 (£10 16s for the year; allowed by master to keep 16p)	Straits of Dover and the Downs (2 pages); The *Royal Charles* (formerly *Naseby*) off Sheveningen, Holland

Dates	Travel (major places)	Employment	Journal illustrations
June–Dec. 1661	Expedition on *Augustine* (under Lord Montagu) to Mediterranean against Barbary pirates	Seaman-apprentice	The *Augustine;* Malaga, Spain; Alicante, Spain; Algiers, Barbary Coast (North Africa); Dolphin and flying fish; Lisbon, Portugal
Dec. 1661 – June 1662	Exchanges onto another ship, the *Martin Galley,* a dispatch vessel for the fleet lying off Tangier; lives a long time aboard ship at Deptford awaiting pay (weekends with his master); travels to Lambeth to see Queen Katherine of Lisbon arrive by water to Whitehall	Seaman-apprentice, exchanged from *Augustine;* odd jobs for master's wife in Whitehall (resented)	Cadiz, Spain; Straits of Gibraltar; The *Martin Galley,* off Cape Spartel and Arzila (NW Africa); Milford Haven (SW Wales)
1662–64 (21 months)	Voyage on *Queen Katherine* to Lisbon, then to Barcelona (on secret mission), and back to Lisbon; on to Rio de Janeiro via Madeira; back to Lisbon via St. Michael, Azores; to Blackwall, London	Seaman-apprentice at 19s a month (paid to master's wife)	The *Queen Katherine;* Barcelona, Spain; Madeira Island; Shark (eating man) and pilot fish; Rio de Janeiro, Brazil (2 pages); Azores Islands
1664 – Nov. 1664	Voyage on merchant and man-of-war ship *Maderas* to Guinea; interrupted by 2nd Dutch War; Barlow turned over to *Monk* frigate	Seaman-apprentice at 26s a month (paid ticket for 1 month, 9 days; given to his master)	The *Maderas*

Dates	Travel (major places)	Employment	Journal illustrations
Nov. 12, 1664 – Nov. 14, 1667	Whole of 2nd Dutch War on *Monk* frigate, cruising for Dutch and French in English Channel, off Land's End, up to Shetland Islands, and along west side of Ireland; early on goes aboard *London* at Portsmouth to visit master (not there), and *Monk* sets sail without him; hops frigate headed for Plymouth; travels 40 miles overland from Plymouth to Falmouth to reunite with *Monk;* after second engagement with Dutch, sent with wounded to Rochester (3-week recuperation); sails again on *Monk* with fleet; winters 1666 aboard ship at Chatham; with peace treaty, travels by land and wherry from Portsmouth to London	Seaman-apprentice (paid Apr. 1666 for 9 out of 18 months worked—£9, sent to his master; winter 1666, the men force purser to pay them each ½ crown of full crown owed them; never received the other 5s); same winter, master discharges Barlow from his apprenticeship, allowing him to keep next 7 months' pay owed to master in place of the master's buying him a suit of clothes; now seaman, receives 1 year's pay; paid for another 10 months and ticket for 5 more to be paid at London Nov. 14, 1667; at sea 3 years and 2 days	Isle of Wight and Portsmouth (2 pages); Plymouth; Falmouth; Battle of Lowestoft, June 1665 (separate insert); Bressay Sound (Shetland); Humber River and Hull; The *Monk;* Kinsale, Ireland
1667	Whitechapel lodgings, 2 weeks	None	None
Jan. 1667 – Apr. 30, 1668	Voyage on merchant ship *Real Friendship,* bound to Tenerife, the Canaries, for wine	Seaman (4 months); pressed upon return into the *Yarmouth* frigate	The *Real Friendship;* Tenerife Island (Canaries)
May 1668 – Apr. 1669	Voyage on *Yarmouth* frigate cruising western part of English Channel looking for French;	Pressed out of *Real Friendship;* seaman	Dieppe, France; Cadiz, Spain; Cagliari, Sardinia (and Lisbon Rock);

Dates	Travel (major places)	Employment	Journal illustrations
	convoys Duke of York's pleasure boat to Dieppe (Normandy); joins fleet for Algiers; returns to Portsmouth		[Tunis—on page lost from MS]; Tripoli (North Africa); Messina, Sicily (with Mt. Aetna); North coast of Sicily (with fighting galleys and volcanic islands); Naples, Italy; Leghorn, Italy; Genoa, Italy; The *Yarmouth*
Apr. 1669 – early 1670	Travels by foot, horse, and water from Portsmouth to London (Whitechapel lodgings); travels with carrier to visit family in Prestwich (70 miles); visits Manchester Fair; stays in Prestwich 12 weeks; on return stays 3–4 months in London	None	None
1670–71	East India voyage on ship *Experiment* (sails from Downs on Mar. 7, 1670) to Surat via Bombay; travels up and down the Malabar Coast of India; sails for England Jan. 15, 1671, via St. Helena and Ascension islands; arrives at Blackwall, London	Seaman; 5 months, 25 days	St. Iago (Cape Verde) and view of it; Birds and fish and views of Devard Islands; Johanna Island and small view of it; Views of Mayotta, Mohella, and Comoro; Bombay, India; Views of Malabar Coast; Surat, India; Karwar, Malabar, and four small islands; Belopatan, Malabar, and views of Krakatau and Bossey (?) islands;

Dates	Travel (major places)	Employment	Journal illustrations
			Ponani and Tannanore, Malabar; Calicut, Malabar; The *Experiment* in a gale; St. Helena Island; Ascension Island and view of it
1671 – Jan. 25, 1674	Second East India voyage on *Experiment* (as Admiral of 3 ships; sails from Gravesend Sept. 27, 1671), bound for Taiwan (Formosa) and Japan via St. Iago and Bantam; from Taiwan to Pescadores Island; returns to Bantam to winter there; ship seized by Dutch in Banka Strait (winter there); Batavia (present-day Jakarta); Bantam; Batavia	Seaman; captured by Dutch in autumn 1672; in June, as prisoner, transferred from ship to ship off Batavia; then to Bantam and back to Batavia; held in East Indies until Jan. 25, 1674	Bantam, Java, with three views of Java Head and island east of it (2 pages); Taiwan/Formosa (2 pages); Capture of *Experiment* in Banka Strait; Prefatory images to journal (begun in captivity): page of verse decorated at the top with dark clouds, a hand holding a quill, and Father Time; and a separate page imaging a sea compass
Jan. 25, 1674 – Sept. 1674	Voyage on Dutch *Leyden Castle* (*Burff van Leiden*) to Helford Sluys, Holland, via Cape of Good Hope and Fernando de Noronha Island; from Helford Sluys by small boat to Amsterdam	Prisoner seaman (8 months passage); paid after peace declared during voyage, £6 13s 4p	The *Leyden Castle;* Batavia (2 pages); Table Bay, Cape of Good Hope; Monster (born to Dutch woman); Fernando de Noronha Island (NW side)
1674	Travels from Amsterdam to Harwich (4 days) on Colonel Stroude's new pleasure boat; then up Thames to Wapping Wall	Seaman on pleasure boat, paid 35s; East India Company paid only 7 months' pay for voyage of 3 years, 2 months; Barlow peddles Bibles and other goods he brought from Holland	Amsterdam; Harwich, England

Dates	Travel (major places)	Employment	Journal illustrations
Nov. 1674 – Apr. 1675	Whitechapel?	?	None
May 1675 – Aug. 23, 1675	Voyage on *Florentine* bound for North Bergen to load stockfish via Amsterdam, then for Leghorn and Venice; wrecked on Goodwin Sands (Aug. 23) off English coast	Gunner	North Bergen, Norway, and the *Florentine;* Wreck of the *Florentine*
Aug. 28, 1675 – May 1676	Voyage on *Marigold* to Straits with pickled herrings from Glasgow; travels to Greenock on Glasgow's Clyde River via Kinsale, Ireland; travels to Marseilles via Lamlash, Cape St. Vincent, Tangier, Alicante, and Toulon; travels to Naples via Arron Island and Leghorn; returns to London via Portsmouth and the Downs	Regular seaman?; 32s a month	The *Marigold* at Greenock and Newark on the Clyde River (of Glasgow); Toulon, France; Marseilles, France; Naples, Italy
May–Sept. 1676	Quarters near the Tower	?	None
Sept. 1676 – Jan. 1677	Voyage on *Mayflower* to Tenerife in Canaries for wine	Regular seaman?; paid £7 for 4 months, 10 days	The *Mayflower*
Jan.–Feb. 1677	Quarters near the Tower?	?	None
Feb.–Aug. 1677	Voyage on pink *Rouen Factor* to Rouen; hired to ship pipe hoops to Tangier and Malaga; travels there via	Boatswain at 40s a month	Havre de Grace and Rouen on the Seine; The *Rouen Factor;* Portland and Wey- mouth, Dorchester

Dates	Travel (major places)	Employment	Journal illustrations
	Portsmouth, Portland, Weymouth, Plymouth, and Cadiz; passage from Tangier to London of 28 days		
Aug.–Nov. 1677	Quarters near the Tower?	?	None
Nov. 1677 – July 1678	Voyage on *Guannaboe* to Jamaica, West Indies; before departing, married at Deal, Kent, to servant maid from London (she returns to her father's house in Gloucestershire and miscarries at Hounds-ditch, London, 14 days before Barlow's return); voyage to Jamaica via Madeira and Barbados; London	2nd mate at 55s a month; at sea 8 months, 10 days	Carlisle Bay and Bridgetown, Barbados, with small sketch of the island
Winter 1678/79	St. Botolph, Bishopsgate	?	None
Mar. 1679 – ca. Nov. 1679	Voyage on *Guannaboe* to Jamaica via Barba-dos; in Jamaica 7 weeks; returns to London via Plymouth	Chief mate; masters ship from Barbados to Jamaica; cheated of his full pay	Port Royal, Jamaica
Winter 1679/80	St. Botolph, Bishopsgate	?	None
Apr. 1680 – Feb. 1681	Voyage on *Cadiz Mer-chant* to Jamaica via Nevis; returns to Lon-don at Ratcliff Cross	2nd mate	The *Cadiz Merchant*; Nevis Island, Caribbean
"A long time" in 1681	St. Botolph, Bishopsgate	?	None

Dates	Travel (major places)	Employment	Journal illustrations
1681 – Jan. 1682	Voyage on *Cadiz Merchant* to Jamaica via Plymouth and Barbados; returns to Gravesend	Chief mate	None
Feb.–Nov. 1682	St. Botolph, Bishopsgate?	?	None
Nov. 1682 – July 1683	Voyage on *Delight* to East Indies via Isle of Wight, Plymouth, and Cape of Good Hope	Chief mate; £6 5s a month; turned ashore at Achin, Sumatra, without payment	Achin, Sumatra; The *Delight*
July–Aug. 1683	Achin, Sumatra	"Made what shift I could, sometimes amongst some English there . . . sometimes amongst the natives"; "destitute"	None
Aug. 19, 1683 – Oct. 1683	Voyage on *Recovery* from Achin to Hooghly River, Bengal; at Balasore Road before the river Ganges; up to Hooghly in boats	Works his passage	Balasore Road, river Ganges, Hooghly, and rhinoceros
Nov. 14, 1683 – June 25, 1684	Voyage on *Kent* from Hooghly to London via Fort St. George, St Helena, and Ascension; arrives Deptford, London	Chief mate; £5 a month; is refused payment from East India Company for time worked on the *Recovery*	Fort St. George (Madras), East Indies
July–Dec. 1684	Holy Trinity, Minories	?	None
Dec. 9, 1684 – July 18, 1687	Voyage on *Kent* for Surat via Fogo (Cape Verde), Karwar, Goa, and Bombay; sails up and down Malabar	Chief mate; £6 a month; at sea 32 months, 7 days; on return, some of pay stopped to crew on charges of running concealed goods	Fogo Island and Tristan da Cunha; Karwar, Malabar; Goa, Malabar; Tellicherri, Malabar;

Dates	Travel (major places)	Employment	Journal illustrations
	Coast; ship hired by native merchant to load pepper along Malabar Coast and ship it to Gomboroon, Persia; more shipments along Malabar; returns to England via St. Helena and Ascension; arrives at Bell Wharf, London, after passage from Calicut of 5 months, 22 days		[Barlow's ship, the *Kent,* on missing leaf]; Gomboroon, Persia
July–Dec. 1687	Holy Trinity, Minories	?	None
Dec. 5, 1687 – Feb. 1690	Voyage on *Rainbow* to Tongking (Tonkin), China, via St. Iago and Batavia; travels by boat up to Cacho; returns via Banka Strait to Batavia; sets sail to Bencoolen, Sumatra, to load pepper; sets sail Apr. 27, 1689, for London via Mauritius and St. Helena; in gale at Downs, Barlow (since captain is off ship) orders ship ashore; Blackwall, London	Chief mate; £6 10s a month	The *Rainbow,* aground in Banka Strait, June 27, 1688; Tongking (Tonkin) River with elephant; Cacho, Tongking, and Bencoolen, Sumatra; Mauritius Island (off SE coast of Africa)
Summer 1690 – Jan. 1691	Travels in late summer to Prestwich to visit his mother; returns Sept. 29; resides at St. Mary, Whitechapel, London	?	None
Feb. 1691 – Oct. 13, 1691	Voyage on *Royal Sovereign* with British fleet on summer cruise in English Channel, off	Volunteer; reckoned as a midshipman at 44s a month; received £19 10s; paid off Oct. 13, 1691	Torbay, Devonshire; The *Royal Sovereign*

Dates	Travel (major places)	Employment	Journal illustrations
	France and off Ireland, looking for French fleet; returns to Chatham		
Oct. 13, 1691 – Nov. 18, 1691	St. Mary, Whitechapel	?	None
Nov. 18, 1691 – Feb. 1695	Voyage on *Sampson* (ships Nov. 18, 1691; sails Mar. 16, 1692) to Fort St. George (Madras) and Bengal via Falmouth, Grand Canary, Cape of Good Hope, and Ceylon; travels from Balasore Road, Bengal, to Hooghly; towed up the river to "Cheteynotey" and winters and summers there; returns to Madras for more goods to ship (having been in Bengal more than 14 months); returns to London via Cape of Good Hope, St. Helena, and Barbados (arriving Plymouth Nov. 24, 1694; cargo out Feb. 1695)	Chief mate; £5 6s a month; 7-month delay in payment on his return	Grand Canary Island; Galle, Ceylon; Views of coastlines of Persia, Arabia, India, and Ceylon; Pulo Condore Island; The *Sampson* in a gale
Feb.–Aug. 1695	St. Mary, Whitechapel	? Awaiting pay for 7 months for last East India Company voyage	None
Aug. 1695 – Aug. 5, 1698	Voyage on *Scepter* (ships in August; sails from Gravesend Sept. 28, 1695; sails from Spithead May 19, 1696) to Surat via Portsmouth,	Chief mate; in command after death of captain on June 12, 1697, on voyage to Mocha; declared commander of ship by president of Surat factory for rest of voyage	Anjengo, Malabar; Cochin, Malabar; Mangalore, Malabar; Mocha, Red Sea; The *Scepter*

Dates	Travel (major places)	Employment	Journal illustrations
	Spithead, Cape of Good Hope, Ceylon, the Malabar Coast, and Bombay; sent to help convoy fleet of Moors' ships to Mocha in Red Sea; returns to Surat, then Bombay; sails the Malabar Coast loading and unloading pepper; sets sail for England from Surat via Bombay, Cape of Good Hope, and St. Helena; arrives Blackwall, London, Aug. 5, 1698		
Aug. 1698 – Oct. 1699	St. Mary, Whitechapel	?	None
Oct. 13, 1699 – Aug. 1701	Voyage on *Wentworth* (sails from Blackwall Oct. 13, 1699) to Canton, China, via St. Iago, Cape of Good Hope, St. Paul's Island (E of the Cape), Batavia, and Macao; winters in Macao and from there trades with Canton; returns to England via island near Java, the Cape of Good Hope, and St. Helena; arrives Blackwall, London	Chief mate	Macao Island; The *Wentworth*
Sept. 1701 – Jan. 1702	St. Mary, Whitechapel?	?	None
Jan. 23, 1702 – July 1703	Voyage on *Fleet Frigate* to Canton, China, via Batavia, Macao, and	Chief mate and then pilot from Batavia to China, with some privileges; captain at first	Canton River, China

Dates	Travel (major places)	Employment	Journal illustrations
	Caberrero Island; sails up Canton River to Boca Tigris, then up to Whampoa; sets sail for England via Pulo Condore, an island near Java, and St. Helena	refuses to pay him for piloting and then cheats him of his promised payment; Barlow argues with captain over use of sails and is ordered off deck; at St. Helena put aboard the *Kingfisher* frigate in charge of East India convoy	
July 21, 1703 – Dec. 1703	Voyage on *Kingfisher* frigate from St. Helena to England via Ascension, Kinsale (Ireland), and Cork Harbor (Ireland); at mouth of the Thames, rides through the Great Storm of Nov. 26, 1703; travels to Gravesend (where he leaves ship); London	Passenger	Cork Harbor, Ireland
Nov. 1703 – 1705	?	?	?
Jan. 7, 1706 – ?	Voyage on *Liampo* to Mocha in the Red Sea; departs from Portsmouth; ship lost off coast of Mozambique, 1706	Captain; Barlow's will is made Nov. 1705, on eve of the voyage; will is proved in 1708	?

Appendix D

Will of Edward Barlow,
Commander of the *Liampo*, 1708

In the name of God amen, know that I Edward Barlow being now bound out to sea of a voyage to Mocha in the Red Sea, being Commander of the good ship [?] called the *Liampo*,[1] in the United East India Company's service, and it being a long voyage and many accidents and changes may happen and knowing that all men are mortal and death certain and this time and place uncertain and not knowing how soon the Almighty God and Lord of life may call me to pay that debt *which is* which is due to death and being now at this writing in perfect health and sound memory I do now make and order this my last Will and Testament. And do now at this present writing revoking and disannulling all other Wills and Testaments in manner and forms as followeth.

In the first place I do give and bequeath my soul to Almighty God that gave it to me,[2] my Savior where and whenever it shall please the Lord to call me out of this transitory life, hoping and believing that through and by the merits and precious blood and death of his son Jesus Christ to receive free pardon and forgiveness of all my sins with an everlasting life in heaven, and as for what worldly goods and estate God hath pleased to give me at this time either in moneys, goods, bonds, debts, dues and demands from any person or persons whatsoever as pertaining to me either by wages or bonds, debts or dues by partnership or any other ways being found any ways whatsoever lawfully

Source: Wills and Probate, Prerogative Court of Canterbury, National Archives, London, PROB11/500

1. The words "Red Sea, being Commander of the good ship called the *Liampo*" appear in the margin. In the text, there is a caret (∧) at the location where, it would seem, these words should have appeared. Apparently, the words in the margin were omitted from the original text and added later.
2. The words "that gave it to me" appear in the margin; there is a caret in the text where they apparently should have appeared.

belonging or appertaining to me. I give and bequeath in manner and form following. First I make and ordain my lawful and loving wife Mary Barlow my true and lawful Attorney for the term of her life, and after her decease I order for my Attorney for me and in my name on Mr. Bankes, a land waiter [customs man in charge of landed cargo] at the custom house of London and on Richard Smith, wine cooper and merchant living in Devonshire Street without Bishopsgate to [execute?][3] this my last Will and Testament. Item I give to my loving wife Mary Barlow for the term of her life all goods and furniture and all manner of utensils for us[e] and ware as household goods in any manner of ways belonging to the house or for the use and wear therein, and likewise I also give to my wife Mary Barlow a third part of my estate in money or in any goods for sale or any dues or sums in any debts, bonds or wages, contracts or demands due from any person or persons whatsoever due, and Item I give another [another third] part of all sum and sums aforesaid to my son Edward Barlow, and moreover half the plate is in my house for wear and use and the other half part of all plate or wrought silver belonging to the house namely one silver tankard, one silver salver, two silver cups, one salt, one silver sugar dish, and one pottinger [soup bowl?], and six silver spoons, and four small tea spoons, and a small silver dram cup, with a third part of my estate nominated as before. I give to my daughter Anne Barlow at her coming to age of 21 years and the same to my son Edward but with proviso to my daughter that if she is not obedient, obliging and willing to take her mother's advice in all things for her good and show herself loving and in all things dutiful as a child ought to be to her parent, that then I give her no more than one quarter of what estate I may appear to be worth at my decease in moneys or goods as aforesaid, and the other moiety of her[4] third part shall go to her brother Edward. But if she proves dutiful and obedient as a child ought to be that then [she] shall have a third as aforesaid but not otherwise. Likewise I give my son Edward the bonds and judgment contest of my cousin Torbell of two hundred and fifty pounds to sue for and receive whenever he can come at the said Torbell and likewise twenty pounds his wife owing me for goods I sold her and never was paid for India chintz [color printed, usually glazed cloth] and [culgees?] and other goods. And this is all I devise to be fulfilled as my last Will and Testament, wishing a long and happy life to my loving wife and children, praying to God that they may all live in his fear, that

3. The words "to execute" (if "execute" *is* the second word — the handwriting here is very hard to make out) appear in the margin; there is a caret in the text where they apparently should have appeared (after the word "Bishopsgate").

4. The word "her" appears in the margin; there is a caret in the text where it apparently should have appeared.

they may all die in his favor, which God of his good grace and mercy grant to us all. And this as my last will and deed I sign and seal this eighteenth day of November in the fifth year [1705] of our Sovereign Lady Queen Anne, Queen of England, Scotland, France and Ireland, Defender of the faith and in the year of our Lord anno one thousand seven hundred and five.

Edward Barlow = sealed in the presence of us = Evan Evans, William Miller, Charles Alexander.

Appendix E

On the Variation of the Compass

The problem of "the variation of the compass" lay in the enigma that the magnetic compass needle varied from true north irregularly (versus proportionately) as seamen sailed eastward or westward. William Borough, in *A Discourse of the Variation of the Compass* (annexed to Robert Norman's *The New Attractive* [1581, 1585]), declares such magnetic variation "to be the cause of many errors and imperfections in navigation." He adds that "in all sea charts generally, which are made without consideration of the variation [neglecting both differing proportions of latitude and compass variations in longitude], are committed great errors and confusion," so that "the form of those coasts is so distorted from the right shape it should bear." Compounding the problem, Borough says, is the practice of altering the compass to account for variation (in the common sea compass of northern seamen, for instance, the needle was offset three-quarters of a point to the east of north to allow for variation in home waters). "This variety of setting the wires," Borough declares, "hath caused great confusion in navigation, and in other accounts of sea causes." If chartmakers "collect notes made by sundry compasses of divers sets," he admonishes, "they ought to reduce all the varieties unto some one certain, and to give notice of the same, in their plate: And not to make a confused mingle mangle by joining together all varieties of observations, notes and reports."[1]

Edward Wright, in the preface to his [*Certain*] *Errors in Navigation* (1599), also decries the false projection of latitudes on plane charts as well as the "neglecting, or not rightly using the variation of the compass," which together make many parts of the charts "like an inextricable labyrinth of error."[2] He reiterates the latter point in his dedications to *The Haven-Finding Art* (1599; translated from the Dutch): chartmakers, he declares, failing to recognize unpredictable variations in the compass, have caused "much deformity and confusion in many parts of the chart." Wright approvingly notes that the Lord Admiral of the United Provinces commanded the translation of the Dutch book into French and Latin as well, so that all seamen could provide themselves with appropriate instruments and "into what place soever they shall come, they may diligently search out the declination of the magnetical needle from the true North (which they commonly call the variation of the compass)." The seamen would then report their findings back home so that the Admiralty might bring their observations "into some good order and method"—what Wright also terms "some certain reason and rule of the variation."[3] Wright here echoes Robert Norman and other writers on navigation, who also wanted to find, in Norman's words, "rules for the solving of the apparent irregularity of the variation."[4]

Only if such a rule or order of the variation of the compass could be ascertained, contemporaries felt, could the related problem of determining longitude be solved. D. W. Waters points out that errors "arose to a considerable extent from ignorance of the length of a degree."[5] But they were compounded by the use of differently set compasses (as we have noted), as well as of a differently set prime meridian—the point marking zero degrees of longitude. Placement of the prime meridian on charts varied widely, depending on the whim of the chartmaker: often it was set somewhere in the Canary Islands or in the Azores, but it also frequently occupied the chartmaker's hometown, such as Amsterdam or London. Concern over such migrations of the prime meridian were really beside the point, however, as J. B. Hewson notes, since its location was not relevant until a method for finding longitude at sea could be perfected. To this end, Charles II established the Greenwich Observatory in 1675.[6] But the accurate determination of longitude had to await better instruments (in particular the reflecting quadrant and the chronometer) that would not be invented until the eighteenth century, together with more information about natural phenomena—such as tides, currents, and winds, as well as magnetic variation—that would not be sufficiently amassed until the nineteenth century.[7] Longitude remained highly elusive in the seventeenth century.

Acknowledging this elusiveness in his commendatory poem to the fifth edition of John Seller's immensely popular *Practical Navigation* (first published in 1669), Nathaniel Friend asserts:

> here we find
> What in this art may please a curious mind,
> The *longitude* excepted: but if we
> Your rules observe, obtained it may be
> For use sufficient; but the same to get

> With certainty, is not discovered yet.
> Which rare performance, if that any can
> Make plainly out, I wish you be the man.[8]

Earlier, in his *A Regiment for the Sea* (1574), William Bourne declared that sea-men "are not able to give any estimation at all, by the varying of the compass, to know any longitude"—hence Blaeu's dismissal of longitude in *The Light of Navigation* (1612) as not only "unprofitable," but even "hurtful and deceit-ful."[9] Writers recognized that compass variations, if known in advance, might aid seamen in determining their positions at sea; and those wrestling with and arguing over this problem—Martin Curtis, William Gilbert, Bourne, Nor-man, Borough, Wright, William Barlow (no relation to our seaman, Edward Barlow), and others—advise masters and pilots to make note of the variation of a place, "which will be a great help," says Bourne, "for them to find that place again."[10] "Although," William Barlow adds cynically (or realistically), in his *Magnetical Advertisements* (1616), "by reason of their diversities of the sets of their compasses, and unfitness and unapt handling of their instruments, they [navigators] very seldom times agree among themselves."[11] Indeed, sea-men often found themselves vexed with the seemingly irrational and mostly unrecorded irregularities of their compasses, especially when so many other aspects of sailing were equally uncertain.

William Dampier (who met Edward Barlow at Tongking in 1688–89 and entrusted him with a packet to deliver to England)[12] recorded at length his perplexities over such irregularities of variation. Two days before he made the Cape of Good Hope on his voyage from the West Indies to the East Indies in 1699, Dampier recorded his variation as 7 degrees, 58 minutes west. His recorded longitude was 43 degrees, 27 minutes east from Cape Salvador (in the absence of a stable prime meridian, seamen often recorded their longi-tude as the difference in longitude from the last well-known place),[13] and he gave his latitude as 35 degrees, 30 minutes south. This put him by his reckon-ing about ninety leagues from the Cape of Good Hope. But the next day he saw a large black bird with a whitish bill, which his East India waggoner said didn't fly above thirty leagues from the Cape. "So that I was in some doubt," Dampier records, "whether these were the right fowls spoken of in the wag-goner; or whether those fowls might not fly farther off shore than is there mentioned; or whether, as it proved, I might not be nearer the Cape than I reckoned my self to be; for I found, soon after, that I was not then above 25 or 30 leagues at most from the Cape." Dampier goes on to try to puzzle out the problem: "Whether the fault were in the charts laying down the Cape too much to the east from Brazil, or were rather in our reckoning, I could not tell." He then gives a very accurate account of the uncertainties that longitude reckoning faced at the time: "But our reckonings are liable to such uncertainties from steerage, log, currents, half-minute-glasses: and sometimes want of care, as in so long a run cause often a difference of many leagues in the whole account."[14] After addressing the care seamen should take to ensure more accurate readings, Dampier returns to the problem of variation. His thoughts so well demonstrate the puzzling problem facing the seaman in regard to the question of variation that they are worth quoting at length:

> Another thing that stumbled me here was the variation, which, at this time, by the last amplitude I had found to be but 7 degrees 58 minutes west whereas the variation at the Cape (from which I found my self not 30 leagues distant) was then computed, and truly, about 11 degrees or more. And yet a while after this, when I was got 10 leagues to the eastward of the Cape, I found the variation but 10 degrees 40 minutes west whereas it should have been rather more than at the Cape. These things, I confess, did puzzle me. Neither was I fully satisfied as to the exactness of the taking the variation at sea. For in a great sea, which we often meet with, the compass will traverse with the motion of the ship; besides the ship may and will deviate somewhat in steering, even by the best helmsmen. And then when you come to take an azimuth [a record of the sun's altitude], there is often some difference between him that looks at the compass, and the man that takes the altitude height of the sun; and a small error in each, if the error of both should be one way, will make it wide of any great exactness. But what was most shocking to me, I found that the variation did not always increase or decrease in proportion to the degrees of longitude east or west, as I had a notion they might do to a certain number of degrees of variation east or west, at such or such particular meridians.[15]

Upon returning home, Dampier takes consolation in discovering his own findings substantiated by a Captain Hally in a chart "wherein are represented the several variations in the Atlantic Sea, on both sides [of] the equator; and there, the line of no variation in that sea is not a meridian line, but goes very oblique, as do those also which shew the increase of variation on each side." Dampier hopes that Hally's chart will advance movement toward "fixing a general scheme or system of the variation everywhere." Toward aiding the "settling or confirming the theory of it," Dampier then offers a table of all the variations he observed on his voyage (in a similar gesture, Wright publishes all the recorded variations he could find for the known world, and Seller publishes charts showing differences in variations observed near London over some one hundred years).[16]

Edward Barlow, in his journal, tells many tales of his own ships finding themselves off course because of miscalculations in their positioning, especially their longitudinal positioning. Often his ships find themselves out of place near the Canary Islands: once the crew mistake the Grand Canary for Tenerife Island (141); another time, they see the Canary Islands when they expected to be further westward (329); yet another time, they expect to see the Canary Islands and then Bonavista, but miss them both (367); yet again, when most of the sailors aboard think themselves west of the Madeira Islands, they find themselves in fact (as Barlow judged) to be east of them and approaching Tenerife (461). Other landfalls are also mistaken, missed, or sighted earlier than expected. When Barlow's ship the *Martin Galley* finally makes England, the men have no idea where they are (later Barlow blames the pilot for not recognizing Milford Haven; p. 73); on a voyage to Jamaica, deciding to stop over in Barbados, they see the island twenty-four hours sooner than expected (344); on returning from China, they run upon St. Helena twenty-four hours earlier than expected as well (403); on another voyage to China, they find themselves one hundred degrees east of their reckoning (465); and on yet another voyage, they arrive further east of Canton than expected (536).

On one voyage to Jamaica, both the master of Barlow's ship and the master of its companion ship make a potentially deadly error: mistaking the land at nightfall, they think they are west of Havana. Barlow and a Dutchman aboard his ship, however, argue that they are in fact east of the city. Finally the masters trust Barlow's experience, and his ship, signposted with a lantern, leads the other on a safe course (Barlow says that if they had set the course according to the masters' reckoning, they would have run aground on shoals; p. 338). On another voyage, Barlow again claims that his commander was off in the ship's course setting, whereas Barlow knew they were much farther east (461). Barlow often criticizes the navigation of his commanders, as when his ship overshoots the Cape of Good Hope in both directions (463). Sometimes, however, he also attributes their mispositioning to stronger-than-expected currents. This was the case, he says, when they overshot the Cape. And on three separate voyages, his ship is carried off course by strong currents around Java (207, 357, 533); the first time, they find themselves sixty degrees too far east (207). On another voyage, returning from Jamaica, the crew made soundings ahead of their reckoning due to a strong easterly current beyond their expectation (317). And on his last recorded voyage (to China), Barlow notes that they miscalculated the Cape by a hundred leagues—but, echoing Dampier's puzzlement in a similar situation, he is unsure whether to blame a stronger-than-expected current or an incorrect half-minute glass (522).

Barlow gives accounts of other ships that were equally—or sometimes, it seems, more hopelessly—displaced. On the voyage where his ship sees the Canary Islands when they expected to be further westward, Barlow adds that the East India Company ships that had been traveling with them would be way off course, "their dead-reckoning for longitude badly adrift" (329). On his way home from a voyage to India, Barlow's ship runs into the *Phoenix* frigate, which, Barlow says, was off her reckoning by one hundred leagues—but the ship would not believe them that it was off course (382). Off the coast of China, they found another ship, the *Halifax,* sailing the wrong way: "She was sailing out of her way," records Barlow, "having sight of some of the Macao Islands and sailing from them, not knowing any of them" (537).

As Barlow gained more experience in both great and common navigation, he became more attentive to details of latitude, longitude, distance traveled, date, and magnetic variation in his efforts accurately to place his ship. During the last voyage chronicled in his journal, as if heeding the calls by writers on navigation to record the magnetic variation of places, he twice makes such a recording (511, 533). As with Dampier, the most notable variation he records occurred around the Cape of Good Hope. Barlow observes that as the ship passed south of the Cape and steered east for Java, "the greatest west variation we made of the compass was 26 degrees and odd minutes in the latitude 38 degrees and about 600 leagues to the eastward of Cape 'Bonsprance' [Cape of Good Hope]" (533). But Barlow's efforts to record the irregularities of magnetic variation, as well as his other carefully recorded "placings" of his ship, were continually undermined (as evidenced by the many displacements of his ships) by the uncertain variations facing navigation in his period. In sum, even as chartmakers increasingly left out sea monsters and sailing ships that represented the seaman's uncertain labor of sailing—as one facet of the seaman's multifaceted experience of unsettledness—the art of navigation was by no means a sure thing. And Barlow knew it.

Notes

Preface

1. Patricia Fumerton, *Cultural Aesthetics: Renaissance Literature and the Practice of Social Ornament* (Chicago: University of Chicago Press, 1991).

2. Essex Record Office, Maldon Borough, D/B 3/3/397/18; also cited in A. L. Beier, *Masterless Men: The Vagrancy Problem in England, 1560–1640* (London: Methuen, 1985), 88.

3. Joan R. Kent, "Population Mobility and Alms: Poor Migrants in the Midlands during the Early Seventeenth Century," *Local Population Studies* 27 (1981): 35.

4. On "the discretionary nature of vagrancy policy," see Steve Hindle, *The State and Social Change in Early Modern England, c. 1550–1640* (New York: St. Martin's Press, 2000), 169.

5. Lawrence Stone, "Social Mobility in England, 1500–1700," *Past and Present* 33 (1966): 16–55.

6. Hindle, *The State and Social Change,* 48; Marcus Rediker, *Between the Devil and the Deep Blue Sea: Merchant Seamen, Pirates, and the Anglo-American Maritime World, 1700–1750* (Cambridge: Cambridge University Press, 1987), 80.

7. Paul Slack, *Poverty and Policy in Tudor and Stuart England* (New York: Longman, 1988), 31.

8. Louis Montrose nicely summarizes the characterization of new historicist methodology as dialectical and defends the methodology from such attacks; see his "New Historicisms," in *Redrawing the Boundaries: The Transformation of English and American Literary Studies,* ed. Stephen Greenblatt and Giles Gunn (New York: Modern Language Association of America, 1992), 402–6.

9. Paul Griffiths, Adam Fox, and Steve Hindle, introduction to *The Experience of Authority in Early Modern England,* ed. Paul Griffiths, Adam Fox, and Steve Hindle (New York: St. Martin's Press, 1996), 7.

10. A. L. Beier, "Poverty and Progress in Early Modern England," in *The First Modern Society: Essays in English History in Honour of Lawrence Stone,* ed. A. L. Beier, David Cannadine, and James M. Rosenheim (Cambridge: Cambridge University Press, 1989), 213.

11. Paul Griffiths and Mark S. R. Jenner, eds., *Londinopolis: Essays in the Cultural and Social History of Early Modern London* (Manchester: Manchester University Press, 2000), 4.

12. See Margaret Pelling, *The Common Lot: Sickness, Medical Occupations, and the Urban Poor in Early Modern England* (London: Longman, 1998), which defines its parameters as 1500–1700 (7); and Paul Slack, *From Reformation to Improvement: Public Welfare in Early Modern*

England; The Ford Lectures Delivered in the University of Oxford, 1994–1995 (Oxford: Clarendon, 1999), in which the period covered stretches into the eighteenth century. Paul Griffiths and Steve Hindle extend their historical gaze from their earlier work in their new volume (edited with Adam Fox), *Experience of Authority*. A. L. Beier offers an early gesture toward this idea of the long seventeenth century in his published PhD dissertation, *Studies in Poverty and Poor Relief in Warwickshire, 1540–1680* (Princeton, NJ: Princeton University, 1970).

13. Beier, "Poverty and Progress," 223–26; Slack, *Poverty and Policy*, 48–55.

14. Beier, *Studies in Poverty*, 201–2.

15. Slack, *Poverty and Policy*, 39.

16. Jeremy Boulton, "Going on the Parish: The Parish Pension and Its Meaning in the London Suburbs, 1640–1724," in *Chronicling Poverty: The Voices and Strategies of the English Poor, 1640–1840*, ed. Tim Hitchcock, Peter King, and Pamela Sharpe (New York: St. Martin's Press, 1997), 24. See also Slack, *Poverty and Policy*, 174.

17. Joan Thirsk, *Economic Policy and Projects: The Development of a Consumer Society in Early Modern England* (Oxford: Clarendon, 1978), 6–9.

18. Margaret Spufford, *The Great Reclothing of Rural England: Petty Chapmen and their Wares in the Seventeenth Century* (London: Hambledon Press, 1984).

19. Pelling, *The Common Lot*, 144.

20. See especially Laura Gowing, "'The Freedom of the Streets': Women and Social Space, 1560–1640," in Griffiths and Jenner, *Londinopolis*, 130–51; and Bernard Capp, "Separate Domains? Women and Authority in Early Modern England," in Griffiths, Fox, and Hindle, *Experience of Authority*, 117–45.

21. Paul Griffiths, "Masterless Young People in Norwich, 1560–1645," in Griffiths, Fox, and Hindle, *Experience of Authority*, 146–86. See also his *Youth and Authority: Formative Experiences in England, 1560–1640* (Oxford: Clarendon Press, 1966), 351–89.

22. Slack, *Poverty and Policy*, 31.

23. Ibid., 45.

24. Peter Linebaugh and Marcus Rediker, *The Many-Headed Hydra: Sailors, Slaves, Commoners, and the Hidden History of the Revolutionary Atlantic* (Boston: Beacon Press, 2000); Rediker, *Between the Devil and the Deep Blue Sea*.

25. Rediker, *Between the Devil and the Deep Blue Sea*, 290.

26. Hitchcock, King, and Sharpe, introduction to *Chronicling Poverty*, 1–18.

27. Ballads cost one penny at the end of the sixteenth century and dropped to half a penny by the end of the seventeenth. Hyder E. Rollins, "The Black-Letter Broadside Ballad," *PMLA* 34 (1919): 296, 304.

Chapter One

1. Essex Record Office, Maldon Borough, D/B 3/3/397/18; also cited in Beier, *Masterless Men*, 88.

2. The noun *minister*, of course, had both secular and religious meanings in the period. Among the secular definitions included in the *Oxford English Dictionary* (*OED*) is "servant" or "attendant" (1b), which would characterize a server of meat and drink. Employable in both secular and religious ways is definition 1a: "A person acting under the authority of another; one who carries out executive duties as the agent or representative of a superior." Definition 2 in the *OED* offers purely "ecclesiastical and related senses" of the term. http://dictionary.oed.com/.

If we see the clerk as intentionally or subconsciously overlaying religious onto secular service, we might better understand his unusual use of the word, for in a survey of the principal occupational groups of male alehouse-keepers in Kent, 1590–1619, and Hertfordshire, 1604–7, Peter Clark found no clergy at all. Some evidence of clerical alehouse-keepers can be found only in the poorer, highland areas of Britain (where grinding poverty drove curates and priests to supplement their incomes and where the traditional link between the church and public drinking was still strong). Clark, *The English Alehouse: A Social History, 1200–1830* (London: Longman, 1983), 74–75. In all areas of the realm, however, it was common for the poorer clergy to frequent alehouses—despite Puritan opposition to them (124).

3. The uncommonly long apprenticeships adhered to by stationers—from eight to as many as fourteen years—may well have been a deciding factor in Spickernell's truncating his term (if, of course, he was not dismissed). Marjorie Plant, *The English Book Trade: An Economic History of the Making and Sale of Books,* 2nd ed. (London: George Allen & Unwin, 1965), 131–32. Paul Griffiths provides statistics on the high rates of dropout from apprenticeships in urban centers (*Youth and Authority,* 330 n. 172).

4. Beier, *Masterless Men,* 89–90. See also Spufford, *The Great Reclothing,* 6–14 and passim. Spufford notes that peddlers in the late seventeenth century often requested adequate licensing in the hope of better distinguishing themselves from rogues and vagabonds (9). On Bassett, see "Register of Passports for Vagrants, 1598–1669" (only a few entries appear after 1638), in *Poverty in Early-Stuart Salisbury,* ed. Paul Slack (Devizes, UK: Wiltshire Record Society, 1975), 63.

5. Beier, *Masterless Men,* 98; see also Peter Burke, *Popular Culture in Early Modern Europe* (London: Maurice Temple Smith, 1978), 99. On Williams, see "Register of Passports," 49.

6. Clark, *The English Alehouse,* 128–31.

7. On religious dissension and vagrancy, see Beier, *Masterless Men,* 140–42; and Christopher Hill, *The World Turned Upside Down: Radical Ideas during the English Revolution* (New York: Viking, 1972), 34–35, 38, 40. See also William C. Carroll, *Fat King, Lean Beggar: Representations of Poverty in the Age of Shakespeare* (Ithaca, NY: Cornell University Press, 1996), 170–71; Elizabeth Hanson, *Discovering the Subject in Renaissance England* (Cambridge: Cambridge University Press, 1998), chap. 3; and Jeffrey Knapp, "Rogue Nationalism," in *Centuries' Ends, Narrative Means,* ed. Robert Newman (Stanford, CA: Stanford University Press, 1996), 138–50. Itinerant bands of Irish were considered to be especially threatening because of their rebellious popery (Beier, *Masterless Men,* 11, 64). It should be noted, however, that the "story" of religious persecution could be turned to one's advantage: poor strangers of the Protestant faith who told narratives of religious persecution at the hands of Catholics might receive one-time or occasional support from local parishes. Claire S. Schen, "Constructing the Poor in Early Seventeenth-Century London," *Albion* 32 (2000): 450–63.

8. Olwen Hufton coined the term "makeshift" to describe the economy of the poor in eighteenth-century France. *The Poor of Eighteenth-Century France, 1750–1789* (Oxford: Clarendon Press, 1974). As my study will show, such a "makeshift" economy was growing in England as early as the late sixteenth century, especially in the laboring practices of poor women.

9. Christopher Pye, "The Theater, the Market, and the Subject of History," *ELH* 61 (1994): 501–3.

10. We should be cautious in our use of the word "new." Change is rarely sudden, and what might appear "new" at any one moment in time might in fact be an old bird in new dressing. My epilogue shall further explore this problematic in discussing the "new" global economy of another mobile workforce active today. A sense of newness may be a response not so much to

actually new phenomena as to an intensifying of already existing institutions and events, as David Harris Sacks has commented. Certainly, mobility, by-employments, and homelessness—the focus of this and the next chapter—were not entirely new in the sixteenth century, any more than were alehouses, which temporally housed and fed the itinerant. It was the burgeoning of such phenomena at the end of the sixteenth century—fueled by the rapid expansion of manufacturing centers, preeminently London, and by growing dependence on credit—that created the impression of an emergent destabilizing "new" economy. David Harris Sacks, "The Nature of Reality: Historical Facts and Fictions" (response to a panel for the North American Conference on British Studies titled "History, the New Historicism, and the Renaissance Literature of Roguery: New Perspectives," Pasadena, Calif., October 13, 2000, in which I participated). I would like to thank Professor Sacks for generously providing me with a copy of his response.

11. Heather Dubrow, *Shakespeare and Domestic Loss: Forms of Deprivation, Mourning, and Recuperation* (Cambridge: Cambridge University Press, 1999), 80–193. Although she discusses the problem of vagrancy, Dubrow is more concerned with loss defined as an *invasion* of the domestic space.

12. *The Statutes of the Realm,* ed. John Raithby et al. (London: Record Commission, 1810–28), 39 Elizabeth 1, c. 4. Steve Rappaport has rejected the generally accepted notion of rising poverty and itinerancy in early modern England; he argues instead for the effectiveness of individual and guild charity, poor laws, and economizing in containing poverty. He thus finds in the sixteenth century not unsettling mobility, but a stable social structure (hence the title of his book, *Worlds within Worlds*); and not anxious hostility to the poor and homeless, but beneficent charity. *Worlds within Worlds: Structures of Life in Sixteenth-Century London* (Cambridge: Cambridge University Press, 1989), especially 1–22. As Theodora A. Jankowski notes, however, Rappaport's evidence and methods of analysis have since come under considerable question by such historians as Ronald Berger, Keith Lindley, and Ian W. Archer. Jankowski, "Historicizing and Legitimating Capitalism: Thomas Heywood's *Edward IV* and *If You Know Not Me, You Know Nobody,*" in *Medieval and Renaissance Drama in England,* vol. 7, ed. Leeds Barroll (New York: AMS Press, 1995), 332–33 n. 7. Archer, for instance, takes issue with Rappaport's use (on p. 5) of London's Bridewell records to prove that in 1600–1601, there were only about 5,500 vagrants out of a total of some 150,000 Londoners (that is, only about 4 percent of the city's population). Rappaport, Archer notes, "fails to appreciate both that more vagrants passed through Bridewell than appear in the court books, and that vagrants might be punished elsewhere, either in special sessions or, crucially after the act of 1598, summarily by local constables." The fact is, as Archer concludes, that "the numbers game is . . . decidedly unhelpful." *The Pursuit of Stability: Social Relations in Elizabethan London* (Cambridge: Cambridge University Press, 1991), 208. Valerie Pearl adopts a stance similar to that of Rappaport, arguing for the effectiveness of private and public charity, in "Change and Stability in Seventeenth-Century London," *London Journal* 5 (1979): 3–34; see also her "Social Policy in Early Modern London," in *History and Imagination: Essays in Honour of H. R. Trevor-Roper,* ed. H. Lloyd-Jones, V. Pearl, and B. Worden (New York: Holmes & Meier, 1982), 115–31. Archer also criticizes Pearl's position (149–50).

13. Peter Clark and Paul Slack, eds., *Crisis and Order in English Towns, 1500–1700: Essays in Urban History* (Toronto: University of Toronto Press, 1972), 152; see also Steve Hindle, "Exclusion Crises: Poverty, Migration and Parochial Responsibility in English Rural Communities, c. 1560–1660," *Rural History* 7 (1996): 125–49.

14. Slack, *Poverty and Policy,* 72.

15. A. L. Beier, "Vagrants and the Social Order in Elizabethan England," *Past and Present* 64 (1974): 23.

16. Paul Slack, "Vagrants and Vagrancy in England, 1598–1664," *Economic History Review,* 2nd ser., 27 (1974): 365; see also A. L. Beier, "Social Problems in Elizabethan London," *Journal of Interdisciplinary History* 9 (1978): 220–21. The exceptions to small groups were Irish and Gypsy bands, although in both cases contemporary reports exaggerated their numbers. See Beier, *Masterless Men,* 57–65. It should also be noted that the average number of persons in a vagrant group increased in the first half of the seventeenth century, especially after 1620 (from 1–2 persons to 3–4). This was because whole families took to the road in response to prolonged economic crisis (ibid., 57). See also Clark and Slack, *Crisis and Order,* 143–44.

John L. McMullen attempts to recuperate the notion of organized, hierarchical, guildlike criminal activity—in London at least—with the emphasized qualification that such organizations were locally based and shifting in nature. However, though his study provides a valuable look at the economics of vagrancy as represented in the literature of the period, his evidence for professional crime is far too dependent on the rogue pamphlets to be trustworthy. McMullen, *The Canting Crew: London's Criminal Underworld, 1550–1700* (New Brunswick, NJ: Rutgers University Press, 1984). A more recent study of rogue communities, which also tends disturbingly to read rogue pamphlets as if they were historical documents (and their characters as if they were real people)—though highly sophisticated theoretically—is Bryan Reynolds's *Becoming Criminal: Transversal Performance and Cultural Dissidence in Early Modern England* (Baltimore: Johns Hopkins University Press, 2002).

17. "Register of Passports," 23, 43.

18. Beier, *Masterless Men,* 52.

19. *Statutes of the Realm,* 7 James 1, c. 4.

20. *The Book of John Fisher, Town Clerk and Deputy Recorder of Warwick, 1580–1588,* ed. Thomas Kemp (Warwick: Henry T. Cooke & Son, n.d.), 106.

21. Dubrow, *Shakespeare and Domestic Loss,* 142–93; Slack, "Vagrants and Vagrancy," 366.

22. I am grateful to Lena Cowen Orlin for pointing out to me the inadequacy of the conventional terms contemporaries and historians have used to describe these modular family units.

23. Spufford, *The Great Reclothing,* 53–54 (quotation from p. 53); see also 23–31. On the inability of chapmen to name where they were, see p. 24. On Barrye, see "Register of Passports," 47.

24. Michael Roberts, "Women and Work in Sixteenth-Century English Towns," in *Work in Towns, 850–1850,* ed. Penelope J. Corfield and Derek Keene (Leicester: Leicester University Press, 1990), 92; Pelling, *The Common Lot,* 115, 150–51. What indicates expediency in the remarriages of the poor is the frequent and large inequality of ages (usually it was a much older man marrying a younger woman, but sometimes the roles were reversed). Faramerz Dabhoiwala finds evidence in the period of "fluid relational patterns that were not solely dependent upon the sanction of marriage, nor very different across ranks." "The Pattern of Sexual Immorality in Seventeenth- and Eighteenth-Century London," in Griffiths and Jenner, *Londinopolis,* 91. But, of course, in the case of the poor, such fluidity was more often a matter of expediency than for other classes.

25. Slack, "Vagrants and Vagrancy," 367.

26. "Register of Passports," 29. See also Slack, "Vagrants and Vagrancy," 367; and Beier, *Masterless Men,* 67.

27. Archer, *The Pursuit of Stability,* 185; Slack, *Poverty and Policy,* 99.

28. *Statutes of the Realm,* 1 Edward 6, c. 3. On parish apprentices, see Pamela Sharpe, "Poor Children as Apprentices in Colyton, 1598–1830," *Continuity and Change* 6 (1991): 1–18.

29. Linebaugh and Rediker, *The Many-Headed Hydra,* 59. On the exportation of child labor to the New World, see also Robert Hume, *Early Child Immigrants to Virginia, 1619–1642* (Baltimore: Magna Carta Book Co., 1986); and Robert C. Johnson, "The Transportation of Vagrant Children

from London to Virginia, 1618–1622," in *Early Stuart Studies: Essays in Honor of David Harris Willson,* ed. Howard S. Reinmuth (Minneapolis: University of Minnesota Press, 1970), 137–51.

30. Slack, *Poverty and Policy,* 99 (where he also cites other instances of family fragmentation).

31. Alice Clark, *Working Life of Women in the Seventeenth Century* (London: George Routledge & Sons; New York: E. P. Dutton & Co., 1919), 81; see also 81–82, 82 n. 2.

32. Clark and Slack, *Crisis and Order,* 143.

33. Beier, *Masterless Men,* 68.

34. Slack, *Poverty and Policy,* 99.

Chapter Two

1. A. L. Beier and Roger Finlay, introduction to *London, 1500–1700: The Making of the Metropolis,* ed. A. L. Beier and Roger Finlay (London: Longman, 1986), 2, 18, 9.

2. Ibid., 15.

3. Beier, "Social Problems in Elizabethan London," 206–7, 214. Of those arrested in London between 1597 and 1608 whose occupations were listed, forty-seven out of sixty-five were listed as servants or apprentices.

4. Beier and Finlay, *London, 1500–1700,* 20.

5. Margaret Pelling, "Skirting the City? Disease, Social Change and Divided Households in the Seventeenth Century," in Griffiths and Jenner, *Londinopolis,* 154, 167.

6. Edward Barlow, *Barlow's Journal of His Life at Sea in King's Ships, East and West Indiamen and Other Merchantmen, from 1659–1703,* transcribed by Basil Lubbock, 2 vols. (London: Hurst & Blackett, 1934), 31.

7. Stone, "Social Mobility in England," 31, 29.

8. Barlow, *Journal,* 31.

9. Archer, *The Pursuit of Stability,* 76. Steve Rappaport, of course, would wholeheartedly agree (*Worlds within Worlds*).

10. Jeremy Boulton, *Neighbourhood and Society: A London Suburb in the Seventeenth Century* (Cambridge: Cambridge University Press, 1987), 246, 210, 212–27. For arguments in favor of a community network in the face of mobility, see especially 228–61.

11. Beier, "Social Problems in Elizabethan London," 215. See also A. L. Beier, "Engine of Manufacture: The Trades of London," in Beier and Finlay, *London, 1500–1700,* 154. The percentage of dependent labor declined from 1540 to 1640 to 1700 (from 53.2% to 39.1% to 22.8%), but it remained a sizable proportion of the city's population (ibid.).

12. Stone, "Social Mobility in England," 53.

13. William C. Carroll, *Fat King, Lean Beggar,* 141 n. 15 (see also 142–43); Archer, *The Pursuit of Stability,* 1–2 (see also 243–44).

14. Griffiths, *Youth and Authority,* 13, 40, 60–61, and passim. On masterless youths, see 351–89. See also Griffiths's "Masterless Young People in Norwich," 146–86.

15. Griffiths, *Youth and Authority,* 378–79.

16. Merry Wiesner, *Women and Gender in Early Modern Europe* (Cambridge: Cambridge University Press, 1993), 99.

17. Griffiths, *Youth and Authority,* 381.

18. Ibid. On accusations of lewdness made against women living independently, see 380–81.

19. Ibid., 381.

20. Ibid., especially 380–81. On the labeling of resident youths as "vagrant," see also Griffiths's "Masterless Young People in Norwich," 179 n. 34.

21. Roughly 40 percent of London's population was below the age of fifteen—an especially youthful population that was "due to the large numbers of young immigrants" (Beier, "Social Problems in Elizabethan London," 213–14). On the small proportion of Londoners that were married, see Beier and Finlay, *London, 1500–1700*, 50. Ilana Krausman Ben-Amos sees family relationships as the strongest support system available to youths, given that their extraordinary mobility precluded strong neighborhood or even peer ties. *Adolescence and Youth in Early Modern England* (New Haven, CT: Yale University Press, 1994), 156–82. She concedes, however, that "once they left the parental home and became servants and apprentices in the households of others, many youths did not see their parents, brothers, sisters, old playmates, or the neighbors with whom they had grown up, sometimes for years" (156).

22. Beier, "Social Problems in Elizabethan London," 216.

23. Beier, "Poverty and Progress in Early Modern England," 227.

24. Roberts, "Women and Work," 92.

25. Pelling, "Skirting the City?" 167. See also her fuller study of this problem in "Apprenticeship, Health, and Social Cohesion in Early Modern London," *History Workshop Journal* 37 (1994): 33–56.

26. Beier, "Social Problems in Elizabethan London," 215. Griffiths provides statistics on the high dropout rates in *Youth and Authority*, 330 n. 172.

27. Steve Rappaport, "Reconsidering Apprenticeship in Sixteenth-Century London," in *Renaissance Society and Culture: Essays in Honor of Eugene F. Rice, Jr.*, ed. John Monfasani and Ronald G. Musto (New York: Italica, 1991), 239–61; see also his *Worlds within Worlds*, 311–15. What I find amazing about Rappaport's argument is his determined suppression of even the *possibility* of unplaced labor. He conjectures that *all* apprentices who were dismissed or left service probably returned with their skills to their homes or other towns in the country. He thus envisions London as a vocational training center and projects a completely contained cycle of labor in which *no one* is unemployed and in which the countryside is repopulated by urban emigration. Archer also takes exception to Rappaport's overly optimistic vision of the apprenticeship system (Archer, *The Pursuit of Stability*, 15). For more on Rappaport's arguments against unsettledness, and on the counterarguments raised against him, see chap. 1, n. 12.

28. *The Book of John Fisher*, 20–26.

29. Ibid., 22.

30. In addition to occasional work in the harvest and coalpits, Barlow tried out an apprenticeship as a whitester in Lancashire, as a tapster in Southwark, and again as a tapster or vintner in Dartford, Kent; he also worked at various odd jobs as a servant. He complained that his whitester master fed him poorer food than the family ate and that he beat his servants. Barlow shared as well Fletcher's fear of being under too many thumbs: that because his master had so many children, "ere long I should have more masters and dames than one" (Barlow, *Journal*, 18). He also complained about the kind of food his Dartford master served him (26).

31. On general problems within master-servant relations, see Beier, "Social Problems in Elizabethan London," 215–17. See also Steven R. Smith, "The Ideal and Reality: Apprentice-Master Relationships in Seventeenth Century London," *History of Education Quarterly* 21 (1981): 449–59, especially 457; Smith, "The London Apprentices as Seventeenth-Century Adolescents," *Past and Present* 61 (1973): 151–53; Ben-Amos, *Adolescence and Youth*, 100–108; Archer, *The Pursuit of Stability*, 216–18; and Griffiths, *Youth and Authority*, 290–350. Frances E. Dolan studies cases where women as mistresses were authorized to exert power over—and even employ violence on—apprentices and servants. "Household Chastisements: Gender, Authority, and 'Domestic Violence,'" in *Renaissance Culture and the Everyday*, ed. Patricia Fumerton and Simon Hunt (Philadelphia: University of Pennsylvania Press, 1999), 204–25. For Tim Meldrum on advice

manuals, see his "London Domestic Servants from Depositional Evidence, 1660–1750: Servant-Employer Sexuality in the Patriarchal Household," in Hitchcock, King, and Sharpe, *Chronicling Poverty*, 50. On the abusive conditions that provoked a high rate of suicides among the servant orders, see Michael MacDonald and Terence R. Murphy, *Sleepless Souls: Suicide in Early Modern England* (Oxford: Clarendon Press, 1990), 252–55. Pelling, in "Apprenticeship," argues that the master-servant relationship was never intended to be an aspect of kinship, where the master functioned as a father figure, but rather a substitute moral structure that was intended to be stronger than the often fragmented family of the period.

 32. On the activities of masterless young men in London, see Beier, "Social Problems in Elizabethan London," 210; on the jobs a displaced apprentice might assume, see Ben-Amos, *Adolescence and Youth*, 218–19.

 33. Sara Mendelson and Patricia Crawford, *Women in Early Modern England, 1550–1720* (Oxford: Clarendon Press, 1998), 278.

 34. Griffiths, "Masterless Young People in Norwich," 160.

 35. Slack, *Poverty and Policy*, 94–95; Ben-Amos, *Adolescence and Youth*, 82; see also 82–83. Ben-Amos has a habit of ending a youth's story with placement as an apprentice, but given the high dropout rate of apprentices, in many cases such placement would be but a stage in a continuous process of displacement.

 36. Margaret Spufford provides the best account of such itinerant sellers in England, in *The Great Reclothing*. Laurence Fontaine notes that the peddler was held in suspicion throughout Europe until the end of the nineteenth century. *History of Pedlars in Europe*, trans. Vicki Whittaker (Durham: Duke University Press, 1996), 2.

 37. Thirsk, *Economic Policy and Projects*, 6.

 38. *Orders Appointed to Be Executed in the Cittie of London, for Setting Roges and Idle Persons to Worke, and for Releefe of the Poore* (London, n.d.), B2v. The *Orders* were probably printed in 1582 or 1586. See also Thirsk, *Economic Policy and Projects*, 65–66.

 39. See, for example, Thirsk, *Economic Policy and Projects*, on the cultivation of woad and the searching out of copperas (3–4, 37)—though Thirsk also notes that poor men as well as women were involved in domestic industries (see, e.g., 45, 103, 161). See also Mendelson and Crawford, *Women in Early Modern England*, 271, 274–75.

 40. Boulton, "Going on the Parish," 24.

 41. Capp, "Separate Domains?" 119. On the importance of the labors of women (and children) for a poor family's survival, see Pelling, *The Common Lot*, 144.

 42. Mendelson and Crawford, *Women in Early Modern England*, 274.

 43. Ibid., 276.

 44. Ibid., 279–80. See also Archer on the extra income poor women and children might garner through "spinning, laundering, and trades like button making" (*The Pursuit of Stability*, 196).

 45. Gowing, "'The Freedom of the Streets,'" 141–42.

 46. Roberts, "Women and Work," 95.

 47. Pelling, *The Common Lot*, 10. Pelling further suggests that occupational diversity on the part of an individual was not necessarily a sign of his or her economic decline (208). Nevertheless, makeshift employment was a necessity for the poor in ways it was not for those capitalizing on diversification.

 48. Thirsk, *Economic Policy and Projects*, 155.

 49. Ibid.

 50. Ibid., 172; see also 3, 7–8, 110–11, 148, and especially 155–57.

51. Boulton, *Neighbourhood and Society*, 72–73. See also Keith Wrightson and David Levine, *Poverty and Piety in an English Village: Terling, 1525–1700* (New York: Academic Press, 1979), 22–23. As Thirsk adds, a "flexible, even casual, attitude to the choice of an occupation" characterized even more well-to-do entrepreneurs in the new domestic trades, who might shift from job to job (*Economic Policy and Projects*, 171, 172). Archer, similarly, observes an increasing tendency toward the end of the sixteenth century for freemen of particular companies in London to take on other trades. For example: "During the first decade of the seventeenth century the Blacksmiths admitted at least three tailors, two hatmakers, two goldsmiths, a coachmaker, a pointmaker, an embroiderer, a carman, and a wheelwright, and it is unlikely that all cases were recorded" (*The Pursuit of Stability*, 115). Such job-shifting by the middling sort suggests that perhaps unsettled economics was truly spacious, extending beyond the itinerant and multitasked laboring poor.

52. A. Hassel Smith, "Labourers in Late Sixteenth-Century England: A Case Study from North Norfolk," pt. 2, *Continuity and Change* 4 (1989): 380–81.

53. Quoted in Thirsk, *Economic Policy and Projects*, 151; she also comments on the inaccurate exaggeration of Smith's portrait.

54. *Statutes of the Realm*, 39 Elizabeth 1, c. 3; 43 Elizabeth 1, c. 2.

55. Beier, *Masterless Men*, 88.

56. Pelling, *The Common Lot*, 166.

57. John F. Pound, ed., *Norwich Census of the Poor, 1570* (Norfolk: Norfolk Record Society, 1971), 28, 72, 29.

58. Slack, *Poverty and Policy*, 31.

59. Paul Slack, *The English Poor Law, 1531–1782* (Macmillan, 1990; repr., Cambridge: Cambridge University Press, 1995), 30.

60. Slack, *From Reformation to Improvement*, 96–97.

61. *Statutes of the Realm*, 7 James 1, c. 4. In *Poverty and Policy*, Slack notes that the concept of the laboring poor can be found as early as a survey of the poor in London in 1552. But frequent references to this shadowy category of poor become prevalent only in the late sixteenth century (27–28). The matter of who was to be counted as a vagrant, he further points out, was "a topic much disputed in the Commons in 1571 and 1572" (*The English Poor Law*, 12). Norwich in 1570 and Ipswich in 1597 were among the first towns to recognize that the resident needy could include the employed and underemployed, not just the disabled, old, and orphaned. Nevertheless, though both towns increased their rates to supplement more workers, the resistance to this notion was strong, and many indigent but "able" workers continued to be deprived of regular relief. Furthermore, transient workers from outside the community were ruthlessly turned away. See Pound, *Norwich Census of the Poor*; John F. Pound, "An Elizabethan Census of the Poor: The Treatment of Vagrancy in Norwich, 1570–1580," *University of Birmingham Historical Journal* 8 (1962): 135–61, where he more clearly delimits the "success story" of Norwich; and John Webb, ed., *Poor Relief in Elizabethan Ipswich* (Ipswich, UK: Suffolk Records Society, 1966). Slack sums up the general situation nationwide: "In the early 17th century," he says, "as it became increasingly difficult to find masters to take on poor apprentices, as the number of the unemployed outgrew the facilities of the small workhouse, and as many in employment also came to require public alms to support their families, the burden on the poor-rate became unmanageable" (*Poverty in Early-Stuart Salisbury*, 4). Many houses of correction, Beier adds, soon lapsed from workhouses into penal institutions (*Masterless Men*, 164–70). On the ways poor foreigners and sympathetic authorities felt compelled to construct "a narrative of legitimacy" that would make immigrants acceptably deserving (telling tales of suffering, such as captivity or religious persecution), see Schen, "Constructing the Poor" (quotation is on p. 456).

62. Archer, *The Pursuit of Stability*, 244–45.

63. Linda Woodbridge, *Vagrancy, Homelessness, and English Renaissance Literature* (Urbana: University of Illinois Press, 2001). As Woodbridge notes, the more positive rendering of this comic treatment of the vagrant was the merry-beggar trope, in which vagrant mobility was idealized as freedom; see her conclusion, "New Place or Noplace?" (239–66). It should be noted that Woodbridge traces the mockery of vagrants through jest books to the early sixteenth century and thus argues that the anxiousness about vagrants in the late sixteenth century was nothing "new." While agreeing, I would add that such anxiousness reached an especially high pitch around this time because of the period's increasing reliance on a fluid money market and mobile workforce, into which vagrants were folded.

64. Those removed under the settlement laws in the eighteenth century, for instance, were now predominantly women and the old—a marked change from the late sixteenth and early seventeenth centuries (Slack, *The English Poor Law*, 31). Boulton, however, finds a different situation in early seventeenth-century Boroughside, Southwark, where "just over two thirds of all inmates and new settlers detected (and often ejected by the searcher for inmates) were single women, mostly pregnant servants" (*Neighbourhood and Society*, 129 n. 28). Boulton's different findings may be in part explained by the tendency of pregnant women to seek refuge or anonymity in the less policed suburbs.

65. Griffiths, *Youth and Authority*, 383–84.

66. Archer, *The Pursuit of Stability*, 244.

67. Hindle, "Exclusion Crises," 141.

68. See Hext's 1596 letter to Burghley, reprinted in Frank Aydelotte, *Elizabethan Rogues and Vagabonds*, vol. 1, Oxford Historical and Literary Studies (Oxford: Clarendon Press, 1913), 168–73.

69. *Statutes of the Realm*, 1 Edward 6, c. 3; 1 James 1, c. 7.

70. Slack, *Poverty in Early-Stuart Salisbury*, 3.

71. Boulton documents badging laws in the 1670s and in 1697 in St. Martin-in the-Fields, though they appear to have been implemented only sporadically after a few years ("Going on the Parish," 34–35).

72. Woodbridge, *Vagrancy*, 116.

73. Beier, "Poverty and Progress," 204–13. For King's estimation of the poor, see 204.

74. Boulton, *Neighbourhood and Society*, 115; Hindle, "Exclusion Crises," 131; Slack, *Poverty in Early-Stuart Salisbury*, 6. Those paying the lowest tax rates were probably also near poverty. Looking at the numbers of poor counted in the Norwich census of 1570 and including those subsequently taxed in the lowest bracket, Pound concludes that "at least 50 per cent of the English population in the city were either poverty stricken or very near it" ("An Elizabethan Census of the Poor," 144).

75. Boulton, *Neighbourhood and Society*, 100, 115.

76. Jonathan Barry, introduction to *The Middling Sort of People: Culture, Society and Politics in England, 1550–1800*, ed. Jonathan Barry and Christopher Brooks (New York: St. Martin's Press, 1994), 17; "independent trading households" is quoted from Shani d'Cruze on p. 2.

77. Hindle, *The State and Social Change*, 50.

78. Ibid., 48.

79. Hindle, "Exclusion Crises," 131. See also Tim Wales, "Poverty, Poor Relief and the Life-Cycle: Some Evidence from Seventeenth-Century Norfolk," in *Land, Kinship and Life-Cycle*, ed. Richard M. Smith (Cambridge: Cambridge University Press, 1984), 351–404. I would like to thank Deborah Harkness for helping me think through the knotty problems of categorizing the poor and mobile.

80. Hitchcock, King, and Sharpe, introduction to *Chronicling Poverty*, 10.

81. Jean-Christophe Agnew, *Worlds Apart: The Market and the Theater in Anglo-American Thought, 1550–1750* (Cambridge: Cambridge University Press, 1986), 41 and passim.

82. Rappaport, for instance, notes that for 53 of the 101 "Brewers, Butchers, and Coopers who did not leave London immediately after their apprenticeships ended[,] . . . journeywork was not only the beginning but also the end of their occupational careers" (*Worlds within Worlds*, 333). Rappaport attempts to ameliorate these figures by explaining that the fifty-three included those journeymen who died or left London before they could become householders (338–43).

83. On traveling painters, artists, and entertainers, see Burke, *Popular Culture in Early Modern Europe,* 91–115; on itinerant masons, see 40–41.

Chapter Three

1. Carroll, *Fat King, Lean Beggar,* 81–82. Variants of "Genings" (Gennins, Genynges, etc.) that appear in the original editions of Harman's work are typically rendered "Jennings" in modern editions. I have consulted the various original editions of the *Caveat,* but for the reader's convenience, I will quote from Arthur F. Kinney's readily available modern edition. I will thus defer to Kinney's spelling of "Jennings"; see, e.g., p. 130 in Kinney, ed., *Rogues, Vagabonds and Sturdy Beggars: A New Gallery of Tudor and Early Stuart Rogue Literature* (Amherst: University of Massachusetts Press, 1990). Text citations of Harman's pamphlet are from Kinney's edition.

It should be noted, however, that Kinney's discussion of the various editions of Harman's tract (p. 296) is misleading, since he conflates the second and third editions of the work into one and so talks about three, not four, editions. Kinney persuasively supports his choice to use the earliest available edition of Harman's tract on the grounds that it is closest to the author's original intent. He thus consults the Bodleian copy of the second edition, *A Caveat for Commen Cursetors Vulgarely Called Vagabones* (Q2), since the first edition is lost. Kinney then supplements his text with footnotes to the 1573 edition, which he calls the third edition. But there was a third edition of the *Caveat* (Q3), which came out in the same year as the second—copies are held at the Folger, Huntington, and British Libraries—and which is slightly different from the second. This edition preceded the 1573 edition (correctly, Q4). See Carroll's extensive discussion of the various editions in *Fat King, Lean Beggar,* 70 n. 1, and throughout his chapter on Harman, 77–96.

2. Stephen Greenblatt, "Invisible Bullets," in *Shakespearean Negotiations: The Circulation of Social Energy in Renaissance England* (Berkeley and Los Angeles: University of California Press, 1988), 21–65 (Harman becomes central to the discussion on pp. 49–52 and 57–58); Hanson, *Discovering the Subject,* chap. 3; Paola Pugliatti, *Beggary and Theatre in Early Modern England* (Aldershot, UK: Ashgate, 2003), 139–52; Carroll, *Fat King, Lean Beggar,* 70–96.

3. Carroll, *Fat King, Lean Beggar,* 180–207 (Carroll discusses 2 *Henry VI* on the road to *Lear,* 127–57); Woodbridge, *Vagrancy,* 205–37; Pugliatti, *Beggary and Theatre,* 149–52; Greenblatt, "Invisible Bullets," 56–65 (Greenblatt glances at Shakespeare's *Henry IV* as well but concentrates his focus on *Henry V*).

4. Early studies that tend to read rogue pamphlets as if they were historical documents, despite occasional qualifications, include Aydelotte, *Elizabethan Rogues and Vagabonds,* 1:76–139; A. V. Judges, *The Elizabethan Underworld* (New York: E. P. Dutton & Co., 1930), xiii–lxiv; and James A. S. McPeek, *The Black Book of Knaves and Unthrifts in Shakespeare and Other Renaissance Authors* (Storrs: University of Connecticut Press, 1965). Later believers include McMullen, *The Canting Crew* (1984); and Gamini Salgado, *The Elizabethan Underworld* (New York: St. Martin's Press, 1992). Though highly sophisticated in his approach, I would also place in this camp Bryan Reynolds (*Becoming Criminal,* 2002).

More-recent studies that are more careful to separate the "history" from the "fiction" of vagrants but that follow a narrative line from vagrancy to drama or theatricality (usually through rogue pamphlets) include Pugliatti, *Beggary and Theatre;* Woodbridge, *Vagrancy;* Dubrow, *Shakespeare and Domestic Loss* (Dubrow discusses Shakespeare's poetry as well as plays); Hanson, *Discovering the Subject,* chap. 3; Garrett A. Sullivan Jr., "Knowing One's Place: The Highway, the Estate, and *A Jovial Crew,*" in *The Drama of Landscape: Land, Property, and Social Relations on the Early Modern Stage* (Stanford, CA: Stanford University Press, 1998), 159–93; Carroll, *Fat King, Lean Beggar;* Knapp, "Rogue Nationalism," 138–50; Jankowski, "Historicizing and Legitimating Capitalism," 305–37; Marcia A. McDonald, "The Elizabethan Poor Laws and the Stage in the Late 1590s," in Barroll, *Medieval and Renaissance Drama,* 121–44; Rosemary Gaby, "Of Vagabonds and Commonwealths: *Beggar's Bush, A Jovial Crew,* and *The Sisters,*" *Studies in English Literature* 34 (1994): 401–24; Greenblatt, "Invisible Bullets," 49–65; and, an early instance of this methodology, Normand Berlin, *The Base String: The Underworld in Elizabethan Drama* (Rutherford, NJ: Fairleigh Dickinson University Press, 1968).

5. Pugliatti, *Beggary and Theatre.*

6. Woodbridge, *Vagrancy,* 116.

7. Craig Dionne, "Fashioning Outlaws: The Early Modern Rogue and Urban Culture," in *Rogues and Early Modern English Culture,* ed. Craig Dionne and Steve Mentz (Ann Arbor: University of Michigan Press, 2004), 40. Karen Helfand Bix sees a marked difference between earlier pamphleteers, such as Harman, and the later "cony-catching" pamphleteers, such as Robert Greene and Thomas Dekker. In these later pamphlets, she finds embrace along with criticism of a more flexible, unregulated economy and of "occupations divorced from traditional vocational regimes and from material productions." "'Masters of Their Occupation': Labor and Fellowship in the Coney-Catching Pamphlets," in Dionne and Mentz, *Rogues,* 179–80. Pugliatti also insists on a distinction between rogue and cony-catching pamphlets (*Beggary and Theatre,* 125–90).

8. Dionne, "Fashioning Outlaws," 55.

9. Linda Woodbridge, "The Peddler and the Pawn: Why Did Tudor England Consider Peddlers to be Rogues?" in Dionne and Mentz, *Rogues,* 143–70.

10. Woodbridge, *Vagrancy.*

11. Thomas Dekker, *The Belman of London* (London, 1608), in *"The Guls Hornbook" and "The Bellman of London" by Thomas Dekker* (Letchworth, UK: Temple Press, 1905), 105.

12. Griffiths, *Youth and Authority,* 330 n. 172; Beier, "Social Problems in Elizabethan London," 214–15. See also the discussion in the previous chapter.

13. Woodbridge, *Vagrancy,* 78 n. 17.

14. Beier and Finlay, introduction to *London, 1500–1700,* 9.

15. Carroll, *Fat King, Lean Beggar,* 82–83.

16. I have here taken and modernized the poem from Harman's 1573 edition, D2r (Kinney's modernized edition, which I cite throughout my discussion, does not reproduce either the woodcut or the verse). My rendering mostly follows that of Judges, in his edition of Harman's pamphlet in *The Elizabethan Underworld,* facing p. 90. Both picture and poem, it should be noted, were cribbed by the author of *The Groundworke of Conny-Catching* (London, 1592). In the 1568 edition of Harman's pamphlet (Q3), the illustration and verse are essentially the same as those in his 1573 edition. The one significant difference in the verse—the last word—is noted below.

17. Agnew, *Worlds Apart,* 66.

18. Ibid.

19. Carroll, *Fat King, Lean Beggar,* 79–80.

20. Woodbridge, *Vagrancy*, 4; Kathleen Pories, "The Intersection of Poor Laws and Literature in the Sixteenth Century: Fictional and Factual Categories," in *Framing Elizabethan Fictions: Contemporary Approaches to Early Modern Narrative Prose*, ed. Constance C. Relihan (Kent, OH: Kent State University Press, 1996), 38; Jodi Mikalachki, "Women's Networks and the Female Vagrant: A Hard Case," in *Maids and Mistresses, Cousins and Queens: Women's Alliances in Early Modern England*, ed. Susan Frye and Karen Robertson (New York: Oxford University Press, 1999), 52–69.

21. The description of vagrancy as a "liberty" that is "sweet" (though also "wicked") is from Edward Hext, in a letter of 1596 (discussed in more detail below), cited in Aydelotte, *Elizabethan Rogues and Vagabonds*, 171. Among those given to vagrant wandering, complains Hext, is the son of a gentleman, with inheritance (171). Reported as pretending to be Gypsies were gentlemen (Judges, *The Elizabethan Underworld*, xxv), a shoemaker (Salgado, *The Elizabethan Underworld*, 155), and yeomen (McPeek, *Black Book of Knaves and Unthrifts*, 263). An official response to the perceived problem was the 1598 "Act for Punishment of Rogues, Vagabonds and Sturdy Beggars," which expands the definition of rogues to include "all such persons not being felons wandering and pretending to be Egyptians, or wandering in the habit, form or attire of counterfeit Egyptians" (*Statutes of the Realm*, 39 Elizabeth 1, c. 4). The latter wording leaves open the possibility that such rogues are pretending to be pretend Gypsies! For more on this phenomenon, see Reynolds, *Becoming Criminal*, 23–63. Vagrants pretending to be legally sanctioned glassmen became such a problem that a statute under James I responded by making glassmen legally vagrant (*Statutes of the Realm*, 1 James 1, c. 7). On vagrants pretending to be servants of nobles, see McPeek, *Black Book of Knaves and Unthrifts*, 10; on Gypsies pretending to be tinkers, etc., see Samuel Rid, *The Art of Juggling or Legerdemain* (London, 1612), in Kinney, *Rogues, Vagabonds and Sturdy Beggars*, 266.

22. Quoted in Aydelotte, *Elizabethan Rogues and Vagabonds*, 169, 168, 173.

23. Ibid., 172.

24. Ibid., 173.

25. Robert Greene, *The Second and Last Part of Conny-Catching* (London, 1591), in Judges, *The Elizabethan Underworld*, 160.

26. See also the preface to the first part of Robert Greene's series, *A Notable Discovery of Coosenage* (London, 1591): "Yet, Gentlemen, am I sore threatened by the hacksters of that filthy faculty that if I set their practices in print, they will cut off that hand that writes the pamphlet; but how I fear their bravados, you shall perceive by my plain painting out of them" (in Judges, *The Elizabethan Underworld*, 122); the preface to Greene's *Second and Last Part of Conny-Catching*: "These cony-catchers . . . [swear] even by God Himself, that they will make a massacre of his bones, and cut off my right hand for penning down their abominable practices. But alas for them, poor snakes! Words are wind, and looks but glances: every thunderclap hath not a bolt, nor every cony-catcher's oath an execution. I live still, and I live to display their villainies" (ibid., 150–51); and Greene's *A Disputation, Betweene a Hee Conny-Catcher, and a Shee Conny-Catcher* (London, 1592): "Let them [cozeners] do what they dare with their Bilbao blades! I fear them not" (ibid., 226). The trope continued to thrive well after Greene and Hext wrote; Luke Hutton invokes it twice in his *The Blacke Dogge of Newgate* (London, [1596]). In his preface to the Lord Chief Justice, Sir John Popham, Hutton heroically declares, "So the work be acceptable in your good opinion, I will not regard the malice of the threatening cony-catcher[s], who hath sworn, if I publish this book, they will do me what mischief they can." And in the body of Hutton's work, he reiterates his bold stance: "The Devil should have his due of these knaves; and I hold it my duty to reveal

whatsoever is to the good of a commonwealth: and so I will, though the cony-catcher swear to give me a cut in the leg for my labor" (in Judges, *The Elizabethan Underworld*, 265, 285).

Chapter Four

1. Beier, "Vagrants and the Social Order," 4.

2. *Statutes of the Realm,* 14 Elizabeth 1, c. 5.

3. "Register of Passports," 43, 34, 37.

4. Cited in Mendelson and Crawford, *Women in Early Modern England*, 298.

5. *The Diary of Roger Lowe of Ashton-in-Makerfield, Lancashire, 1663-74,* ed. William L. Sachse (New Haven, CT: Yale University Press, 1938), 2.

6. Paul Delany, *British Autobiography in the Seventeenth Century* (London: Routledge & Kegan Paul, 1969), 17. On spiritual autobiographers specifically from the lower orders, see also Margaret Spufford, "First Steps in Literacy: The Reading and Writing Experiences of the Humblest Seventeenth-Century Spiritual Autobiographers," *Social History* 4 (1979): 407–35. On religious autobiographers generally, see Dean Ebner, *Autobiography in Seventeenth-Century England: Theology and Self* (The Hague: Mouton, 1971).

7. Katharine Eisamen Maus, *Inwardness and Theater in the English Renaissance* (Chicago: University of Chicago Press, 1995). For my review of Maus's fine book, see *Shakespeare Studies* 26 (1998): 395.

8. The only other poor seaman's story of the period that I know of is the autobiography of Edward Coxere, covering the period of his life from 1647 to 1685; see *Adventures by Sea of Edward Coxere,* ed. E. H. W. Meyerstein (Oxford: Clarendon Press, 1945). However, Coxere's manuscript properly belongs in the company of spiritual autobiographies, or conversion narratives, since two-thirds of the way through his story (beginning in 1659), Coxere focuses on his conversion to and persecution for Quakerism. His account is also significantly shorter—about one-fifth the length of Barlow's.

9. Smith, "London Apprentices," 157–61; see also his "The Ideal and Reality." For Erikson on the experience of adolescence, see Erik H. Erikson, *Childhood and Society,* 2nd ed. (New York: Norton, 1963), 261–63; and his *Identity, Youth and Crisis* (New York: Norton, 1968), 128–35, 156–57. On the range of apprentice literature as well as its political significance, see Mark Thornton Burnett, "Apprentice Literature and the 'Crisis' of the 1590s," *Yearbook of English Studies* 21 (1991): 27–38; and Burnett's recent book, *Masters and Servants in English Renaissance Drama and Culture: Authority and Obedience* (New York: St. Martin's Press, 1997). Steve Rappaport, in "Reconsidering Apprenticeship," offers a much more reassuring and stable picture of the apprentice's situation than does Smith or Burnett. For criticism of Rappaport's position, see chap. 1, n. 12.

10. Ben-Amos, *Adolescence and Youth,* 206. See also Martin Ingram, *Church Courts, Sex and Marriage in England, 1570–1640* (Cambridge: Cambridge University Press, 1987), 354, 365.

11. Griffiths, *Youth and Authority,* 113–22; quotations are on p. 114.

12. See especially Stephen Greenblatt's *Renaissance Self-Fashioning: From More to Shakespeare* (Chicago: University of Chicago Press, 1980); and his "Invisible Bullets."

13. Agnew, *Worlds Apart,* 52, 99; see also 101–48.

14. Judith Butler, *Gender Trouble: Feminism and Subversion of Identity* (London: Routledge, 1990), 134–41. Thus Butler's objection to "identity politics," that is, the notion of a stable and coherent agent or producer of acts: "My argument is that there need not be a 'doer behind the deed,' but that the 'doer' is variably constructed in and through the deed" (142). Because of his or her continual mobility, the physically unsettled subject, one might say, epitomizes such displaced

doing. I might add that while I see "low" subjectivity as experienced by both genders, I also see it marked as specifically male at various moments in the act of displacement, particularly those moments of temporarily "siting" unsettledness in alehouses (a subject I explore more fully in "Not Home: Alehouses, Ballads, and the Vagrant Husband in Early Modern England," in "Renaissance Materialities," ed. Maureen Quilligan, special issue, *Journal of Medieval and Early Modern Studies* 32 [2002]: 493–518).

15. Hill, *The World Turned Upside Down*, 32–45. Hill cites Brome's play *A Jovial Crew* on p. 39.

16. Beier and Finlay, introduction to *London, 1500–1700,* 21. On vagrancy as "feminine emancipation," see, for instance, Clark and Slack, *Crisis and Order*, 153.

17. Steven Mullaney, *The Place of the Stage: License, Play, and Power in Renaissance England* (Chicago: University of Chicago Press, 1988).

18. Yi-Fu Tuan, *Space and Place: The Perspective of Experience* (Minneapolis: University of Minnesota Press, 1977); Michel de Certeau, *The Practice of Everyday Life,* trans. Steven Rendall (Berkeley and Los Angeles: University of California Press, 1984); Henri Lefebvre, *The Production of Space,* trans. Donald Nicholson-Smith (Oxford: Blackwell, 1991).

19. Gowing, "'The Freedom of the Streets,'" 133.

20. Mendelson and Crawford, *Women in Early Modern England,* 341.

21. Ibid., 209. Gowing notes that women frequently testified in church depositions about witnessing a disruption from the vantage point of their doorsteps. *Domestic Dangers: Women, Words, and Sex in Early Modern London* (Oxford: Clarendon Press, 1996), 236, 239. Lena Cowen Orlin observes the relative absence of women placing themselves at windows in such depositions and attributes such absence to the negative valence associated with women at windows (conventionally linked with female promiscuity). This leads her to question the accuracy of place in the depositions. Did women merely say they were on doorsteps, because such a liminal place was acceptable, when in fact they might have been at a window or even "on the street 'gadding' and gathering"? "Women on the Threshold," *Shakespeare Studies* 25 (1997): 56.

22. Gowing, "'Freedom of the Streets,'" 141–42. Quotation is on p. 142.

23. Andrew McRae, "The Peripatetic Muse: Internal Travel and the Production of Space in Pre-Revolutionary England," in *The Country and the City Revisited: England and the Politics of Culture, 1550–1850,* ed. Gerald MacLean, Donna Landry, and Joseph P. Ward (Cambridge: Cambridge University Press, 1999), 41–57.

24. De Certeau, *The Practice of Everyday Life,* 103.

25. *The Book of John Fisher,* 106.

26. Jean Baudrillard, "Simulacra and Simulations," in *Jean Baudrillard: Selected Writings,* ed. Mark Poster (Stanford, CA: Stanford University Press), 166–84.

27. *All the Works of John Taylor the Water Poet* (first published 1630; London: Scolar Press, 1973), 99.

28. Tuan, *Space and Place,* 3.

29. Francis Barker, *The Tremulous Private Body: Essays on Subjection* (London: Methuen, 1984); Jonathan Dollimore, *Radical Tragedy: Religion, Ideology and Power in the Drama of Shakespeare and His Contemporaries* (Chicago: University of Chicago Press, 1984); Catherine Belsey, *The Subject of Tragedy: Identity and Difference in Renaissance Drama* (London: Methuen, 1985); Greenblatt, *Renaissance Self-Fashioning;* Jonathan Goldberg, *James I and the Politics of Literature: Jonson, Shakespeare, Donne, and Their Contemporaries* (Baltimore: Johns Hopkins University Press, 1983); Fumerton, *Cultural Aesthetics;* Debora Kuller Shuger, *The Renaissance Bible: Scholarship, Sacrifice, and Subjectivity* (Berkeley and Los Angeles: University of California Press, 1994); Maus, *Inwardness and Theater.*

30. Belsey, in *The Subject of Tragedy,* not only seeks to differentiate female fragmented subjectivity from the male projection of a unified self, but also cites some popular antifeminist debate pamphlets (i.e., more-lowly—though at six pence on average, still relatively expensive—literary fare). Nevertheless, she mostly shares the preoccupation of the other critics with drama (and theatricality) and their neglect of "low" street literature (chapbooks, ballads, pamphlets, etc.). Only Shuger, in *The Renaissance Bible,* constructs her subject outside of drama.

31. For Maus's insightful recognition that subjectivity need not be consistent, see *Inwardness and Theater,* 29–30. Following this reasoning, Maus also here makes a distinction between "subjectivity" and "inwardness," which, she argues, are not always commensurate.

32. Rediker, *Between the Devil and the Deep Blue Sea,* 80.

33. Ibid., 290.

Chapter Five

1. Barlow, *Journal,* 20–21. In addition to the 1934 transcription of Barlow's journal by Basil Lubbock, there also exists a loose narrative summary of the journal published by Captain A. G. Course under the title *A Seventeenth-Century Mariner* (London: Frederick Muller, 1965). All citations to the text of Barlow's manuscript (which was not published during his lifetime) will be to Lubbock's complete modern publication—the two volumes of which are continuously paginated—and will hereafter appear in the body of my study. Lubbock, in addition to having transcribed the original manuscript, was also a previous owner of it. In April 1939, he presented the manuscript to the National Maritime Museum in Greenwich, London, where it still resides. Only recently, however (in fall 2000), was it made available to scholars for study—finally allowing me to confirm my argument about Barlow's illustrations by studying them *in toto.* Some twelve pages (including at least two illustrations) are lost from the original manuscript. Of the 279 extant pages of the manuscript (278 pages plus the insert illustration of the Battle of Lowestoft), 147 include watercolor and pencil illustrations (the latter mostly "views" of land). The Lubbock edition prints only eighty of these images, eight of them in color—hence the pressing need to study the original manuscript. I should add that Lubbock counts the illustrations differently than I do. He identifies 182, not 147, illustrations—"127 in color . . . and 55 in pencil" (p. 11). In coming up with this number, Lubbock must have counted multiple representations on a single page as more than one illustration. However, because it is often difficult to decide which illustrations on a page should be considered separate, I count each page of illustrations as a single illustration, even if, as is often the case, the page includes more than one representation—say, a view of a harbor but also an inset view of an island or an elephant. I also count any page with some wash of color, even if the illustration is predominantly in pencil, as a color illustration. Applying this standard, I find that only three out of the 147 pages of illustrations are solely pencil drawings.

Barlow opens his account of his life in 1656, at around age thirteen, with his going "a-liking" (i.e., on a trial basis) as apprentice to a local whitester, or linen bleacher. He liked it not and soon returned home. It was shortly after this trial apprenticeship that he set off on his own for London.

2. *The Life of Adam Martindale,* ed. Richard Parkinson (n.p.: Chetham Society, 1845), 6–7. I am grateful to Mark Thornton Burnett for drawing my attention to this passage and for pointing out how we can hear Jane's voice in Adam's text; he also discusses the first passage in his book, *Masters and Servants,* 127. It should be noted that Jane eventually did quite well for herself (by the period's standards), marrying a "gentleman" (though of little means); however, her fate

was very uncertain for a while. Destitute at one point, she contemplated selling her hair (Martindale, *Life*, 7)—and it is clear that she could as easily have turned out unsettled in the most extreme sense: homeless and living on the streets.

3. As Peter Clark observes, alehouses offered a space of temporary repose not only for itinerants, but also for local journeymen and older single men, including widowers, and thus "filled an important gap in employment and family cycles" (*The English Alehouse*, 136). By the eighteenth century, the alehouse, as a place of "call" for labor, began to operate as a replacement to the guild system (230).

4. Rediker, *Between the Devil and the Deep Blue Sea*, 8.

5. For Barlow's baptism, see *The Registers of the Parish Church of Prestwich; Baptisms, Burials, and Weddings, 1603–1688*, transcribed by Henry Brierley (Cambridge: Cambridge University Press for the Lancashire Parish Register Society, 1909), 34:40. Baptisms usually occurred soon after a birth (within a few days). Until 1752, dates in parish registers were recorded according to the old calendar, by which a new year begins March 25. I have thus here written the date with a slash to indicate the old-style date (before the slash) as well as the new-style date (after the slash). Lubbock, in his edition of Barlow's journal, records all dates in the new style (with a running header at the top of each page indicating the date of that page's journal entry). When quoting from Lubbock's edition, I shall follow his method of modern dating; when quoting from archives of the period, however, I shall indicate dates that occurred between January 1 and March 24 with a slash, as in my chart of Barlow's family tree (app. A).

6. "Notes," appended to the Barlow MS, in the National Maritime Museum, Greenwich, England. JOD/4.

7. Delany, *British Autobiography*, 115. The autobiographer, notes Delany, was particularly concerned with his reputation, especially if he intended to publish during his lifetime. This explains why no secular autobiography published in the seventeenth century admits to any serious misdeed or indiscretion (155).

8. Barlow lived with various masters with whom he tried out apprenticeships, with his uncle in Southwark, and in the two different households of his naval master in London until the completion of his seaman's apprenticeship. For a time after that he lived, between sailings, in Whitechapel, but there his self-placing ends. From archival records, discussed below, we also know that he lived for a time in the Minories and in Bishopsgate, London.

9. See app. A, note a.

10. Hearth Tax Returns, Lancashire, Salford Hundred, 1664, Lancashire County Record Office, E179/250/11 part 6.

11. Overseers Accounts, 1646–83, Parish Record of Prestwich, St. Mary, Manchester Local Studies Unit, Archives, L160/2/1. The status of these allotments is not indicated on the records; they would appear to have been occasional doles.

12. Inventory of George Barlow, of Pilkington in the Parish of Prestwich, February 19, 1686, Infra Wills and Probate (proved in Chester), Lancashire County Record Office, WCW1686.

13. Griffiths, *Youth and Authority*, 39.

14. Delany, *British Autobiography*, 21.

15. Barlow's need to test "friends" is strong. When his ship the *Florentine* is wrecked, he asks the captain of his new ship, the *Marigold*, to lend him money, even though he actually managed to save some of his money from the shipwreck; the captain agrees to the loan (264).

16. Barlow may be referring here to a specific moving event "seven years before"; if so, I cannot determine what that event might have been. Only two other times earlier has he expressed grief: (1) he sheds some tears on saying good-bye to his father twelve years previously—Barlow

dropped by the field where his father was working, since, he says, it was "on the way that I did intend to go" and he wanted to sell his father his share of a fowling gun for six shillings; and (2) he declares "great grief" three years previously on hearing about the death of his brother George, who died from the plague along with numerous other relatives, friends, and acquaintances (112). Another possibility is that Barlow here means that he shed more tears than in the past seven years combined; but, then, why seven years remains a mystery.

17. Lubbock, the editor of Barlow's journal, occasionally renders words in Barlow's own spelling (as here) in order to convey some sense of the original writing.

18. The *International Genealogical Index* (Salt Lake City: Genealogical Department of the Church of Jesus Christ of Latter-Day Saints, 1991) gives their baptism dates as follows: Hester, November 20, 1679; Mary, November 16, 1682; Edward, March 23, 1685 (Barlow's text makes it clear that his son was in fact born the year before, according to the old-style calendar); Ann, June 21, 1688; and Martha, July 8, 1691. *IGI*, Middlesex, sheet A1220, pp. 8250, 8258, 8273; sheet A1221, pp. 8287, 8288. The baptisms are confirmed by the registers of the parish of St. Botolph, Bishopsgate, and the parish of Holy Trinity, Minories, Guildhall Library, London, MS4516/1 and MS9238; and by the register of the parish of St. Mary, Whitechapel, London Metropolitan Archives, P93/MRY1. The dates of the children's deaths (at least those that we know) are recorded by Barlow in his journal (310–11, 367, 385, 454).

19. Will of Edward Barlow, Commander of the *Liampo*, 1708 (the date the will was proved), Wills and Probates, Prerogative Court of Canterbury, National Archives, London, PROB11/500. See appendix D.

20. See *Adventures by Sea of Edward Coxere*. It is a sign of Coxere's inclination to maintain some connectivity, even in his many sea wanderings, that his sea journal becomes a spiritual autobiography and he converts to the tight community of Quakerism. See also chap. 4, n. 8.

21. Richard Helgerson, "'I Miles Philips': An Elizabethan Seaman Conscripted by History," *PMLA* 118 (2003): 573–80.

Chapter Six

1. C. G. Cruickshank, *Elizabeth's Army*, 2nd ed. (Oxford: Clarendon Press, 1966), 26, 29; on searching fairs, see p. 27.

2. Christopher Lloyd, *The British Seaman, 1200–1860: A Social Survey* (London: Collins, 1968), 59–60; quotation is on p. 61. On the Dutch Wars, see pp. 76–100. On the navy's growth, see pp. 31, 80. Sir William Petty put the estimated number of seamen at 48,000 in the 1670s, and Gregory King put it at 50,000 in 1688. That represented about 1 percent of the country's population. Ralph Davis, "Merchant Shipping in the Economy of the Late Seventeenth Century," *Economic History Review*, 2nd ser., 9 (1956): 71.

3. J. D. Davies, *Gentlemen and Tarpaulins: The Officers and Men of the Restoration Navy* (Oxford: Clarendon Press, 1991), 67.

4. Lloyd, *The British Seaman*, 122–23. On the problem of desertion, see pp. 70–71, and on the institution of peddling necessities to the crew, see pp. 63–64. The first maritime regiment was not formed until 1664; by 1702, there were six regiments amounting to 40,000 men. "Though such regiments were disbanded after every war," Lloyd notes, "there is a fairly continuous record of service on the part of the Marines from this date" (82); nevertheless, the government still had to resort to vigorous impressment fully to man its ships.

5. William Shakespeare, *2 Henry IV*, in *The Riverside Shakespeare*, ed. G. Blakemore Evans (Boston: Houghton Mifflin Co., 1974), 3.2.112–13, 150.

6. Lloyd, *The British Seaman*, 39, 61, 61–62, 85.

7. Bernard Capp, *Cromwell's Navy: The Fleet and the English Revolution, 1648–1660* (Oxford: Clarendon Press, 1989), 266.

8. Davies, *Gentlemen and Tarpaulins*, 74–75.

9. Captain Woodes Rogers, *A Cruising Voyage round the World* (London, 1712), 3. Subsequent references to Rogers's voyage are given in the text.

10. Captain George Shelvocke, *A Voyage round the World by the Way of the Great South Sea* (London, 1726), 4.

11. Beier, *Masterless Men*, 93, 95.

12. Lloyd, *The British Seaman*, 96–97.

13. Quoted in Davies, *Gentlemen and Tarpaulins*, 78.

14. Ibid. On unpaid seamen literally starving in the streets in 1665, see p. 137. The problem of delayed payment extended through the seventeenth century.

15. Lloyd, *The British Seaman*, 55; see also 39, 56.

16. Ralph Davis, *The Rise of the English Shipping Industry in the Seventeenth and Eighteenth Centuries* (London: Macmillan, 1962), 116; quoted in Rediker, *Between the Devil and the Deep Blue Sea*, 82–83.

17. Davis, "Merchant Shipping," 71, including n. 7.

18. D. C. Coleman, "Naval Dockyards under the Later Stuarts," *Economic History Review*, 2nd ser., 6 (1953): 135–38.

19. Ibid., 142.

20. Ibid., 144.

21. Ibid., 145.

22. Quoted in Lloyd, *The British Seaman*, 93.

23. Peter Kemp, *The British Sailor: A Social History of the Lower Deck* (London: J. M. Dent, 1970), 63.

24. Michael J. Power, "The East London Working Community in the Seventeenth Century," in *Work in Towns, 850–1850*, ed. Penelope J. Corfield and Derek Keene (Leicester: Leicester University Press, 1990), 109.

25. Rediker, *Between the Devil and the Deep Blue Sea*, 158–59.

26. Capp, *Cromwell's Navy*, 252.

27. Valerie Burton, "The Myth of Bachelor Jack: Masculinity, Patriarchy and Seafaring Labour," in *Jack Tar in History: Essays in the History of Maritime Life and Labour*, ed. Colin Howell and Richard J. Twomey (Fredericton, New Brunswick: Acadiensis Press, 1991), 177–98.

28. Linebaugh and Rediker, *The Many-Headed Hydra*; Rediker, *Between the Devil and the Deep Blue Sea*; David Armitage and Michael J. Braddick, eds., *The British Atlantic World, 1500–1800* (Houndsmills, Hampshire: Palgrave Macmillan, 2002), 14–15.

29. Rediker, *Between the Devil and the Deep Blue Sea*, especially 1–152.

30. Ibid., 82–83. On the "fractured" and "diverse" nature of the seaman's community, see especially p. 155.

31. On the seaman's "simple" patriotism, see Davies, *Gentlemen and Tarpaulins*, 85; on the percentage of foreigners legally allowed on English ships, see Lloyd, *The British Seaman*, 53 (and on impressing foreigners, see p. 84); on the seaman's alienation and the landman's suspicion of him, see Rediker, *Between the Devil and the Deep Blue Sea*, 161, 200, 203.

32. Rediker, *Between the Devil and the Deep Blue Sea*, 199–200.

33. Ibid., 207.

34. Linebaugh and Rediker, *The Many-Headed Hydra*, 150.

35. Rediker, *Between the Devil and the Deep Blue Sea*, 245−49.

36. Ibid., 243−53; Linebaugh and Rediker, *The Many-Headed Hydra*, especially chaps. 5−7.

37. Linebaugh and Rediker, *The Many-Headed Hydra*, 116.

38. Rediker, *Between the Devil and the Deep Blue Sea*, 16 (including the quotation from Petty's *Political Arithmetic*). See also Linebaugh and Rediker, *The Many-Headed Hydra*, 146−47.

39. *Statutes of the Realm*, 1 Edward 6, c. 3; 1 James 1, c. 7. See also the 1743/44 vagrancy act, which specified that after being punished, "any male vagrant over the age of 12 years could be sent for service in His Majesty's army or navy." Robert Humphreys, *No Fixed Abode: A History of Responses to the Roofless and the Rootless in Britain* (New York: St. Martin's Press, 1999), 72.

40. Cited in Lloyd, *The British Seaman*, 58.

41. Rediker, *Between the Devil and the Deep Blue Sea*, 50, 47.

42. Ibid., 231.

43. Linebaugh and Rediker, *The Many-Headed Hydra*, 157; see also Lloyd, *The British Seaman*, 150−72.

44. Linebaugh and Rediker, *The Many-Headed Hydra*, 211; see also 211−14.

45. Capp, *Cromwell's Navy*, 282−84. On higher merchant pay in wartime, see also Davies, *Gentlemen and Tarpaulins*, 84.

46. Rediker, *Between the Devil and the Deep Blue Sea*, 101.

47. Linebaugh and Rediker, *The Many-Headed Hydra*, 58.

48. Land Tax Assessment, 1693/94, St. Mary's, Whitechapel, Corporation of London Record Office. Other records were searched in the places where the family resided and for the times they might have resided there; but they revealed no further reference to Edward Barlow or his family. Searched records included Seventeen Months Tax, 1678 (St. Botolph, Bishopsgate); Poll Tax, 1678 (St. Botolph, Bishopsgate); Eighteen Months Tax, 1679/80 (Bishopsgate Ward Without); Six Months Tax, 1680 (Bishopsgate Ward Within); Six Months Assessment, 1680 (Bishopsgate Ward Without); Names of Householders and Lodgers, 1683 (Bishopsgate Ward Without); Inhabitants, Lodgers and Apprentices Absent from Abode, 12/7/1685 (St. Botolph, Bishopsgate); Inhabitants, Lodgers and Apprentices Absent from Abode, 13/7/1685 (Portsoken Ward); Arrears, Ship Money, 1688 (Portsoken Ward); Poll Tax, 1689 (Portsoken Ward Assessment); and Rent Paid to Landlords by the Year, 1693 (Portsoken Ward).

49. M. J. Power, "East London Housing in the Seventeenth Century," in Clark and Slack, *Crisis and Order*, 258.

50. Correspondence with Jayne Stevenson, Red Rose Research.

51. Will of Mary Barlow, 1715, Wills and Probate, Commissary Court of London, Guildhall Library, 9171/57. Mary leaves the tankard to her son Edward and remits a debt of 250 pounds that is owed to her by him. The residue of her estate she leaves to her daughter and son-in-law, James and Ann Sussex. Given the large amount of the debt Edward owed his mother, Mary may have sold off some of the other silver items to fund Edward's needs.

52. Lloyd, *The British Seaman*, 88−90.

53. For more on the problem of advancement for common tars during the seventeenth century and the favoring of gentlemen officers, see Davies, *Gentlemen and Tarpaulins*. Davies concludes that the gentleman-tarpaulin divide has been exaggerated and certainly became more blurred in the early 1660s. It was most problematic during peacetime, when demand for prestigious officer posts exceeded need (233).

54. Barlow also briefly captains the *Guannaboe* from Barbados to Jamaica in 1679 when the master of the ship falls ill (320−21).

55. Rowan Hackman documents that the *Liampo* was purchased on July 27, 1705, by Captain Edward Barlow "for her last voyage." *Ships of the East India Company* (Gravesend, Kent: World Ship Society, 2001), 33. Anthony Farrington notes that the vessel left Portsmouth on January 7, 1706, for Mokha (Mocha) and was "lost off Mozambique." *Catalogue of East India Company Ships' Journals and Logs, 1600–1834* (London: British Library, 1999), 382. The English East India Company Ships Web site gives the date of wreckage as 1705. http://www.eicships.info/eic/lost/lost_l.htm (accessed November 21, 2003). Given the date of departure, however, 1706 (new-style calendar) would appear to be the correct wreckage date. I am grateful to Andrea Cordani, webmaster of the East India Company Ships Web site, for help in locating this information and for confirming, in correspondence with me, the 1706 date for the wreck of the *Liampo*.

56. The other most notable and very disappointing instance of thwarted ambition occurs around the same time as this event, while Barlow is holding out for the position of commander: Barlow pays one hundred pounds for the command of the *Maderas,* which he believed he had got, only to find out later that the ship had been taken up into the East India service and that he was outbid for the position of commander by a less experienced man who had influential backing and who offered twice the amount (506–7).

57. Davies, *Gentlemen and Tarpaulins,* 104–16.

58. See especially the rogue pamphlets of Robert Greene and Thomas Dekker.

Chapter Seven

1. See chap. 5, n. 1, on the character and number of Barlow's illustrations. As I mention in that note, "counting" the illustrations (and even deciding whether to describe individual illustrations as watercolor or pencil pictures) is not an exact science. Sometimes Barlow illustrates one locale over two pages of the manuscript, as in the case of Messina (MS 58v and 59r); only the left, harbor side of the representation is reproduced here, in fig. 13. Sometimes Barlow illustrates two or more different locales on a single page, as in the case of his sketching the two harbors of Ponani and Tannanore, both on the Malabar Coast, on MS 73r. Sometimes, as in this last instance, it is difficult to classify a sketch as "harbor" or "silhouette of land mass"; Ponani and Tannanore are really both. The same multiple representation occurs in the case of strange creatures and even sometimes emblems of ships.

In counting the number of illustrations in the book, then, I have chosen the most inclusive definition: number of pages illustrated. In determining the number of illustrations of harbors, I have done the same: I count the number of pages on which harbors are illustrated, whether singly, multiply, or as a continuation of a previous scene/page.

2. Richard Helgerson, "The Land Speaks," in *Forms of Nationhood: The Elizabethan Writing of England* (Chicago: University of Chicago Press, 1992), 105–47. See also his study of the representation of maps in Dutch domestic painting, in his more recent *Adulterous Alliances: Home, State, and History in Early Modern European Drama and Painting* (Chicago: University of Chicago Press, 2000), 79–119. Helgerson also offers an excellent overview of cartographic studies in the references listed in his introduction to "Literature and Geography," ed. Richard Helgerson and Joanne Woolway Grenfell, special issue no. 3, *Early Modern Literary Studies* 4 (1998), http://www.shu.ac.uk/emls/04-2/04-2toc.html.

3. Edward Lynam, *The Mapmaker's Art: Essays on the History of Maps* (London: Batchworth Press, 1953), 57.

4. Christopher Saxton made the first atlas of England and Wales [1580], and John Norden produced the first English County Handbooks, in *Speculum Britanniae* (1593–98). Much of

Saxton's and Norden's topographical material was adopted by John Speed for his *Theatre of the Empire of Great Britaine* (1612), which became the most famous atlas of the time. John Ogilby's *Britannia* (1675) was the first English road atlas. See Lynam, *The Mapmaker's Art*, 61–75, 79–90, 97–98; on Ogilby, see p. 20. On such chorographic efforts in England, see especially Helgerson, "The Land Speaks"; for estate surveys and the problematic line between estate and road in particular, see Sullivan, *The Drama of Landscape*, 31–193.

5. J. B. Hewson, *A History of the Practice of Navigation* (Glasgow: Brown, Son & Ferguson, 1951), 40.

6. D. W. Waters posits that Drake himself probably saw to it that the principal landfalls on his voyage were recorded by a painter, such as he had carried with him on his voyage around the world in 1577–80. "The Art of Navigation in the Age of Drake," appendix to *The Last Voyage of Drake & Hawkins*, ed. Kenneth R. Andrews (Cambridge: Cambridge University Press, 1972), 263. Andrews reproduces six of the artist's drawings in the plates immediately preceding Waters's essay. On the Earl of Sandwich's sketches, see *The Journal of Edward Mountagu, First Earl of Sandwich, Admiral and General at Sea, 1659–1665*, ed. R. C. Anderson, Publications of the Navy Records Society, vol. 64 (London: Navy Records Society, 1929), ix; see also the reproduction of Sandwich's sketch of the naval action at the Bay of North Bergen in 1665, facing p. 262. The Dampier illustrations can be found in William Dampier, *A Collection of Voyages* (London, 1729), vol. 1, facing p. 384.

7. J. H. Parry, *The Age of Reconnaissance: Discovery, Exploration and Settlement, 1450 to 1650* (London, 1963; repr., Berkeley and Los Angeles: University of California Press, 1981), 85.

8. The first comprehensive collection of *portolani*, the *Compasso da Navigare* (late thirteenth century), included directions for open-sea crossings of seven or eight hundred miles in length (ibid.).

9. D. W. Waters, *The Art of Navigation in England in Elizabethan and Early Stuart Times* (New Haven, CT: Yale University Press, 1958), 11–14; quotation is on p. 14. See also Waters, *The Rutters of the Sea: The Sailing Directions of Pierre Garcie; A Study of the English and French Printed Sailing Directions; With Facsimile Reproductions* (New Haven, CT: Yale University Press, 1967).

10. Robert Norman's *The Safegard of Sailers* (London, 1587) was translated from Cornelis Antoniszoon, *Het Leeskaartbock van Wisbuy* (1581). Norman's work was revised and republished by Edward Wright in 1605 and by John Tapp in 1612. Waters, *The Art of Navigation in England*, 321.

11. Waters, "The Art of Navigation in the Age of Drake," 263–65.

12. Lucas Janszoon Waghenaer, *The Mariners Mirrour*, trans. Sir Anthony Ashley (London, 1588).

13. See Waters, *The Art of Navigation in England*, 168–75. The key to markers in the *Mirrour* is given on p. 1 of the first atlas.

14. For the publication history of these works, see R. A. Skelton's introduction to the facsimile edition of Willem Janszoon (William Johnson) Blaeu, *The Light of Navigation* (Amsterdam: N. Israel, 1964), v–ix. Ashley's 1588 translation of Waghenaer's *Mariners Mirrour* was brought out again in 1605, but in this edition the plates only were in English (the text was in Dutch); Waters, *The Art of Navigation in England*, 321. Blaeu's *The Sea-Mirrour* was translated by Richard Hynmers (London, 1625).

In addition to my study of the original texts of Blaeu, the information on his works given in this chapter is indebted to Skelton's introduction, as well as to Waters, *The Art of Navigation in England*, 322–28, 457–62; and Hewson, *History of the Practice of Navigation*, 20–24.

15. Blaeu, "To the Reader," in *The Light of Navigation;* Waters, *The Art of Navigation in England*, 323–24.

16. For entering Falmouth harbor from the east side of the rock, Blaeu advises: "Within in the haven [of Falmouth] standeth on the land a white chalky spot, also a little wood of trees. Keep them over the north point of the fore said high west land [on which the castle stands], and sail so right in with them, keeping them so until you come near them" (*The Sea-Mirrour,* 48–49).

17. On Blaeu's cartouches in *The Sea-Mirrour,* see Waters, *The Art of Navigation in England,* 460. Blaeu's cartouches are much more florid in *The Light of Navigation* than in his later *Sea-Mirrour,* which reflects a gradual movement toward restrained ornamentality.

18. Skelton, introduction to *The Light of Navigation,* vii. Blaeu added a latitude scale in charts of the western seas in *The Light of Navigation* and in his more general maps in *The Sea-Mirrour.*

19. Greenvile Collins, *Great Britain's Coasting-Pilot* (London, 1693).

20. Edward Lynam, *British Maps and Map-Makers* (London: William Collins, 1947), 36.

21. Collins also includes a separate two-page set of views at the end of the first part of his book showing twenty-nine different coastal elevations, seen as one travels along the southern coast of England from South Foreland to Milford Haven. Another set of coastal views stands alone on the last page of his book.

22. Collins, *Great Britain's Coasting-Pilot,* 1.

23. Waters, *The Art of Navigation in England,* 322; Skelton, introduction to *The Light of Navigation,* x.

24. Hewson, *History of the Practice of Navigation,* 24–28. Hack's drawings are based on a Spanish *derrotero,* or route book, captured by Captain Bartholomew Sharp. For Hack's drawings, see also *A Buccaneer's Atlas: Basil Ringrose's South Sea Waggoner,* ed. Derek Howse and Norman J. W. Thrower (Berkeley and Los Angeles: University of California Press, 1992). I am grateful to Roy Ritchie at the Huntington Library for directing me to the Hack drawings. On the use of Portuguese and Spanish pilots, see Waters, *The Art of Navigation in England,* 81–82.

25. De Certeau, *The Practice of Everyday Life,* 121. Not only did the representation of ships reflect the charting eye/I, but also, as Waters observes of Ashley's edition, such drawings could provide useful information about the type of vessel met with off various stretches of seacoast and could thus facilitate position finding (*The Art of Navigation in England,* 174–75).

26. Hack's use of pictorial watercolors and hatching, however, belongs to an earlier age of decorative manuscripts (as do Collins's cartouches).

27. Waghenaer, *The Mariners Mirrour,* A2r.

28. Ashley, "Dedication to Christopher Hatton," ibid.

29. Blaeu, *The Light of Navigation,* E3v. See also his other urgings in this section of his work that the young seaman or pilot make sketches: "When you sail out of any river or haven, you must reckon every course along the reach from town to town, or from beacon to beacon, which you must keep well and perfectly and write it in a book, and some times draw the situation in manner of a card [chart] . . . and counterfeit with a pen upon several strokes of the compass, as they change their form of standing by sailing along by them . . . then take the counterfeit or form thereof with a pen, to know in what manner they shew themselves upon such strokes of the compass . . . and when you see any marks or towers, you must note them with a pen" (E3v).

30. Norman J. W. Thrower, *Maps & Civilization: Cartography in Culture and Society* (Chicago: University of Chicago Press, 1996), 64.

31. John Smith, *The Generall Historie of Virginia, New-England, and the Summer Isles* (London, 1624); cited in Waters, *The Art of Navigation in England,* 259–60.

32. See also Barlow's list of the duties of a mate, which include ordering "what course should be steered" (though, he says, that should come mostly from the master) and keeping "an account

of the courses and ship's runs, and shifting of winds, and trimming of sails according as the wind veers to and fro" (327–28).

33. Blaeu, *The Sea-Mirrour,* A3r. John Seller makes a similar distinction in his *Practical Navigation,* 5th ed. (1669; London, 1683) and privileges oceanic navigation as the true "art of navigation" (B1r–v).

34. Not all of Collins's maps are bare of ships, but the number of ships has significantly decreased in comparison to earlier charts, such as those by Waghenaer.

35. See Hewson, *History of the Practice of Navigation,* 41–42.

36. *Journal of Edward Mountagu,* for example, 134–36. In these cases of discrepant readings, the earl usually preferred his own.

37. Edward Wright, trans., *The Haven-Finding Art* (London, 1599), B3v. Translated from the Dutch *De Havenvending,* by Simon Stevin.

38. Blaeu, "To the Reader," in *The Light of Navigation.* Blaeu somewhat revised his position in *The Sea-Mirrour,* where he includes a section titled "Of the Variation of the Compasse" (44–46).

39. Lloyd, *The British Seaman,* 82, 274–75. The men lined up on board the *Augustine* may in fact be soldiers being transported by this naval vessel. During the Civil War, "red breeches seem to have become the sign of a soldier," and the New Model army "adopted a red coat for the uniform of its regiments." Cecil C. P. Lawson, *A History of the Uniforms of the British Army: From the Beginnings to 1760,* vol. 1 (London: Peter Davies, 1940), 9, 11. But military uniform was not regularized until the reign of Charles II, and even then red coats for regiments were not universal (12, 16). Lawson notes that the first marine regiment, raised in 1664, was "dressed in yellow coats faced red, red breeches and stockings and hats bound with gold colored lace"; in 1685 "the uniform was changed to red coats lined yellow, dark grey breeches and white stockings" (54). The uniforms of marine regiments underwent other color transformations until 1710, when the regiments were disbanded (55–56). Though their cut and color varied, the "slops," or clothes sold by the purser aboard ship to the common seamen, could sometimes be red as well, though blue was also a favored color (Lloyd, *The British Seaman,* 235).

Chapter Eight

1. On Pepys's advancement to the position of secretary to Montagu and his activities surrounding the preparations for and voyage of the *Naseby* to retrieve Charles, see Claire Tomalin, *Samuel Pepys: The Unequaled Self* (New York: Penguin-Viking, 2002), 101–109. Pepys was related to Montagu via Montagu's mother, Paulina, née Pepys, who was sister to Talbot Pepys and great-aunt to Samuel Pepys (family tree, pp. vi–vii).

2. Martin Parker, "A Description of a Strange (and Miraculous) Fish" [1630s], in Hyder E. Rollins, ed., *A Pepysian Garland: Black-Letter Broadside Ballads of the Years 1595–1639* (Cambridge: Cambridge University Press, 1922), 438–42; "Prides Fall; or, A Warning for All English Women. By the Example of a Strange Monster, Born Late in Germany, by a Merchants Proud Wife at Geneva" [1650], in *The Pepys Ballads,* ed. W. G. Day, facsimile edition, 5 vols., from *Catalogue of the Pepys Library at Magdalene College, Cambridge* (Wolfeboro, NH: D. S. Brewer, 1987), 2:66–67. For an interesting discussion of Parker's ballad, see Mark W. Booth, "Broadside: 'Description of a Strange Fish,'" in *The Experience of Songs* (New Haven, CT: Yale University Press, ca. 1981), 97–113.

3. "The *Benjamin*'s Lamentation for Their Sad Loss at Sea, by Storms and Tempests," *Pepys,* 4:200. The ballad is dated in the printed Roxburghe collection as probably 1670–83/84. *The Roxburghe Ballads,* 9 vols. in 8, ed. W. Chappell (vols. 1–3) and J. Woodfall Ebsworth (vols. 4–9) (Hertford: Stephen Austin & Sons, 1869–1901; repr., New York: AMS Press, 1966), 7:529–31.

4. Harold Francis Watson, *The Sailor in English Fiction and Drama, 1550–1800* (New York: Columbia University Press, 1931). Passing references to sea chanteys are made on p. 62 and again on pp. 65–66.

5. Natascha Wurzbach, *The Rise of the English Street Ballad, 1550–1650*, trans. Gayna Walls (Cambridge: Cambridge University Press, 1990), 26.

6. Tessa Watt, *Cheap Print and Popular Piety, 1550–1640* (Cambridge: Cambridge University Press, 1991), 5.

7. See the appendix in Wurzbach, *Rise of the English Street Ballad,* 253–84.

8. Garrett A. Sullivan Jr. and Linda Woodbridge, "Popular Culture in Print," in *The Cambridge Companion to English Literature, 1500–1600,* ed. Arthur F. Kinney (Cambridge: Cambridge University Press, 2000), 271–72; Leslie Shephard is quoted on p. 271. See also Shephard's *The Broadside Ballad* (London: Herbert Jenkins, 1962).

9. Rollins, "The Black-Letter Broadside Ballad," 296, 304.

10. My study is based primarily on the many extant naval ballads in the Pepys and Roxburghe collections. The five-volume Pepys collection, which resides at Magdalene College, Cambridge, was published in 1987 in a wonderfully complete, five-volume facsimile edition (cited in n. 2 above). The four-volume Roxburghe collection, which is held at the British Library, London, has been published more haphazardly in an eight-volume edition, cited in n. 3 above (the early volumes of the edition begin by following the order of the ballads in the original collection but later volumes move to thematic gatherings of the ballads, so that it is hard to track the originals; the edition also modernizes the verse and reproduces only some of the woodcuts). For the reader's ease of access, these two printed editions will be my primary sources for quoting the ballads. Also consulted were the sea ballads in the Bagford and Euing collections: *The Bagford Ballads: Illustrating the Last Years of the Stuarts,* ed. Joseph Woodfall Ebsworth, 2 vols. (Hertford: Ballad Society, 1878); and *The Euing Collection of English Broadside Ballads in the Library of the University of Glasgow,* introduction by John Holloway (Glasgow: University of Glasgow Publications, 1971). I am assuming that these collections, taken together, are representative of the time, though I recognize that the preferences and eccentricities of the individual collector could have influenced what has been preserved. Pepys, for instance, was most likely an avid collector of naval ballads because he was secretary of the admiralty under Charles II and James II.

11. Wurzbach, *Rise of the English Street Ballad,* 56–57, 236–41. The godly ballad, of course, continued to be disseminated, though it suffered a decline in the course of the seventeenth century (Watt, *Cheap Print and Popular Piety,* 39–73).

12. "The Seamans Sorrowful Bride," *Pepys,* 4:193. Another edition of this ballad (with slightly different woodcuts) appears in the Pepys original in vol. 3, on the verso of p. 58; published in the *Pepys* facsimile in vol. 5, app. 2, p. 42.

13. To make such a claim is not to deny that this harbor scene—like most ballad woodcuts— was probably used again and again to illustrate other ballads, some of them probably not even about love. Such is the nature of cheap ballad production. The blank scroll at the top right of this worn and cracked woodcut indicates that the image served several uses; the printer was to fill in the scroll with the appropriate designator of place for the harbor scene, which he here forgot to do (or thought unnecessary). Despite the practice of reusing such woodcut images, however, the printer could choose from his box of woodcuts carefully, and in the case of the woodcut under discussion here, he chose a most appropriate image to supplement the song.

14. "The Seamans Return to His Sweetheart; or, The Constant Lovers Happy Agreement," *Pepys,* 4:175.

15. "A Dainty New Ditty of a Saylor and His Love, / How One the Others Constancy Did Prove," ibid., 157.

16. The more propagandistic pressing songs translate such enforced partings into acts of free will—for example, "Like noble hearts of gold, / now freely enter / Your names on board the fleet, / all friends forsaking." "The Boatswains Call; or, The Couragious Marriners Invitation to All His Brother Sailers, to Forsake Friends and Relations, for to Fight in the Defence of Their King and Country," *Pepys*, 4:206.

17. "The Unfeigned Lover; or, The Loyal Seamans Kind Farewell to His Beloved Nancy," *Pepys*, 4:169.

18. "The Faithful Lover's Farewell; or, Private Newes from Chatham," London, [ca. 1673], *Roxburghe*, 7:544–45.

19. "The Sea-Mans Leave Taken of His Sweetest Margery," [ca. 1685–88], *Euing*, no. 326, pp. 538–39.

20. "A Dainty New Ditty of a Saylor and His Love, / How One the Others Constancy Did Prove," *Pepys*, 4:157.

21. "The Mothers Kindness, Conquer'd by Her Daughters Vindication of Valiant and Renowned Seamen; Concluding with the Mothers Kind Acknowledgement," *Pepys*, 4:212; "The Cruel Lover; or, The False-Hearted Saylor," ibid., 5:372.

22. "The Mariner's Delight; or, The Seaman's Seven Wives," *Roxburghe*, 7:490.

23. Another example is "The Seamans Deceit; or, The Wanton Wench of Wapping," *Pepys*, 4:220.

24. "Jack Robinson," in Thomas Hudson, *Comic Songs* (London: Gold & Walton, 1818–27), 32–34. A more serious version of such forsaking is "The Young Seaman's Misfortune; or, The False-Hearted Lass of Lymus," *Pepys*, 4:224. In the latter ballad, what newly compels the seaman to leave is despair: "Now must I wander in despair."

25. Alexandra Halasz, *The Marketplace of Print: Pamphlets and the Public Sphere in Early Modern England* (Cambridge: Cambridge University Press, 1997), 49. In a kind of deconstructive version of Watt's "shared values," Halasz sees popular print, including ballads, as breaking down cultural distinctions. Speaking of Anthony Now-Now's complaint against ballad mongers in Henrie Chettle's *Kind-Heartes Dreame* (1592), Halasz observes that "ballads and ballad singers come to function as tropes precisely because the ballad singer breaks down temporal and vocational distinctions—between oral and written, performance and text, author, printer, publisher, and seller. The ambiguities of the trade can be stabilized and abjected in the figure of the ballad singer" (56). I am more interested in how ballads destabilize the actual personae or subject positions of the singer and audience (who often sing along).

26. The first two ballads appeared as the first and second parts of a single story in a contemporary collection titled *Neptune's Fair Garland* (London: J. M. [John Millet] for J[onah] Deacon, 1686). The first part is "A New Song of Nelly's Sorrow at the Parting with Her Well-Beloved Henry, That Was Just Ready to Set Sail to Sea," and the second part is "A New Song of Henry Setting Forth to Sea; With an Account of Their Unhappy Voyage, Wherein Their Ship Was Cast Away, and Most of Their Men Drowned; But Henry Escaping with Some Few More, through Many Difficulties Is Returned to Fair Nelly His Love, Where Their Joys Was at Length Compleated." The third ballad, which can also be found in *Pepys*, 5:217, is titled "An Excellent New Song, Call'd Nelly's Constancy; or, Her Unkind Lover. Who, after Contract of Marriage, Leaves His First Mistress, for the Sake of a Better Fortune" (London: Charles Barnet, ca. 1686). The fourth ballad, from the Earl of Jersey's Osterley Park Collection, 3:42, is titled "The Seaman's

Answer to His Unkind Lover" (London: T. Staples, ca. 1686). The fifth ballad, which can be found in *Roxburghe*, 3:441; *Pepys*, 5:361; and the Jersey collection, 3:67, is titled "The Faithful Marriner; or, A Copy of Verses, Writ by a Seaman on Board the *Britannia*, in the Streights, and Directed to Fair Isabel His Loyal Love, in the City of London" (London: J. Blare, probably 1692–93). All appear in the appendix to *Roxburghe*, 6:789–94.

27. "A New Song of Nelly's Sorrow at the Parting with Her Well-Beloved Henry," *Roxburghe*, 6:789.

28. "A New Song of Henry Setting Forth to Sea," *Roxburghe*, 6:790.

29. *Roxburghe*, 6:790, note.

30. "An Excellent New Song, Call'd Nelly's Constancy," *Roxburghe*, 6:791–92.

31. Ibid., 792. I here read the last two lines as meaning, "it shall never be said, boys, when we are dead, that jolly seamen rarely breed." Other possible meanings are "it shall never be said, boys, when we are dead, that jolly seamen are rarely born" or "it shall never be said, boys, when we are dead, that jolly seamen are of a rare [uncommon] breed." However, my preferred reading—that this is a call for the jolly seamen to come ashore and breed in their own likeness—fits with the song's depiction of seamen as inconstant; and, of course, seamen were legendary for having one-night stands while on leave ashore. Whichever meaning we prefer, the last word of the song undeniably leaves us with thoughts of breeding.

32. "The Seaman's Answer to His Unkind Lover," *Roxburghe*, 6:792.

33. Ibid.

34. Ibid.

35. "The Faithful Marriner," *Roxburghe*, 6:793.

36. Other ballads play with this idea of exchangeability between the different seamen by having the seaman return to his love in disguise with news that her seaman lover has died and, in dying, told him to wed her in his place. Only after she refuses does the lover reveal himself to be in fact alive and the man standing before her. See "A Pleasant New Song between a Seaman and His Love: Shewing Though, at First, in Misery His Time He Spent, / He Met His Love at Last, with Joy and Sweet Content," *Roxburghe*, 3:127–31.

37. The captain, for instance, speaks in "The Seaman's Adieu to His Dear" (ca. 1665), *Roxburghe*, 7:524–26. The ship is the narrator of "An Excellent New Song, Entituled, A Hot Engagement between a French Privateer, and an English Fire-Ship" (1691), *Pepys*, 5:386. That a ship could be perceived as human (an idea still alive today in the traditional designation of a ship as "she") reminds us that Barlow, in his paintings of individual ships, rendered the seamen aboard as if they were part of the ship's identity (not vice versa).

38. "A Jobb for a Journeyman-Shoomaker, with a Kind-Hearted Seamans Wife, His Landlady," *Pepys*, 4:180.

39. "Neptunes Raging Fury; or, The Gallant Seamans Sufferings," *Pepys*, 4:201; also in *Roxburghe*, 2:543, 6:432; *Bagford*, 2:81; and *Euing*, no. 239, pp. 390–91.

40. "The Seaman's Compass; or, A Dainty New Ditty Composed and Pend / The Deeds of Brave Seamen to Praise and Commend," *Bagford*, 1:269. See also *Euing*, no. 325, pp. 536–37; and *Pepys*, 4:191. (I cite the Bagford ballad because it is more legible than the Pepys.)

41. "The Seaman's Compass," *Bagford*, 1:267–71.

42. "The Fair Maids Choice; or, The Seamans Renown," *Bagford*, 1:289–91.

43. *The Midship-Man's Garland* (London, [1692–1703]), in *Bagford*, 1:109–20.

44. Sean Shesgreen, "The First London Cries," *Print Quarterly* 10 (1993): 367–68. I am indebted to Professor Shesgreen for calling my attention to the Cries and specifically to *The Town*

Crier (which he discusses in the article just cited). Much of what I say here is consonant with Shesgreen's argument, though I lay more stress on the estrangement or alienation imaged in the broadsheet (and less on its figuring a utopian and theatrical dignity). See also Shesgreen, *The Criers and Hawkers of London: Engravings and Drawings by Marcellus Laroon* (Stanford, CA: Stanford University Press, 1990), as well as his recent *Images of the Outcast: The Urban Poor in the Cries of London* (New Brunswick, NJ: Rutgers University Press, 2002).

45. Shesgreen, *Images of the Outcast,* 7–12.

46. Shesgreen, "The First London Cries," 371–72.

47. "Turners Dish of Lentten Stuffe; or, A Galymaufery," London, [1612], in *Pepys,* 1:206–7. The woodcut accompanying this ballad shows humans interacting with rabbits at cards, a rabbit with sword and buckler in the foreground, and a gallows in the background—clearly references to the rogue pamphlets about cheating citizens, called cony-catching pamphlets, that were so popular at the end of the sixteenth and beginning of the seventeenth centuries (and largely precipitated by Harman's *Caveat*).

48. Griffiths, *Youth and Authority,* 206.

49. Shesgreen, "The First London Cries," 364.

Epilogue

1. Bill Clinton, "Remarks Concluding the First Roundtable Discussion of the Forest Conference in Portland," April 2, 1993, in *Weekly Compilation of Presidential Documents,* from the 1993 Presidential Documents Online via GPO Access, http://frwebgate1.access.gpo.gov/ cgi-bin/waisgate.cgi?WAISdocID=9613717391+30+0+0&WAISaction=retrieve (accessed August 1, 2001).

2. Bill Clinton, interview with the New York and New Jersey Press, July 22, 1993, in *Weekly Compilation of Presidential Documents,* from the 1993 Presidential Documents Online via GPO Access, http://frwebgate3.access.gpo.gov/cgi-bin/waisgate.cgi?WAISdocID=9908732497+37+0+ 0&WAISaction=retrieve (accessed November 1, 2000).

3. Joseph H. Boyett and Henry P. Conn, *Workplace 2000: The Revolution Reshaping American Business* (New York: Dutton, 1991; New York: Plume-Penguin, 1992), 3.

4. Charles Piller, "A Rising Force of Mercenaries," *Los Angeles Times,* November 6, 2000, C1.

5. Ibid., C9.

6. Gregory Acs, Katherin Ross Phillips, and Daniel McKenzie, "Playing by the Rules but Losing the Game: America's Working Poor," *Urban Institute,* May 2000, 24, http://www.urban.org/ workingpoor/ playingtherules.html (accessed November 1, 2000).

7. Ibid., 28. Because this report was written before the economic decline that began in 2000, the figures are, if anything, conservative.

8. Bill Clinton, "Remarks on the Welfare to Work Initiative," January 25, 1999, in *Weekly Compilation of Presidential Documents,* from the 1999 Presidential Documents Online via GPO Access, http://frwebgate5.access.gpo.gov/cgi-bin/waisgate.cgi?WAISdocID=081936299+3+0+0& WAISaction=retrieve (accessed November 1, 2000).

9. Beier, *Masterless Men,* 88.

10. Pound, *Norwich Census of the Poor,* 7. See also Pound's article about the Norwich census, "An Elizabethan Census of the Poor"; and William Hudson and John Cottingham Tingey, eds., *The Records of the City of Norwich* (Norwich: Jarrold & Sons, 1910), 2:343–58.

11. Pound, *Norwich Census of the Poor,* 30, 35, 67, 81.

12. Ibid., 19.

13. Out of some 790 families recorded as poor, 272 persons received relief after 1570 (ibid., 8, 20).

14. Pound considers Norwich's approach to its newly found working poor a success story (ibid., 20–21). But it is an indication of just how fragile the system was that it collapsed under the influx of poor Dutch and Walloon refugees, which resulted in outbreaks of plague in 1579, 1583–86, and 1590–93, ultimately wiping out most of the city's poor. Vagrants once again become a nuisance in the 1590s. See Pound, "An Elizabethan Census of the Poor," 149–50.

15. Of course, implied in this statement is the fact that what was new in the early modern period could itself have been in crucial ways a revisiting and reworking of earlier happenings. See chap. 1, n. 10.

Appendix E

1. William Borough, *A Discours of the Variation of the Cumpas, Or Magneticall Needle* (London, 1581), star2r, F2r, F4r. Borough's *Discours* is annexed, with a separate title page, as part 2 to Robert Norman's text *The Newe Attractive* (London, 1581) and again to the second edition of Norman's work in 1585.

2. Edward Wright, "The Preface to the Reader," in *[Certaine] Errors in Navigation* (London, 1599). This is a reissue, with cancelled title page, of *Certaine Errors of Navigation* (London, 1599).

3. Wright, *The Haven-Finding Art*, B3v, A3r, B2v.

4. Robert Norman, dedication to *The Newe Attractive*, 2nd ed. (London, 1585), A2v. Many advances in mathematics made longitude-finding on land more viable (though it still remained a problem at sea); thus, when the printer John Tapp brought out a new edition of Norman's work in 1614, Tapp "omitted Borough's concluding comments on variation, putting in their place six and a half pages of examples of mathematical navigation" (Waters, *The Art of Navigation in England*, 399).

5. Waters, *The Art of Navigation in England*, 290.

6. Hewson, *History of the Practice of Navigation*, 9–16.

7. Waters, *The Art of Navigation in England*, 476; Hewson, *History of the Practice of Navigation*, 35–36. For a fascinating account of the discovery of longitude, see Dava Sobel, *Longitude: The True Story of a Lone Genius Who Solved the Scientific Problem of His Time* (New York: Walker Publishing Co., 1995; London: Fourth Estate Limited, 1996).

8. Nathaniel Friend, "On the *Practical Navigation* of My Very Good Friend, Mr. John Seller," prefatory poem to Seller's *Practical Navigation*, 5th ed. (London, 1683; first published 1669).

9. William Bourne, *A Regiment for the Sea* (London, 1574), 63r (Q3r); Blaeu, "To the Reader," in *The Light of Navigation*.

10. Bourne, *A Regiment for the Sea*, 63v (Q3v).

11. William Barlow, *Magneticall Advertisements* (London, 1616), 54. In 1618, a second edition appeared together with Mark Ridley's *Magneticall Animadversions* (1617).

12. Dampier records in his journal that he asked Barlow to deliver the packet to the owners of the *Cygnet* (introduction to Barlow, *Journal*, 11). The packet may have been lost when the longboat, which stored the goods Barlow had acquired on his voyage, sank in a storm at sea (406).

13. See Seller, *Practical Navigation*, 231; and Hewson, *History of the Practice of Navigation*, 13. This method of position finding was favored by Edward Barlow, who usually records a port's latitude as well as its bearing and distance from London.

14. Dampier, *A Collection of Voyages*, 3:67–68.

15. Ibid., 3:68–69.

16. Ibid., 3:69–74; Wright, *The Haven-Finding Art*, 8–9; Seller, *Practical Navigation*, 136–39.

Selected Bibliography

Primary Sources

Manuscripts

Bibliothèque Nationale, Paris
  Paris Profiles, f. 13, Nombre de Dios. Manuscrits Anglais, 51.
British Library, London
  Exeter and Devon coast, anonymous English chart, ca. 1536. MS. Cotton Aug.I.i.39.
Corporation of London Record Office
  Land Tax Assessment, 1693/94, St. Mary's, Whitechapel.
Essex Record Office
  Maldon Borough. D/B 3/3/397/18.
Guildhall Library, London
  Parish Register, St. Botolph, Bishopsgate. MS4516/1.
  Parish Register, Holy Trinity, Minories. MS9238.
  Will of Mary Barlow, 1715, Wills and Probate, Commissary Court of London. 9171/57.
Huntington Library, San Marino, California
  William Hack's South Sea waggoner. HM265.
Lancashire County Record Office
  Hearth Tax Returns, Lancashire, Salford Hundred, 1664. E179/250/11, part 6.
  Inventory of George Barlow of Pilkington, Parish of Prestwich, 1686, Infra Wills and Probate
    (proved in Chester). WCW1686.
London Metropolitan Archives
  Parish Register, St. Mary, Whitechapel. P93/MRY1.
Manchester Local Studies Unit, Archives
  Overseers Accounts, 1646–83, Parish Record of Prestwich, St. Mary. L160/2/1.
National Archives, London
  Will of Edward Barlow, Commander of the *Liampo*, 1708. Wills and Probate, Prerogative
    Court of Canterbury. PROB11/500.
National Maritime Museum, Greenwich, London
  Edward Barlow's Journal. JOD/4.

Suffolk Record Office, Ipswich
  John Norden's survey of Orford Ness, 1601. Sheet 22, from 28 colored maps in Norden's "An
    Ample and Trew Description and Survey of the Manors, Lordships, Townes and Parishes of
    Staverton, Eyke, Bromswall, Wantesden, Chilsforde, Sudburn, Orforde and Dunningworth
    with Parcell of Tunstall in the Countie of Suffolk, Parcell of the Landes of the Right Wor-
    shipfull Sir Michaell Stanhop." EE5/11/1.

Printed Primary Sources

Antoniszoon, Cornelis. *The Safegard of Sailers.* Translated by Robert Norman. London, 1587.
The Bagford Ballads: Illustrating the Last Years of the Stuarts. Edited by Joseph Woodfall Ebsworth.
    2 vols. Hertford: Ballad Society, 1878.
Barlow, Edward. *Barlow's Journal of His Life at Sea in King's Ships, East and West Indiamen and
    Other Merchantmen, from 1659–1703.* Transcribed by Basil Lubbock. 2 vols. London: Hurst
    & Blackett, 1934.
Barlow, William. *Magneticall Advertisements.* London, 1616.
Blaeu, Willem Janszoon. *The Light of Navigation.* Edited by R. A. Skelton. Amsterdam: N. Israel,
    1964. First published 1612.
———. *The Sea-Mirrour.* Translated by Richard Hynmers. London, 1625.
Borough, William. *A Discours of the Variation of the Cumpas, Or Magneticall Needle.* London,
    1581; 2nd ed., 1585. Annexed as part 2 to Norman, *The Newe Attractive.*
Bourne, William. *A Regiment for the Sea.* London, 1574.
Clinton, Bill. Interview with the New York and New Jersey press, July 22, 1993. In *Weekly Com-
    pilation of Presidential Documents,* from the 1993 Presidential Documents Online via GPO
    Access, http://frwebgate3.access.gpo.gov/cgi-bin/waisgate.cgi?WAISdocID=9908732497+37+
    0+0&WAISaction=retrieve (accessed November 1, 2000).
———. "Remarks Concluding the First Roundtable Discussion of the Forest Conference in Port-
    land," April 2, 1993. In *Weekly Compilation of Presidential Documents,* from the 1993 Presi-
    dential Documents Online via GPO Access, http://frwebgate1.access.gpo.gov/cgi-bin/wais-
    gate.cgi?WAISdocID=9613717391+30+0+0&WAISaction=retrieve (accessed August 1, 2001).
———. "Remarks on the Welfare to Work Initiative," January 25, 1999. In *Weekly Compilation
    of Presidential Documents,* from the 1999 Presidential Documents Online via GPO Access,
    http://frwebgate5.access.gpo.gov/cgi-bin/waisgate.cgi?WAISdo-
    cID=081936299+3+0+0&WAISaction=retrieve (accessed November 1, 2000).
Collins, Greenvile. *Great Britain's Coasting-Pilot.* London, 1693.
Coxere, Edward. *Adventures by Sea of Edward Coxere.* Edited by E. H. W. Meyerstein. Oxford:
    Clarendon Press, 1945.
Dampier, William. *A Collection of Voyages.* 4 vols. London, 1729.
Dekker, Thomas. *The Belman of London.* London, 1608. In *"The Guls Hornbook" and "The Bell-
    man of London" by Thomas Dekker.* Letchworth, UK: Temple Press, 1905.
The Euing Collection of English Broadside Ballads in the Library of the University of Glasgow.
    Introduction by John Holloway. Glasgow: University of Glasgow Publications, 1971.
Fisher, John. *The Book of John Fisher, Town Clerk and Deputy Recorder of Warwick, 1580–1588.*
    Edited by Thomas Kemp. Warwick: Henry T. Cooke and Son, n.d.
Friend, Nathaniel. "On the *Practical Navigation* of My Very Good Friend, Mr. John Seller."
    Prefatory poem to Seller, *Practical Navigation.*

Greene, Robert. *A Disputation, Betweene a Hee Conny-Catcher, and a Shee Conny-Catcher.* London, 1592. In Judges, *The Elizabethan Underworld.*

————. *A Notable Discovery of Coosenage.* London, 1591. In Judges, *The Elizabethan Underworld.*

————. *The Second and Last Part of Conny-Catching.* London, 1591. In Judges, *The Elizabethan Underworld.*

The Groundworke of Conny-Catching. London, 1592.

Harman, Thomas. *A Caveat for Commen Cursetors, Vulgarly Called Vagabones.* London, 1568. Printed, along with 1573 additions, in Kinney, *Rogues, Vagabonds and Sturdy Beggars.*

Hudson, Thomas. *Comic Songs.* London: Gold & Walton, 1818–27.

Hudson, William, and John Cottingham Tingey, eds. *The Records of the City of Norwich.* Vol. 2. Norwich: Jarrold & Sons, 1910.

Hutton, Luke. *The Blacke Dogge of Newgate.* London, [1596]. In Judges, *The Elizabethan Underworld.*

International Genealogical Index. Salt Lake City: Genealogical Department of the Church of Jesus Christ of Latter-Day Saints, 1991.

Lowe, Roger. *The Diary of Roger Lowe of Ashton-in-Makerfield, Lancashire, 1663–74.* Edited by William L. Sachse. New Haven, CT: Yale University Press, 1938.

Martindale, Adam. *The Life of Adam Martindale.* Edited by Richard Parkinson. N.p.: Chetham Society, 1845.

The Midship-Man's Garland. London, [1692–1703]. In *The Bagford Ballads,* 1:109–20.

Mountagu, Edward. *The Journal of Edward Mountagu, First Earl of Sandwich, Admiral and General at Sea, 1659–1665.* Edited by R. C. Anderson. Publications of the Navy Records Society, vol. 64. London: Navy Records Society, 1929.

Neptune's Fair Garland. London: J. M. [John Millet] for J[onah] Deacon, 1686.

Norden, John. *Orford Ness* (1601). Cambridge: W. Heffer & Sons, 1966.

————. *Speculum Britanniae. The first Parte.* London, 1593.

Norman, Robert. *The Newe Attractive.* London, 1581; 2nd ed., 1585. Part 2 of both editions is Borough, *A Discours of the Variation of the Cumpas.*

Orders Appointed to Be Executed in the Cittie of London, for Setting Roges and Idle Persons to Worke, and for Releefe of the Poore. London, n.d.

The Pepys Ballads. Edited by W. G. Day. Facsimile edition. 5 volumes. From *Catalogue of the Pepys Library at Magdalene College, Cambridge.* Wolfeboro, NH: D. S. Brewer, 1987.

Piller, Charles. "A Rising Force of Mercenaries." *Los Angeles Times,* November 6, 2000, C1, C9.

Pound, John F., ed. *Norwich Census of the Poor, 1570.* Norfolk: Norfolk Record Society, 1971.

The Registers of the Parish Church of Bury in the County of Lancaster; Christenings, Burials, and Weddings, 1590–1616. Transcribed and edited by Rev. W. J. Lowenberg and Henry Brierley. Rochdale: Lancashire Parish Register Society, 1898.

The Registers of the Parish Church of Prestwich; Baptisms, Burials, and Weddings, 1603–1688. Transcribed by Henry Brierley. Cambridge: Cambridge University Press for the Lancashire Parish Register Society, 1909.

The Registers of the Parish Church of Prestwich in the County of Lancaster; Baptisms and Burials, 1689–1711, Weddings to 1712. Transcribed by Henry Brierley. Cambridge: Cambridge University Press for the Lancashire Parish Register Society, 1913.

"Register of Passports for Vagrants, 1598–1669." In Slack, *Poverty in Early-Stuart Salisbury.*

Rid, Samuel. *The Art of Juggling or Legerdemaine.* London, 1612. In Kinney, *Rogues, Vagabonds and Sturdy Beggars.*

Rogers, Captain Woodes. *A Cruising Voyage round the World.* London, 1712.

Rollins, Hyder E., ed. *A Pepysian Garland: Black-Letter Broadside Ballads of the Years 1595–1639.* Cambridge: Cambridge University Press, 1922.

The Roxburghe Ballads. 9 vols. in 8. Edited by W. Chappell (vols. 1–3) and J. Woodfall Ebsworth (vols. 4–9). Hertford: Stephen Austin & Sons, 1869–1901. Reprint, New York: AMS Press, 1966.

Saxton, Christopher. *Atlas of the Counties of England and Wales.* London, [1580].

Seller, John. *The English Pilot.* London, 1671.

———. *Practical Navigation.* 5th ed. London, 1683. First published 1669.

Shakespeare, William. *2 Henry IV.* In *The Riverside Shakespeare,* edited by G. Blakemore Evans. Boston: Houghton Mifflin Co., 1974.

Shelvocke, Captain George. *A Voyage round the World by the Way of the Great South Sea.* London, 1726.

The Statutes of the Realm. Edited by John Raithby et al. London: Record Commission, 1810–28.

Taylor, John. *All the Works of John Taylor the Water Poet.* First published 1630. London: Scolar Press, 1973.

The Town Crier (or *The Bellman of London*). London, 1590s.

Waghenaer, Lucas Janszoon. *The Mariners Mirrour.* Translated by Sir Anthony Ashley. London, 1588.

Wright, Edward. [*Certaine*] *Errors in Navigation.* London, 1599. A reissue, with cancelled title page, of *Certaine Errors of Navigation.* London, 1599.

———, trans. *The Haven-Finding Art.* London, 1599. Translated from the Dutch *De Havenvending* by Simon Stevin.

Secondary Works

Acs, Gregory, Katherin Ross Phillips, and Daniel McKenzie. "Playing by the Rules but Losing the Game: America's Working Poor." *Urban Institute,* May 2000, 1–28, http://www.urban.org/workingpoor/playingtherules.html (accessed November 1, 2000).

Agnew, Jean-Christophe. *Worlds Apart: The Market and the Theater in Anglo-American Thought, 1550–1750.* Cambridge: Cambridge University Press, 1986.

Andrews, Kenneth R., ed. *The Last Voyage of Drake and Hawkins.* Cambridge: Cambridge University Press, 1972.

Archer, Ian W. *The Pursuit of Stability: Social Relations in Elizabethan London.* Cambridge: Cambridge University Press, 1991.

Armitage, David, and Michael J. Braddick, eds. *The British Atlantic World, 1500–1800.* Houndsmills, Hampshire: Palgrave Macmillan, 2002.

Aydelotte, Frank. *Elizabethan Rogues and Vagabonds.* Vol. 1. Oxford Historical and Literary Studies. Oxford: Clarendon Press, 1913.

Barker, Francis. *The Tremulous Private Body: Essays on Subjection.* London: Methuen, 1984.

Barry, Jonathan, and Christopher Brooks, eds. *The Middling Sort of People: Culture, Society and Politics in England, 1550–1800.* New York: St. Martin's Press, 1994.

Baudrillard, Jean. "Simulacra and Simulations." In *Jean Baudrillard: Selected Writings,* edited by Mark Poster. Stanford, CA: Stanford University Press, 1988.

Beier, A. L. "Engine of Manufacture: The Trades of London." In Beier and Finlay, *London, 1500–1700.*

———. *Masterless Men: The Vagrancy Problem in England, 1560–1640.* London: Methuen, 1985.

———. "Poverty and Progress in Early Modern England." In Beier, Cannadine, and Rosenheim, *The First Modern Society.*

———. "Social Problems in Elizabethan London." *Journal of Interdisciplinary History* 9 (1978): 203–21.

————. *Studies in Poverty and Poor Relief in Warwickshire, 1540–1680.* PhD diss. Princeton, NJ: Princeton University, 1970.

————. "Vagrants and the Social Order in Elizabethan England." *Past and Present* 64 (1974): 3–29.

Beier, A. L., David Cannadine, and James M. Rosenheim, eds. *The First Modern Society: Essays in English History in Honour of Lawrence Stone.* Cambridge: Cambridge University Press, 1989.

Beier, A. L., and Roger Finlay, eds. *London, 1500–1700: The Making of the Metropolis.* London: Longman, 1986.

Belsey, Catherine. *The Subject of Tragedy: Identity and Difference in Renaissance Drama.* London: Methuen, 1985.

Ben-Amos, Ilana Krausman. *Adolescence and Youth in Early Modern England.* New Haven, CT: Yale University Press, 1994.

Berlin, Normand. *The Base String: The Underworld in Elizabethan Drama.* Rutherford: Fairleigh Dickinson University Press, 1968.

Bix, Karen Helfand. "'Masters of Their Occupation': Labor and Fellowship in the Coney-Catching Pamphlets." In Dionne and Mentz, *Rogues and Early Modern English Culture.*

Booth, Mark W. "Broadside: 'Description of a Strange Fish.'" In *The Experience of Songs.* New Haven, CT: Yale University Press, ca. 1981.

Boulton, Jeremy. "Going on the Parish: The Parish Pension and Its Meaning in the London Suburbs, 1640–1724." In Hitchcock, King, and Sharpe, *Chronicling Poverty.*

————. *Neighbourhood and Society: A London Suburb in the Seventeenth Century.* Cambridge: Cambridge University Press, 1987.

Boyett, Joseph H., and Henry P. Conn. *Workplace 2000: The Revolution Reshaping American Business.* New York: Dutton, 1991; New York: Plume-Penguin, 1992.

Burke, Peter. *Popular Culture in Early Modern Europe.* London: Maurice Temple Smith, 1978.

Burnett, Mark Thornton. "Apprentice Literature and the 'Crisis' of the 1590s." *Yearbook of English Studies* 21 (1991): 27–38.

————. *Masters and Servants in English Renaissance Drama and Culture: Authority and Obedience.* New York: St. Martin's Press, 1997.

Burton, Valerie. "The Myth of Bachelor Jack: Masculinity, Patriarchy and Seafaring Labour." In *Jack Tar in History: Essays in the History of Maritime Life and Labour,* edited by Colin Howell and Richard J. Twomey. Fredericton, New Brunswick: Acadiensis Press, 1991.

Butler, Judith. *Gender Trouble: Feminism and Subversion of Identity.* London: Routledge, 1990.

Capp, Bernard. *Cromwell's Navy: The Fleet and the English Revolution, 1648–1660.* Oxford: Clarendon Press, 1989.

————. "Separate Domains? Women and Authority in Early Modern England." In Griffiths, Fox, and Hindle, *The Experience of Authority.*

Carroll, William C. *Fat King, Lean Beggar: Representations of Poverty in the Age of Shakespeare.* Ithaca, NY: Cornell University Press, 1996.

Certeau, Michel de. *The Practice of Everyday Life.* Translated by Steven Rendall. Berkeley and Los Angeles: University of California Press, 1984.

Clark, Alice. *Working Life of Women in the Seventeenth Century.* London: George Routledge & Sons; New York: E. P. Dutton, 1919.

Clark, Peter. *The English Alehouse: A Social History, 1200–1830.* London: Longman, 1983.

Clark, Peter, and Paul Slack, eds. *Crisis and Order in English Towns, 1500–1700: Essays in Urban History.* Toronto: University of Toronto Press, 1972.

Coleman, D. C. "Naval Dockyards under the Later Stuarts." *Economic History Review,* 2nd ser., 6 (1953): 134–55.

Course, Captain A. G. *A Seventeenth-Century Mariner.* London: Frederick Muller, 1965.

Cruickshank, C. G. *Elizabeth's Army.* 2nd ed. Oxford: Clarendon Press, 1966.

Dabhoiwala, Faramerz. "The Pattern of Sexual Immorality in Seventeenth- and Eighteenth-Century London." In Griffiths and Jenner, *Londinopolis.*

Davies, J. D. *Gentlemen and Tarpaulins: The Officers and Men of the Restoration Navy.* Oxford: Clarendon Press, 1991.

Davis, Ralph. "Merchant Shipping in the Economy of the Late Seventeenth Century." *Economic History Review,* 2nd ser., 9 (1956): 59–73.

———. *The Rise of the English Shipping Industry in the Seventeenth and Eighteenth Centuries.* London: Macmillan, 1962.

Delany, Paul. *British Autobiography in the Seventeenth Century.* London: Routledge & Kegan Paul, 1969.

Dionne, Craig. "Fashioning Outlaws: The Early Modern Rogue and Urban Culture." In Dionne and Mentz, *Rogues and Early Modern English Culture.*

Dionne, Craig, and Steve Mentz, eds. *Rogues and Early Modern English Culture.* Ann Arbor: University of Michigan Press, 2004.

Dolan, Frances E. "Household Chastisements: Gender, Authority, and 'Domestic Violence.'" In *Renaissance Culture and the Everyday,* edited by Patricia Fumerton and Simon Hunt. Philadelphia: University of Pennsylvania Press, 1999.

Dollimore, Jonathan. *Radical Tragedy: Religion, Ideology, and Power in the Drama of Shakespeare and His Contemporaries.* Chicago: University of Chicago Press, 1984.

Dubrow, Heather. *Shakespeare and Domestic Loss: Forms of Deprivation, Mourning, and Recuperation.* Cambridge: Cambridge University Press, 1999.

Ebner, Dean. *Autobiography in Seventeenth-Century England: Theology and Self.* The Hague: Mouton, 1971.

Farrington, Anthony. *Catalogue of East India Company Ships' Journals and Logs, 1600–1834.* London: British Library, 1999.

Fontaine, Laurence. *History of Pedlars in Europe.* Translated by Vicki Whittaker. Durham, NC: Duke University Press, 1996.

Fumerton, Patricia. *Cultural Aesthetics: Renaissance Literature and the Practice of Social Ornament.* Chicago: University of Chicago Press, 1991.

———. "Not Home: Alehouses, Ballads, and the Vagrant Husband in Early Modern England." In "Renaissance Materialities," edited by Maureen Quilligan. Special issue, *Journal of Medieval and Early Modern Studies* 32 (2002): 493–518.

———. Review of *Inwardness and Theater in the English Renaissance,* by Katharine Eisamen Maus. *Shakespeare Studies* 26 (1998): 395.

Gaby, Rosemary. "Of Vagabonds and Commonwealths: *Beggar's Bush, A Jovial Crew,* and *The Sisters.*" *Studies in English Literature* 34 (1994): 401–24.

Goldberg, Jonathan. *James I and the Politics of Literature: Jonson, Shakespeare, Donne, and Their Contemporaries.* Baltimore: Johns Hopkins University Press, 1983.

Gowing, Laura. *Domestic Dangers: Women, Words, and Sex in Early Modern London.* Oxford: Clarendon Press, 1996.

———. "'The Freedom of the Streets': Women and Social Space, 1560–1640." In Griffiths and Jenner, *Londinopolis.*

Greenblatt, Stephen. "Invisible Bullets." In *Shakespearean Negotiations: The Circulation of Social Energy in Renaissance England.* Berkeley and Los Angeles: University of California Press, 1988.

————. *Renaissance Self-Fashioning: From More to Shakespeare.* Chicago: University of Chicago Press, 1980.

Griffiths, Paul. "Masterless Young People in Norwich, 1560–1645." In Griffiths, Fox, and Hindle, *The Experience of Authority.*

————. *Youth and Authority: Formative Experiences in England, 1560–1640.* Oxford: Clarendon Press, 1996.

Griffiths, Paul, Adam Fox, and Steve Hindle, eds. *The Experience of Authority in Early Modern England.* New York: St. Martin's Press, 1996.

Griffiths, Paul, and Mark S. R. Jenner, eds. *Londinopolis: Essays in the Cultural and Social History of Early Modern London.* Manchester: Manchester University Press, 2000.

Hackman, Rowan. *Ships of the East India Company.* Gravesend, Kent: World Ship Society, 2001.

Halasz, Alexandra. *The Marketplace of Print: Pamphlets and the Public Sphere in Early Modern England.* Cambridge: Cambridge University Press, 1997.

Hanson, Elizabeth. *Discovering the Subject in Renaissance England.* Cambridge: Cambridge University Press, 1998.

Helgerson, Richard. *Adulterous Alliances: Home, State, and History in Early Modern European Drama and Painting.* Chicago: University of Chicago Press, 2000.

————. "'I Miles Philips': An Elizabethan Seaman Conscripted by History." *PMLA* 118 (2003): 573–80.

————. Introduction to "Literature and Geography," edited by Richard Helgerson and Joanne Woolway Grenfell. Special issue no. 3, *Early Modern Literary Studies* 4 (1998), http://www.shu.ac.uk/emls/04-2/04-2toc.html.

————. "The Land Speaks." In *Forms of Nationhood: The Elizabethan Writing of England.* Chicago: University of Chicago Press, 1992.

Hewson, J. B. *A History of the Practice of Navigation.* Glasgow: Brown, Son & Ferguson, 1951.

Hill, Christopher. *The World Turned Upside Down: Radical Ideas during the English Revolution.* New York: Viking, 1972.

Hindle, Steve. "Exclusion Crises: Poverty, Migration and Parochial Responsibility in English Rural Communities, c. 1560–1660." *Rural History* 7 (1996): 125–49.

————. *The State and Social Change in Early Modern England, c. 1550–1640.* New York: St. Martin's Press, 2000.

Hitchcock, Tim, Peter King, and Pamela Sharpe, eds. *Chronicling Poverty: The Voices and Strategies of the English Poor, 1640–1840.* New York: St. Martin's Press, 1997.

Howse, Derek, and Norman J. W. Thrower, eds. *A Buccaneer's Atlas: Basil Ringrose's South Sea Waggoner.* Berkeley and Los Angeles: University of California Press, 1992.

Hufton, Olwen. *The Poor of Eighteenth-Century France, 1750–1789.* Oxford: Clarendon Press, 1974.

Hume, Robert. *Early Child Immigrants to Virginia, 1619–1642.* Baltimore: Magna Carta Book Co., 1986.

Humphreys, Robert. *No Fixed Abode: A History of Responses to the Roofless and the Rootless in Britain.* New York: St. Martin's Press, 1999.

Jankowski, Theodora A. "Historicizing and Legitimating Capitalism: Thomas Heywood's *Edward IV* and *If You Know Not Me, You Know Nobody.*" In *Medieval and Renaissance Drama in England,* vol. 7, edited by Leeds Barroll. New York: AMS Press, 1995.

Johnson, Robert C. "The Transportation of Vagrant Children from London to Virginia, 1618–1622." In *Early Stuart Studies: Essays in Honor of David Harris Willson,* edited by Howard S. Reinmuth. Minneapolis: University of Minnesota Press, 1970.

Judges, A. V. *The Elizabethan Underworld.* New York: E. P. Dutton, 1930.

Kemp, Peter. *The British Sailor: A Social History of the Lower Deck.* London: J. M. Dent, 1970.

Kent, Joan R. "Population Mobility and Alms: Poor Migrants in the Midlands during the Early Seventeenth Century." *Local Population Studies* 27 (1981): 35–51.

Kinney, Arthur F., ed. *Rogues, Vagabonds and Sturdy Beggars: A New Gallery of Tudor and Early Stuart Rogue Literature.* Amherst: University of Massachusetts Press, 1990.

Knapp, Jeffrey. "Rogue Nationalism." In *Centuries' Ends, Narrative Means,* edited by Robert Newman. Stanford, CA: Stanford University Press, 1996.

Lawson, Cecil C. P. *A History of the Uniforms of the British Army: From the Beginnings to 1760.* Vol. 1. London: Peter Davies, 1940.

Lefebvre, Henri. *The Production of Space.* Translated by Donald Nicholson-Smith. Oxford: Blackwell, 1991.

Linebaugh, Peter, and Marcus Rediker. *The Many-Headed Hydra: Sailors, Slaves, Commoners, and the Hidden History of the Revolutionary Atlantic.* Boston: Beacon Press, 2000.

Lloyd, Christopher. *The British Seaman, 1200–1860: A Social Survey.* London: Collins, 1968.

Lynam, Edward. *British Maps and Map-Makers.* London: William Collins, 1947.

———. *The Mapmaker's Art: Essays on the History of Maps.* London: Batchworth Press, 1953.

MacDonald, Michael, and Terence R. Murphy. *Sleepless Souls: Suicide in Early Modern England.* Oxford: Clarendon Press, 1990.

Maus, Katharine Eisamen. *Inwardness and Theater in the English Renaissance.* Chicago: University of Chicago Press, 1995.

McDonald, Marcia A. "The Elizabethan Poor Laws and the Stage in the Late 1590s." In *Medieval and Renaissance Drama in England,* vol. 7, edited by Leeds Barroll. New York: AMS Press, 1995.

McMullen, John L. *The Canting Crew: London's Criminal Underworld, 1550–1700.* New Brunswick, NJ: Rutgers University Press, 1984.

McPeek, James A. S. *The Black Book of Knaves and Unthrifts in Shakespeare and Other Renaissance Authors.* Storrs: University of Connecticut Press, 1965.

McRae, Andrew. "The Peripatetic Muse: Internal Travel and the Production of Space in Pre-revolutionary England." In *The Country and the City Revisited: England and the Politics of Culture, 1550–1850,* edited by Gerald MacLean, Donna Landry, and Joseph P. Ward. Cambridge: Cambridge University Press, 1999.

Meldrum, Tim. "London Domestic Servants from Depositional Evidence, 1660–1750: Servant-Employer Sexuality in the Patriarchal Household." In Hitchcock, King, and Sharpe, *Chronicling Poverty.*

Mendelson, Sara, and Patricia Crawford. *Women in Early Modern England, 1550–1720.* Oxford: Clarendon Press, 1998.

Mikalachki, Jodi. "Women's Networks and the Female Vagrant: A Hard Case." In *Maids and Mistresses, Cousins and Queens: Women's Alliances in Early Modern England,* edited by Susan Frye and Karen Robertson. New York: Oxford University Press, 1999.

Montrose, Louis. "New Historicisms." In *Redrawing the Boundaries: The Transformation of English and American Literary Studies,* edited by Stephen Greenblatt and Giles Gunn. New York: Modern Language Association of America, 1992.

Mullaney, Steven. *The Place of the Stage: License, Play, and Power in Renaissance England.* Chicago: University of Chicago Press, 1988.

Orlin, Lena Cowen. "Women on the Threshold." *Shakespeare Studies* 25 (1997): 50–58.

Parry, J. H. *The Age of Reconnaissance: Discovery, Exploration and Settlement, 1450 to 1650.* London, 1963. Reprint, Berkeley and Los Angeles: University of California Press, 1981.

Pearl, Valerie. "Change and Stability in Seventeenth-Century London." *London Journal* 5 (1979): 3–34.

———. "Social Policy in Early Modern London." In *History and Imagination: Essays in Honour of H. R. Trevor-Roper,* edited by H. Lloyd-Jones, V. Pearl, and B. Worden. New York: Holmes & Meier, 1982.

Pelling, Margaret. "Apprenticeship, Health, and Social Cohesion in Early Modern London." *History Workshop Journal* 37 (1994): 33–56.

———. *The Common Lot: Sickness, Medical Occupations, and the Urban Poor in Early Modern England.* London: Longman, 1998.

———. "Skirting the City? Disease, Social Change and Divided Households in the Seventeenth Century." In Griffiths and Jenner, *Londinopolis.*

Plant, Marjorie. *The English Book Trade: An Economic History of the Making and Sale of Books.* 2nd ed. London: George Allen & Unwin, 1965.

Pories, Kathleen. "The Intersection of Poor Laws and Literature in the Sixteenth Century: Fictional and Factual Categories." In *Framing Elizabethan fictions: Contemporary Approaches to Early Modern Narrative Prose,* edited by Constance C. Relihan. Kent, OH: Kent State University Press, 1996.

Pound, John F. "An Elizabethan Census of the Poor: The Treatment of Vagrancy in Norwich, 1570–1580." *University of Birmingham Historical Journal* 8 (1962): 135–61.

Pound, John F., and A. L. Beier. "Debate: Vagrants and the Social Order in Elizabethan England." *Past and Present* 71 (1976): 126–34.

Power, Michael J. "East London Housing in the Seventeenth Century." In Clark and Slack, *Crisis and Order in English Towns.*

———. "The East London Working Community in the Seventeenth Century." In *Work in Towns, 850–1850,* edited by Penelope J. Corfield and Derek Keene. Leicester: Leicester University Press, 1990.

Pugliatti, Paola. *Beggary and Theatre in Early Modern England.* Aldershot, UK: Ashgate, 2003.

Pye, Christopher. "The Theater, the Market, and the Subject of History." *ELH* 61 (1994): 501–22.

Rappaport, Steve. "Reconsidering Apprenticeship in Sixteenth-Century London." In *Renaissance Society and Culture: Essays in Honor of Eugene F. Rice, Jr.,* edited by John Monfasani and Ronald G. Musto. New York: Italica, 1991.

———. *Worlds within Worlds: Structures of Life in Sixteenth-Century London.* Cambridge: Cambridge University Press, 1989.

Rediker, Marcus. *Between the Devil and the Deep Blue Sea: Merchant Seamen, Pirates, and the Anglo-American Maritime World, 1700–1750.* Cambridge: Cambridge University Press, 1987.

Reynolds, Bryan. *Becoming Criminal: Transversal Performance and Cultural Dissidence in Early Modern England.* Baltimore: Johns Hopkins University Press, 2002.

Roberts, Michael. "Women and Work in Sixteenth-Century English Towns." In *Work in Towns, 850–1850,* edited by Penelope J. Corfield and Derek Keene. Leicester: Leicester University Press, 1990.

Rollins, Hyder E. "The Black-Letter Broadside Ballad." *PMLA* 34 (1919): 258–338.

Salgado, Gamini. *The Elizabethan Underworld.* New York: St. Martin's Press, 1992.

Schen, Claire S. "Constructing the Poor in Early Seventeenth-Century London." *Albion* 32 (2000): 450–63.

Sharpe, Pamela. "Poor Children as Apprentices in Colyton, 1598–1830." *Continuity and Change* 6 (1991): 1–18.

Shephard, Leslie. *The Broadside Ballad.* London: Herbert Jenkins, 1962.

Shesgreen, Sean. *The Criers and Hawkers of London: Engravings and Drawings by Marcellus Laroon.* Stanford, CA: Stanford University Press, 1990.

———. "The first London Cries." *Print Quarterly* 10 (1993): 364–73.

———. *Images of the Outcast: The Urban Poor in the Cries of London.* New Brunswick, NJ: Rutgers University Press, 2002.

Ships of the East India Company. Webmaster Andrea Cordani. Mounted 1999–2005. http://www.eicships.info/eic/lost/lost_l.htm.

Shuger, Debora Kuller. *The Renaissance Bible: Scholarship, Sacrifice, and Subjectivity.* Berkeley and Los Angeles: University of California Press, 1994.

Skelton, R. A. Introduction to the facsimile edition of Willem Janszoon (William Johnson) Blaeu, *The Light of Navigation.* Amsterdam: N. Israel, 1964.

Slack, Paul. *The English Poor Law, 1531–1782.* Macmillan, 1990. Reprint, Cambridge: Cambridge University Press, 1995.

———. *From Reformation to Improvement: Public Welfare in Early Modern England; The Ford Lectures Delivered in the University of Oxford, 1994–1995.* Oxford: Clarendon, 1999.

———. *Poverty and Policy in Tudor and Stuart England.* New York: Longman, 1988.

———, ed. *Poverty in Early-Stuart Salisbury.* Devizes, UK: Wiltshire Record Society, 1975.

———. "Vagrants and Vagrancy in England, 1598–1664." *Economic History Review,* 2nd ser., 27 (1974): 360–79.

Smith, A. Hassel. "Labourers in Late Sixteenth-Century England: A Case Study from North Norfolk." Pt. 2. *Continuity and Change* 4 (1989): 367–94.

Smith, Richard M., ed. *Land, Kinship and Life-Cycle.* Cambridge: Cambridge University Press, 1984.

Smith, Steven R. "The Ideal and Reality: Apprentice-Master Relationships in Seventeenth Century London." *History of Education Quarterly* 21 (1981): 449–59.

———. "The London Apprentices as Seventeenth-Century Adolescents." *Past and Present* 61 (1973): 149–61.

Sobel, Dava. *Longitude: The True Story of a Lone Genius Who Solved the Scientific Problem of His Time.* New York: Walker Publishing Co., 1995; London: Fourth Estate Limited, 1996.

Spufford, Margaret. "First Steps in Literacy: The Reading and Writing Experiences of the Humblest Seventeenth-Century Spiritual Autobiographers." *Social History* 4 (1979): 407–35.

———. *The Great Reclothing of Rural England: Petty Chapmen and their Wares in the Seventeenth Century.* London: Hambledon Press, 1984.

Stone, Lawrence. "Social Mobility in England, 1500–1700." *Past and Present* 33 (1966): 16–55.

Sullivan, Garrett A., Jr. *The Drama of Landscape: Land, Property, and Social Relations on the Early Modern Stage.* Stanford, CA: Stanford University Press, 1998.

Sullivan, Garrett A., Jr., and Linda Woodbridge. "Popular Culture in Print." In *The Cambridge Companion to English Literature, 1500–1600,* edited by Arthur F. Kinney. Cambridge: Cambridge University Press, 2000.

Thirsk, Joan. *Economic Policy and Projects: The Development of a Consumer Society in Early Modern England.* Oxford: Clarendon Press, 1978.

Thrower, Norman J. W. *Maps and Civilization: Cartography in Culture and Society.* Chicago: University of Chicago Press, 1996.

Tomalin, Claire. *Samuel Pepys: The Unequaled Self.* New York: Penguin-Viking, 2002.

Tuan, Yi-Fu. *Space and Place: The Perspective of Experience.* Minneapolis: University of Minnesota Press, 1977.

Wales, Tim. "Poverty, Poor Relief and the Life-Cycle: Some Evidence from Seventeenth-Century Norfolk." In Smith, *Land, Kinship and Life-Cycle.*

Waters, D. W. *The Art of Navigation in England in Elizabethan and Early Stuart Times.* New Haven, CT: Yale University Press, 1958.

———. "The Art of Navigation in the Age of Drake." Appendix to Andrews, *The Last Voyage of Drake and Hawkins.*

———. *The Rutters of the Sea: The Sailing Directions of Pierre Garcie; A Study of the English and French Printed Sailing Directions; With Facsimile Reproductions.* New Haven, CT: Yale University Press, 1967.

Watson, Harold Francis. *The Sailor in English Fiction and Drama, 1550–1800.* New York: Columbia University Press, 1931.

Watt, Tessa. *Cheap Print and Popular Piety, 1550–1640.* Cambridge: Cambridge University Press, 1991.

Webb, John, ed. *Poor Relief in Elizabethan Ipswich.* Ipswich, UK: Suffolk Records Society, 1966.

Wiesner, Merry. *Women and Gender in Early Modern Europe.* Cambridge: Cambridge University Press, 1993.

Woodbridge, Linda. "The Peddler and the Pawn: Why Did Tudor England Consider Peddlers to be Rogues?" In Dionne and Mentz, *Rogues and Early Modern English Culture.*

———. *Vagrancy, Homelessness, and English Renaissance Literature.* Urbana: University of Illinois Press, 2001.

Wrightson, Keith, and David Levine. *Poverty and Piety in an English Village: Terling, 1525–1700.* New York: Academic Press, 1979.

Wurzbach, Natascha. *The Rise of the English Street Ballad, 1550–1650.* Translated by Gayna Walls. Cambridge: Cambridge University Press, 1990.

Index

Acs, Gregory, 210n.6

acts. *See* laws; settlement laws; vagrancy laws

Adams, Anthony, 10, 11, 47, 49

adolescents. *See* youths

aesthetics, 117, 127, 146

Agnew, Jean-Christophe, 30, 42–43, 52, 53

agricultural prices, 6

alehouses: alehouse-keepers, 3–4, 185n.2; space of temporary repose, 7, 8, 199n.3; upsurge in number of, 6

aliases, 7

alienation. *See* detachment

Anderson, R. C., 204n.6

Andrews, Kenneth R., 204n.6

Anne, Queen, 90

antifeminist debate pamphlets, 198n.30

Antoniszoon, Cornelius, *The Safeguard of Sailors* (Norman translation), views of coastlines from, 110, 204n.10, Fig. 25

apprentices: abandoned in times of disease, 18; abuse of, 19–20; adolescent lifestyle, 49–50; "a-liking," 19; arrested for vagrancy in London, 12, 15; ballads and stories of, 50; barred from establishing their own families, 17; detachment, 17; encouraged to be celibate, 17; gender roles in contracts, 19–20; high dropout rate of, 19, 190n.35; as immigrants, 12; important economic place in London, 15; job-shifting, 20–22, 30–31; numbers of, 15; parish, 10, 18, 26; role experimentation, 50; runaway, 18–19; unsettledness, 18–22; viewed as having a "vagrant will," 15; as vulnerable to displacement, 20, 22, 49. *See also* servants

Archer, Ian W.: on by-employments of poor women and children, 190n.44; disagreement with Rappaport on apprentice system, 186n.12,

189n.27; on neighborhood obligations, 14; on separation of poor families by parish, 9; on tendency for freemen of particular companies in London to take on other trades, 191n.51

aristocratic subjectivity, xiii

Armitage, David, 92, 201n.28

Ashley, Sir Anthony, 111, 112, 115–16

"at-home" work, 16, 23, 30, 34

atlases, 111, 203n.4. *See also* charts, coastal; maps

Atlas of the Countries of England and Wales, Fig. 21

Augustine (ship), 98, 101, 163, 206n.39

authorities: difficulty in distinguishing between variably employed and idle poor, 27; effect of rogue pamphlets on, 43–44; fears over physically unsettled poor, 27–28

autobiographies: self-conscious performativity, 67; spiritual, 48, 196n.6. *See also* journals

Aydelotte, Frank, 192n.68, 193n.4, 195nn. 21, 22

badging laws, 28, 192n.71

Bagford Ballads: Illustrating the Last Years of the Stuarts, 207n.10

ballads: about street peddlers, 148–52; broadside street ballads, xxi, 45–46, 58, 131–32, 133; godly, 207n.11; price of, 148, 184n.27; selling of "free" unsettled subjectivity, xxi, 146, 152; shift from religious topics to secular ones, 135

ballads, seaman: about love, 135–46; audience, 132–34; four types, 135; idea of exchangeability between the different seamen, 209n.36; images of unsettledness, 137–39, 146; "low" perspective, 135; marketing of "freedom" and "variety" of identity, 146; multiple roles of seamen as lovers in, 141–46; seaman as a metaphor for an unsettled subjectivity, 146; seaman's lover as inconstant in, 140–41; seamen as inconstant